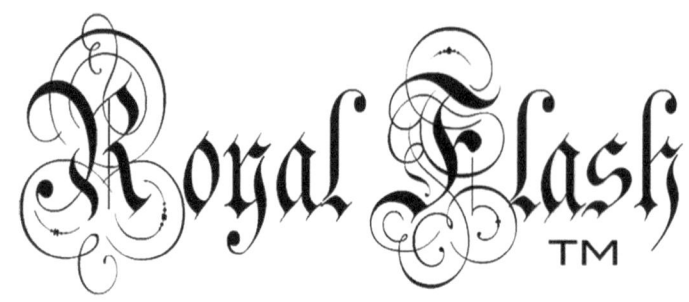

Presents

"Polynesian Skateboards and Posters"

All Artwork and
Photography by

Cort Bengtson

Published by
Cort's Royal Ink Tattoo Comapny
Commentary, Book Design and Layout
by Cort Bengtson

Copyright 2017
All images are on file with
The Library of Congress

All rights reserved. No part of this publication may be reproduced, stored in a digital format or reproduced in any form or by any means,electronical,mechanical,photographing or any other method of reproduction without advanced written permission from the publisher. ISBN # 9781948187268, 1948187264

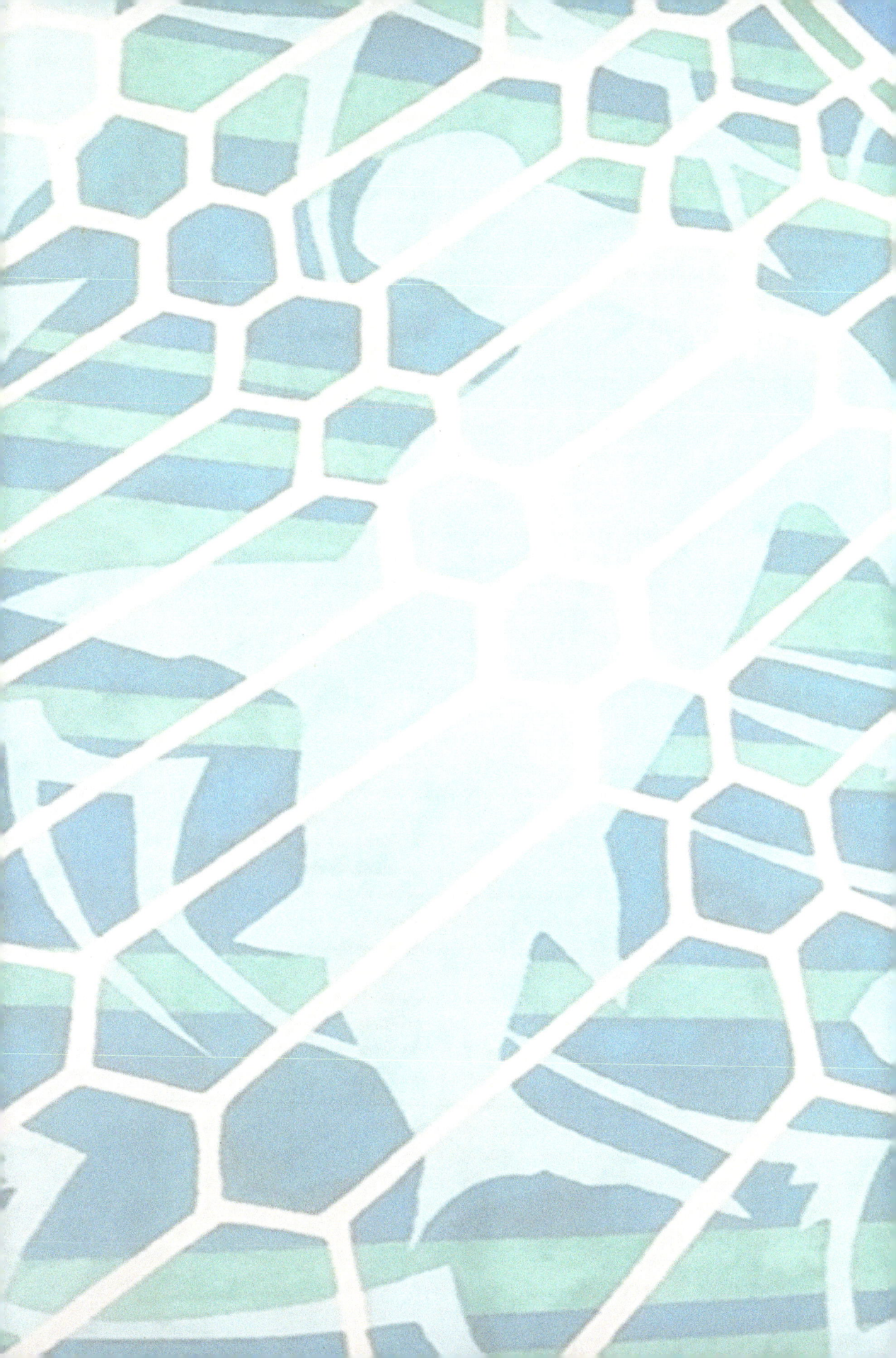

Decks foward

It is easy to believe that the surge in popularity and social acceptance of tattooing can be directly traced to the bold magnanimous and charismatic celebrities and sports personalities of our time sporting this particular style of art generally referred to as "Polynesian" or simply put "Tribal".

And although some consider this surge in popularity somewhat of a new trend, it has been around for thousands of years and is probably one of the oldest forms of art there is.

The art itself was defined not only by the very simple tools that were used to accomplish the act of tattooing but by the need for simplistic, bold graphic type representations that would withstand the ever changing and deteriorating epidermis.

Symbols of nature and family life gives legitimate claim that tattooing was very much a way of transfering knoledge through the ages as well as ones claim to thier own personal independence, individuallity, social hierarchy and coming of age.

This book is a collection of polynesian art from internationally published award winning New York Tattoo artist Cort Bengtson which can be broken into two categories. The first half of this book contains 20 different longboards and pintail skateboard decks that were hand painted with one shot enamel and cleared with a two part epoxy clear for durability and finish quality. Although tribal is usually considered of black rendering these decks explore this age old art in mostly other than black but does so consistent with the positive/negative definition normally associated with tribal polynesian art.

The second is all about art on paper including marker renderings, watercolor projects and some a combination of both. Ranging in sizes up to 40"-50", they include a diverse use of patterns and shapes sure to let anyone read into it and see a story of thier own making. Some are marker right to paper, some took hours just to layout. Some of the water color explore the slightly more sublte side. Some were drawn on the spot some pieces were started one day and finished later.

To be so simple that the shapes can be read
and understood without the need for language,
this is the job of a graphic artist.
As a tattooist you have to create a tapestry for
the skin that will rival time itself.

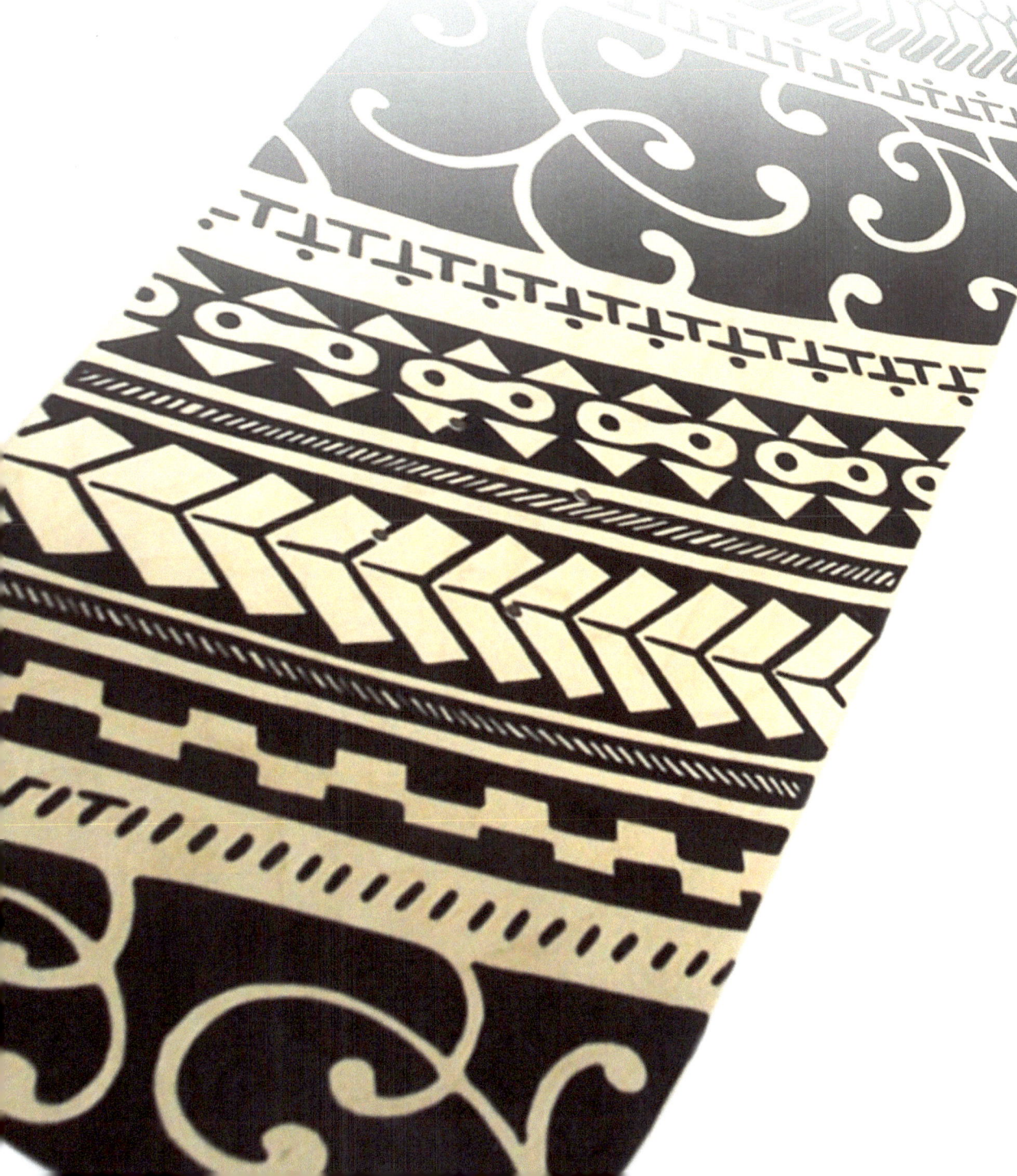

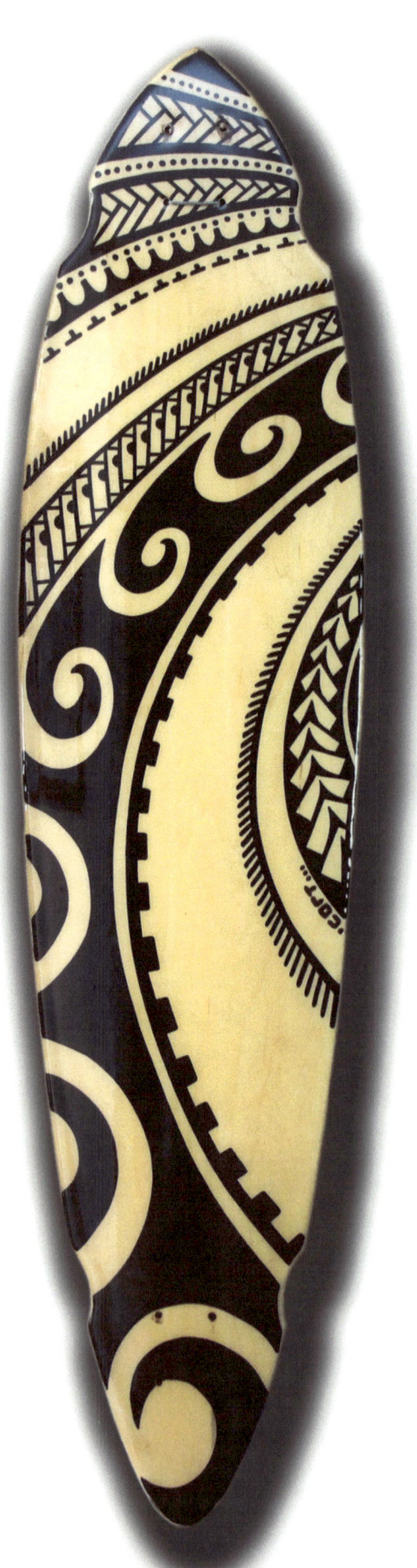

Funny things happen when you put some of your own intrests in your art work. I don't think aboriganese ever knew what a clutch plate or sprocket was but as you can see they fit quite well.

After all, are we ever inventing anything or just reinventing what we see in nature.

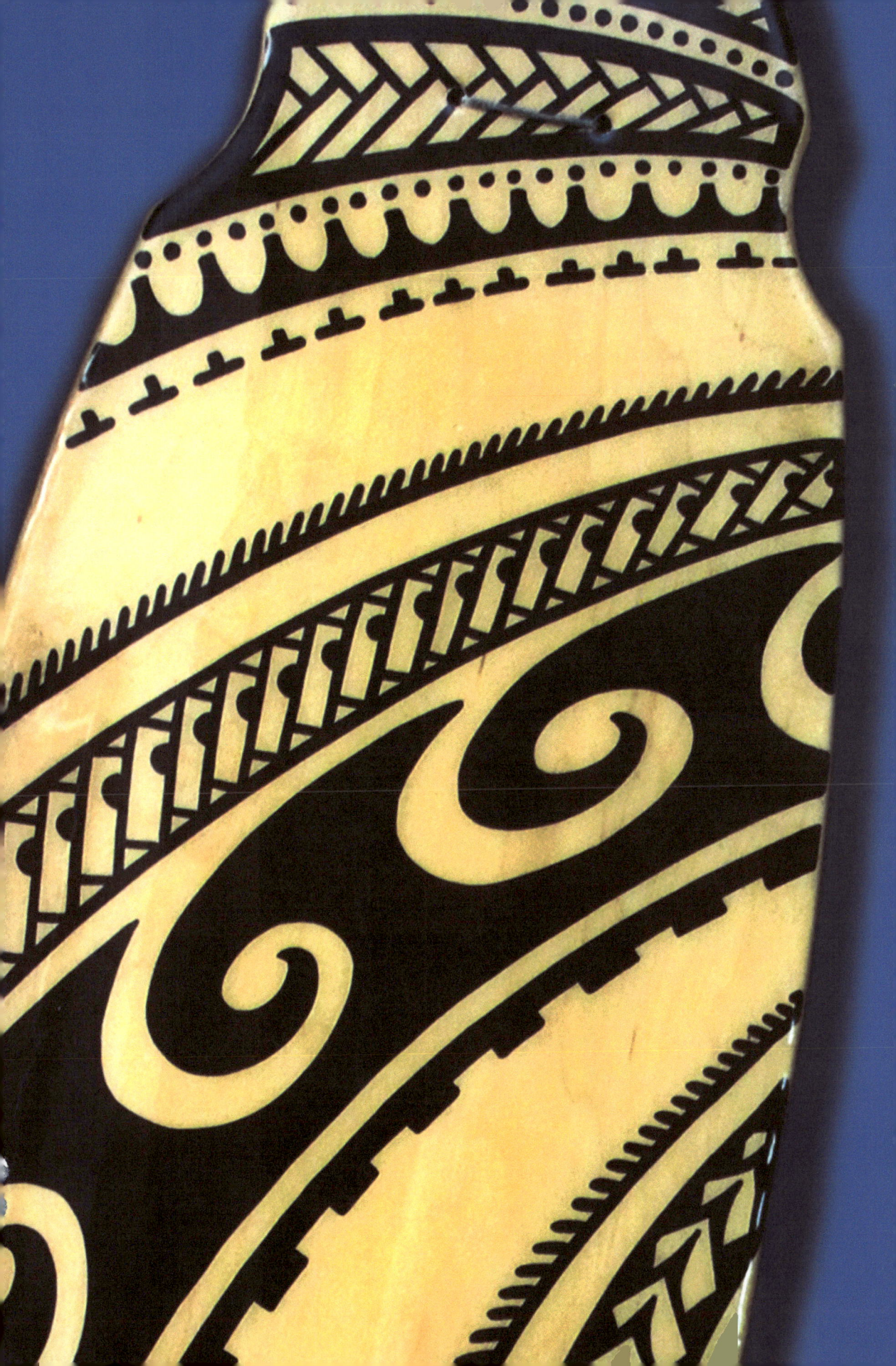

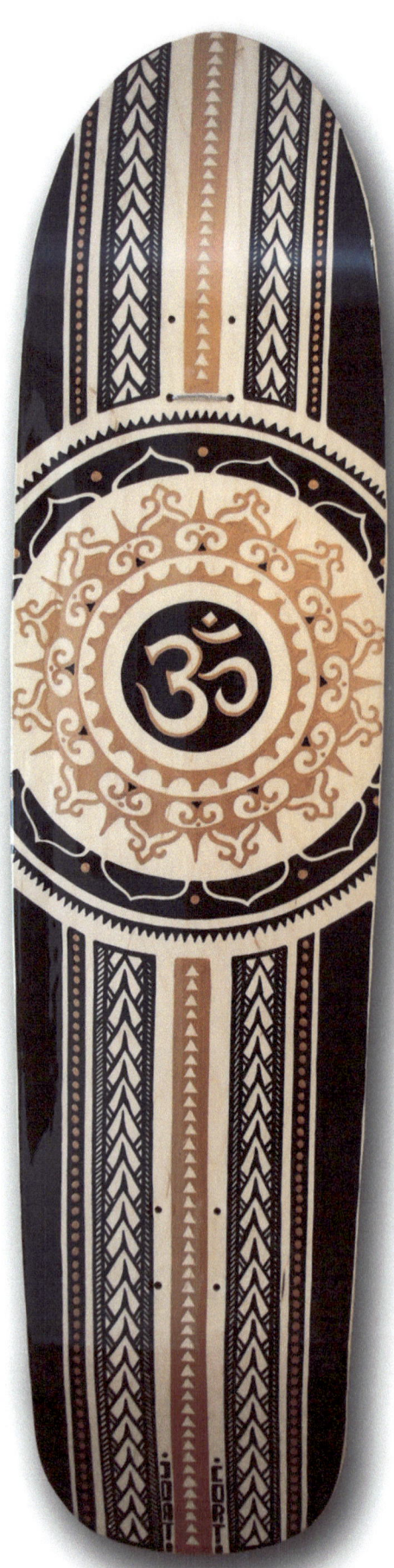

All the decks in this book have had images drawn on the boards with light pencil and then hand painted with brushes and enamel. This is basically car paint, and stinks really bad and dries very quick. Extremely durable though. A bunch of them, this one included, had an abundance of hand poured 2 part epoxy resin applied for protection and durability.

The overall design was inspired by a cigar wrapper. The detail was inspired by sprokets, clock gears, and Lotus Flower pedals. Time is represented by the 12 points. The inner circles radiates like a sun.

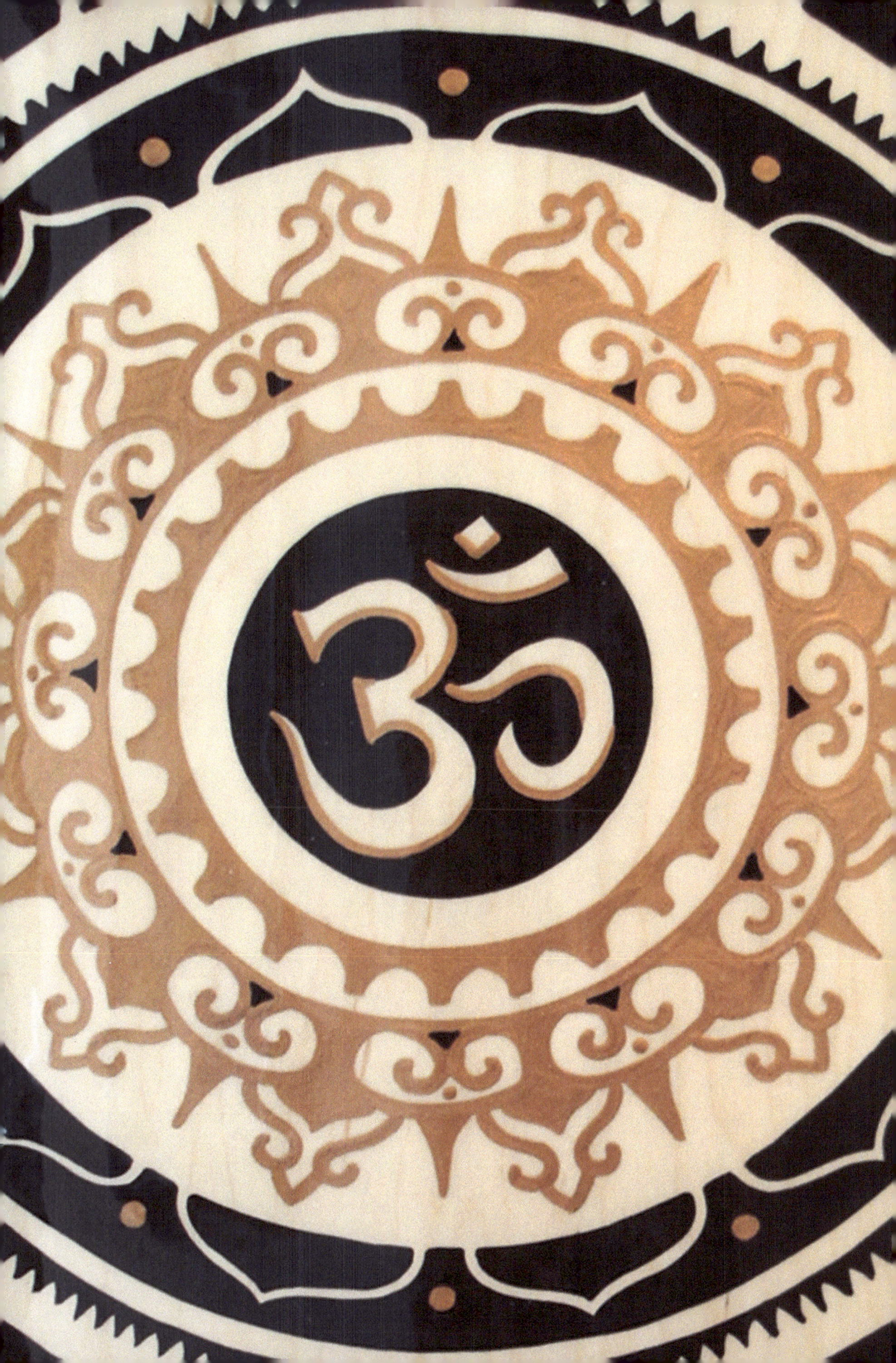

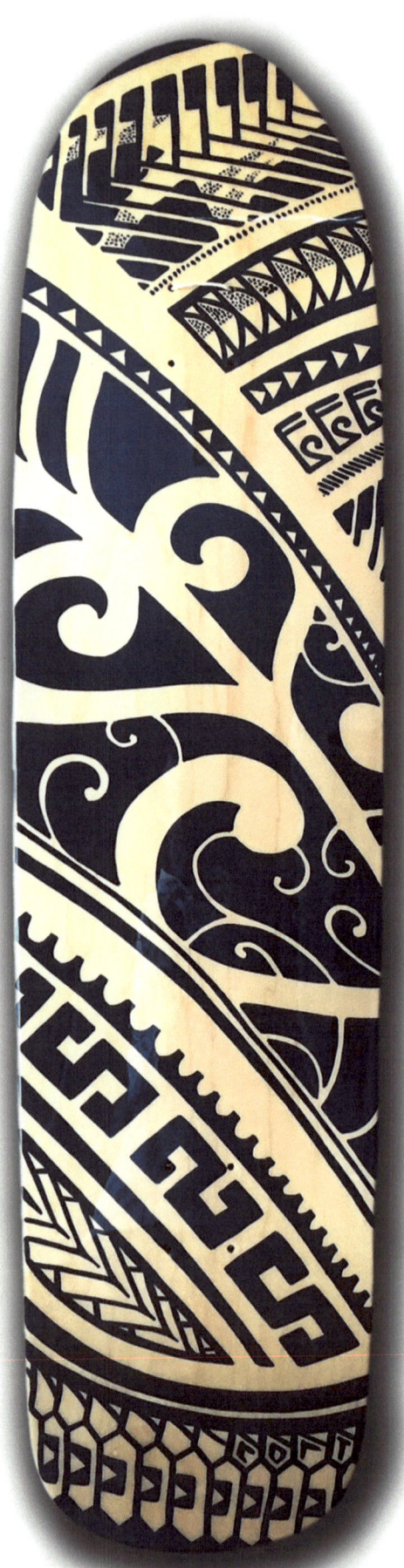

Learning to draw so negative space becomes the shape is very challenging. This board uses negative space for shapes in the middle as well as for borders between the groups of shapes.

It is kind of funny how if you think about it, we are only adding shadow to reveal what was already there. And what was there is and always be an infinite amount of possibilities.

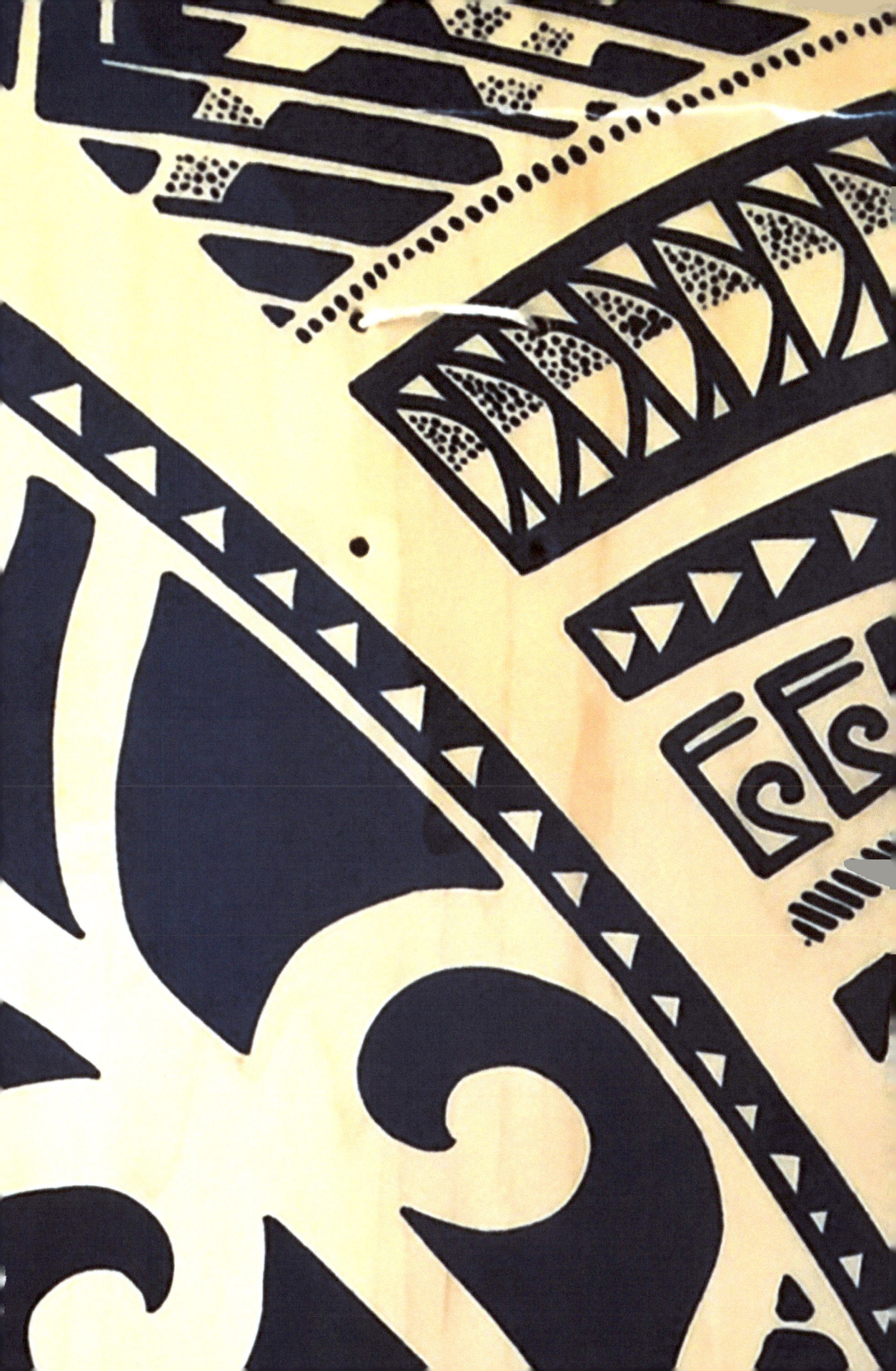

Sketches are so much fun because you don't have to comitt to doing the whole drawing, the dark to light mock up is so much easier and quicker to establish and you take chances when your sketching because you are only spending a minute or two a piece. And thats if you decide to finish the sketch at all.

This page and the next shows about 15 minutes worth of sketching that produced a bunch of ideas I use through out the book.

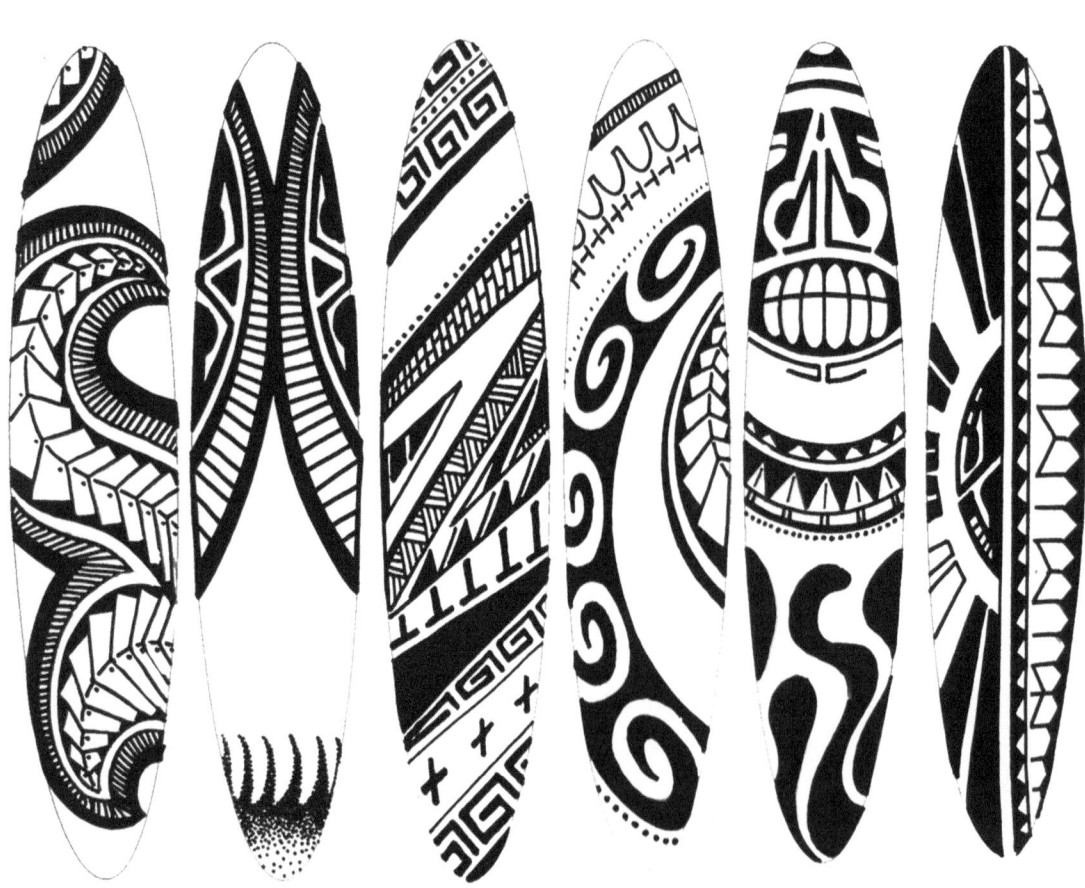

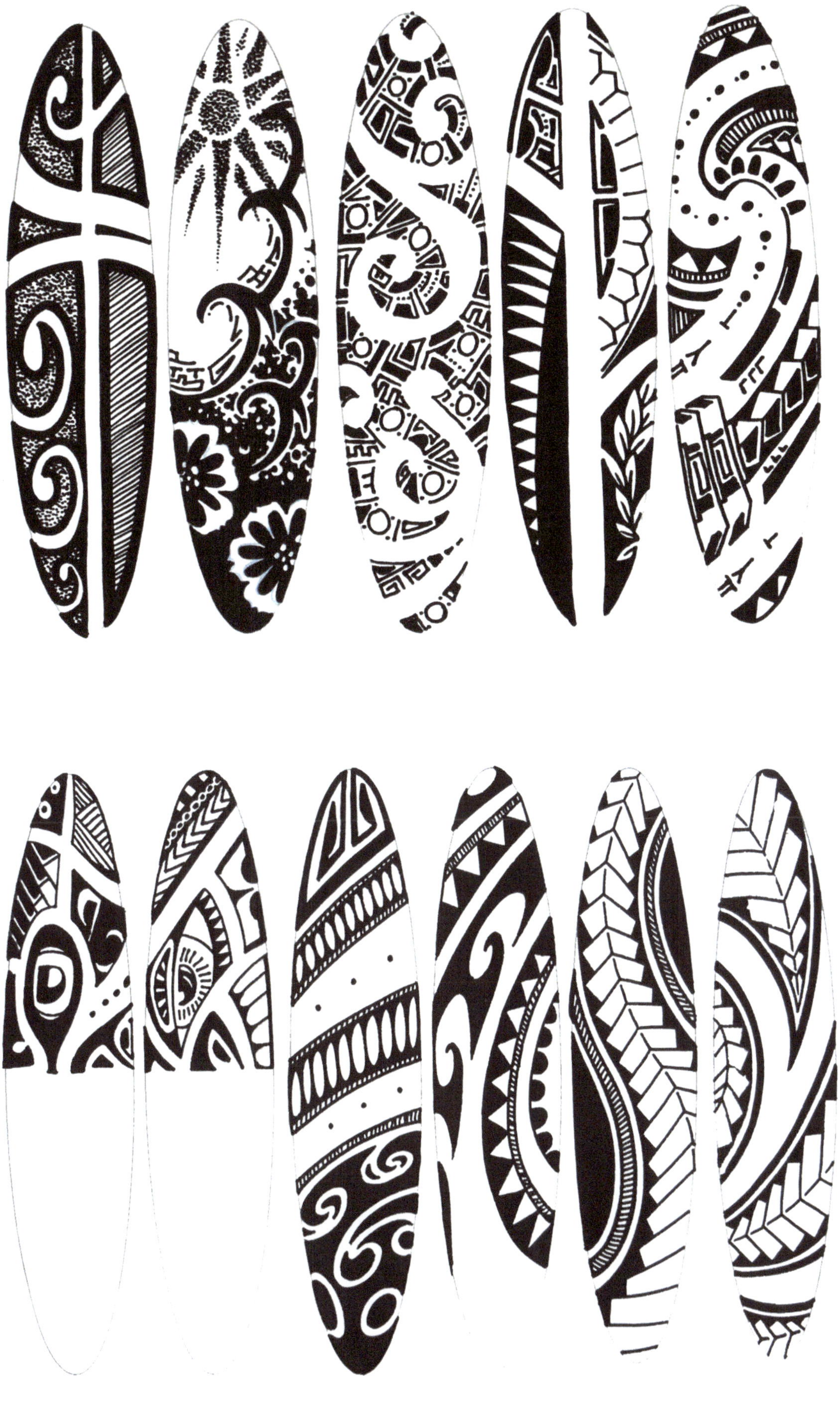

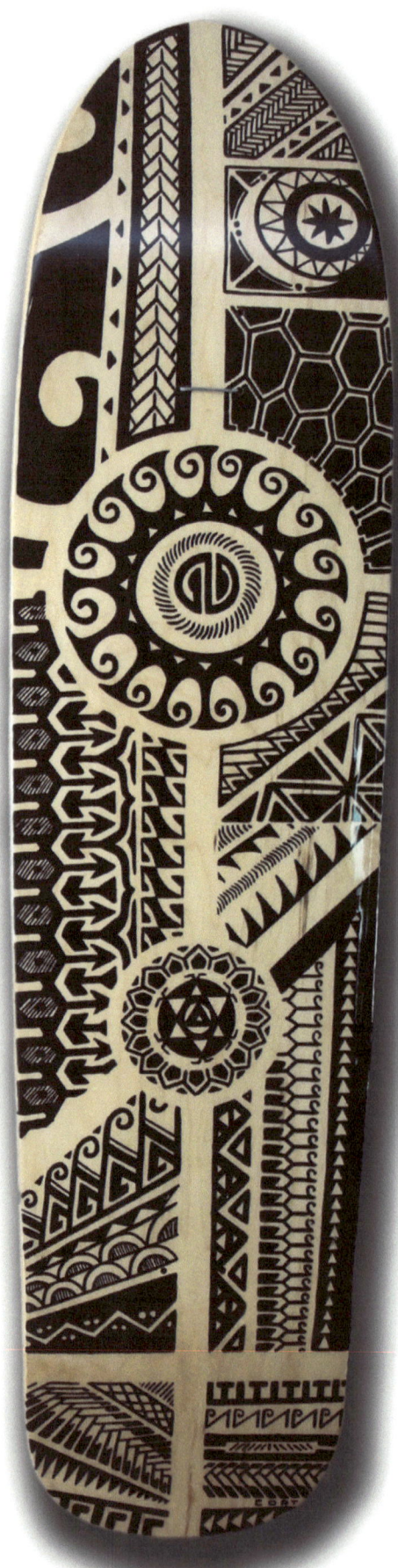

The inspiration for this board was that of a great city layout viewed from above.

The bigger circle in the center represents the capital. That is why I used the sun as the pictoral for it. Because all energy radiates from it.

The smaller one represents the next in command. Or the hierchy of president to vice president theory.

And then all of the other subdivisions represent not only how different quadrants of the city have different members and functions but how each can be made up of different elements within itself.

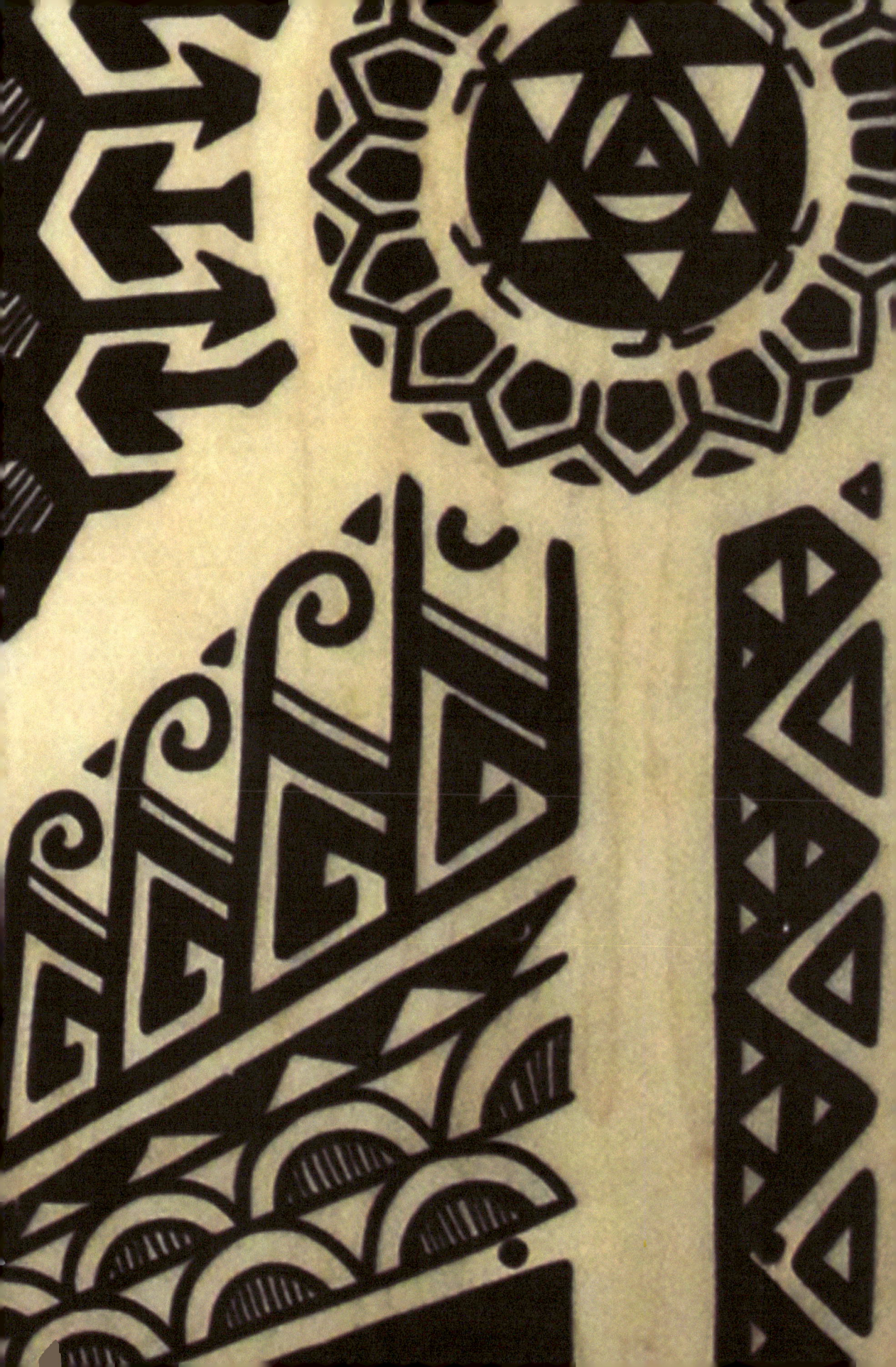

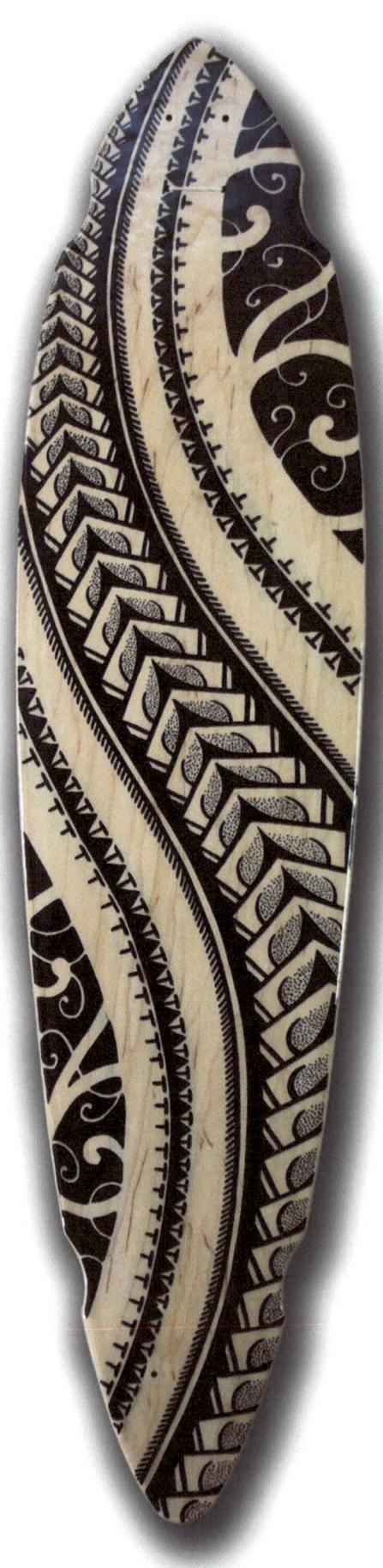

Dividing up the picture plane in dark and light to create balance is always a prime function of tribal art.

The center design of arrows represents movement and flow of energy.

The bordering thin lines represents the biological entity known as cilia cells which are there to represent feelers or reseptors.

The next layer outward ended up reminding me of bulldozer track.

And the darker area outside of that represents the outer of what the inner flows through.

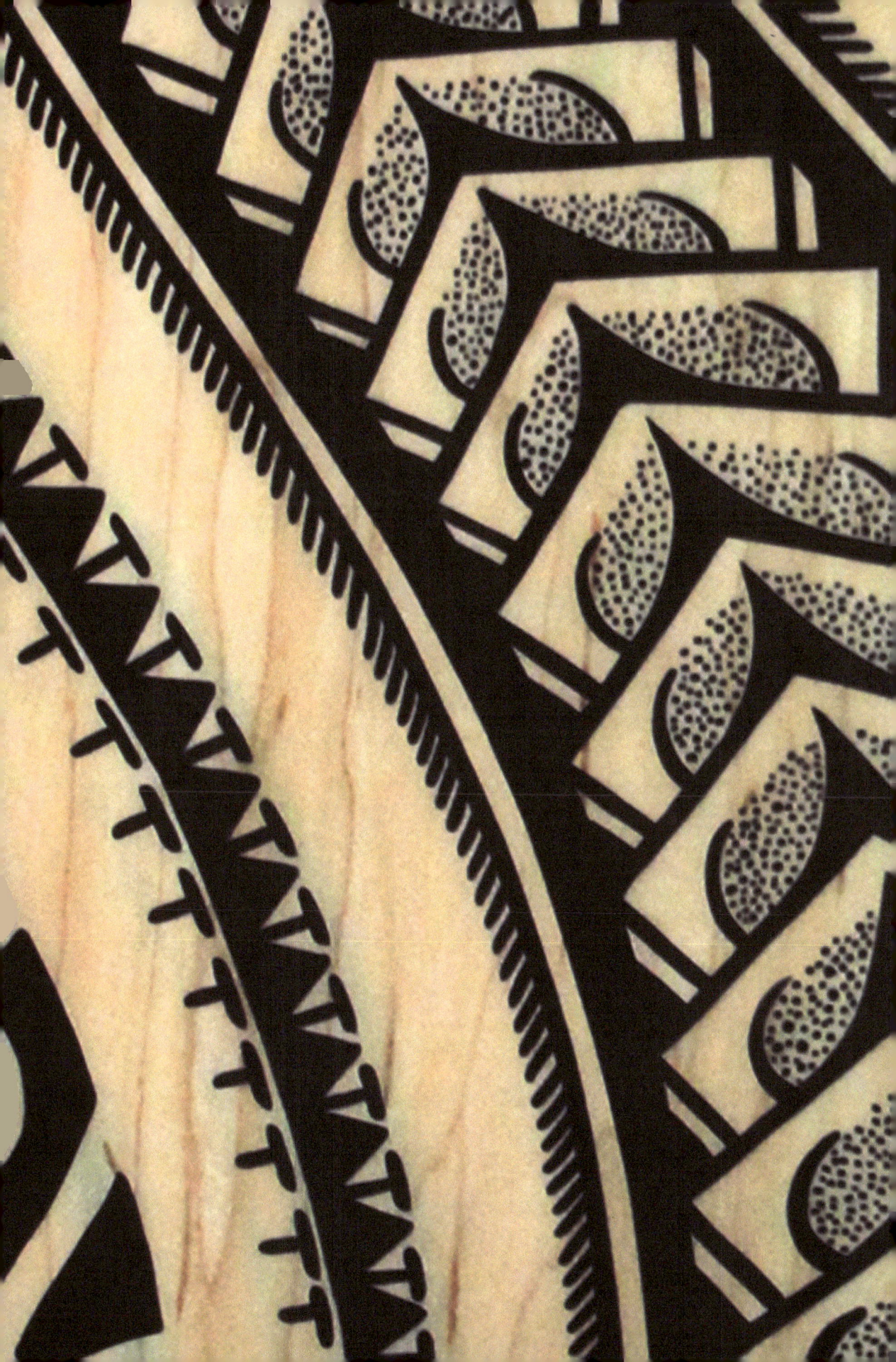

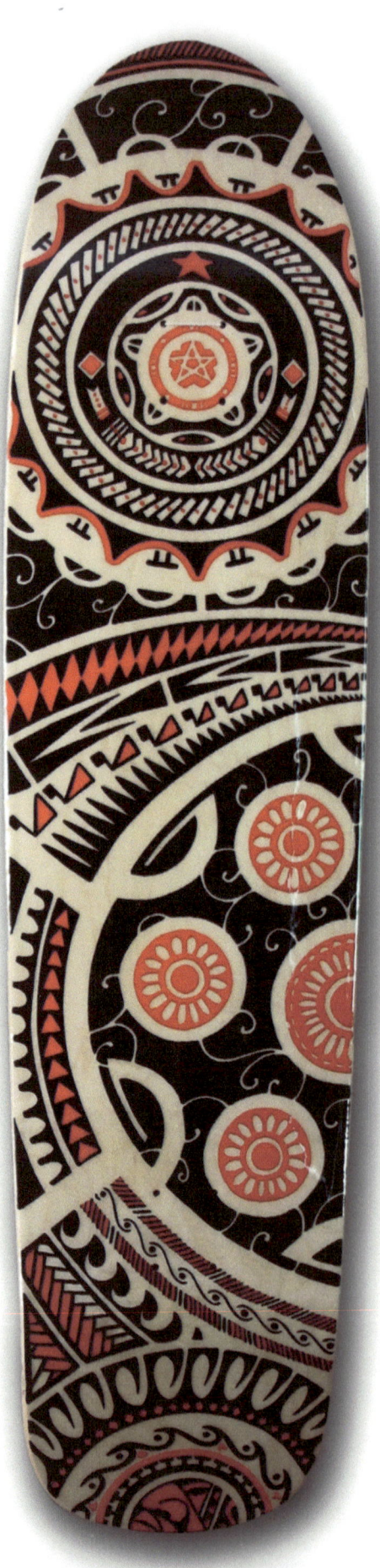

Sometimes I will just combine simple shapes and the repedative nature tells a story. Sometimes I use a theory like the internals of a revolver for the circle within a circle at the lower part of this deck. Maybe the ducks in a row over reeds just above it. Sometimes I will think of a letter in the alphabet and alter it. Then there is no substitute for doing research studying what came before and seeing what other great artist have done. When you are dealing with abstraction and simplification of shapes being generic enough for people to see thier own story is paramount.

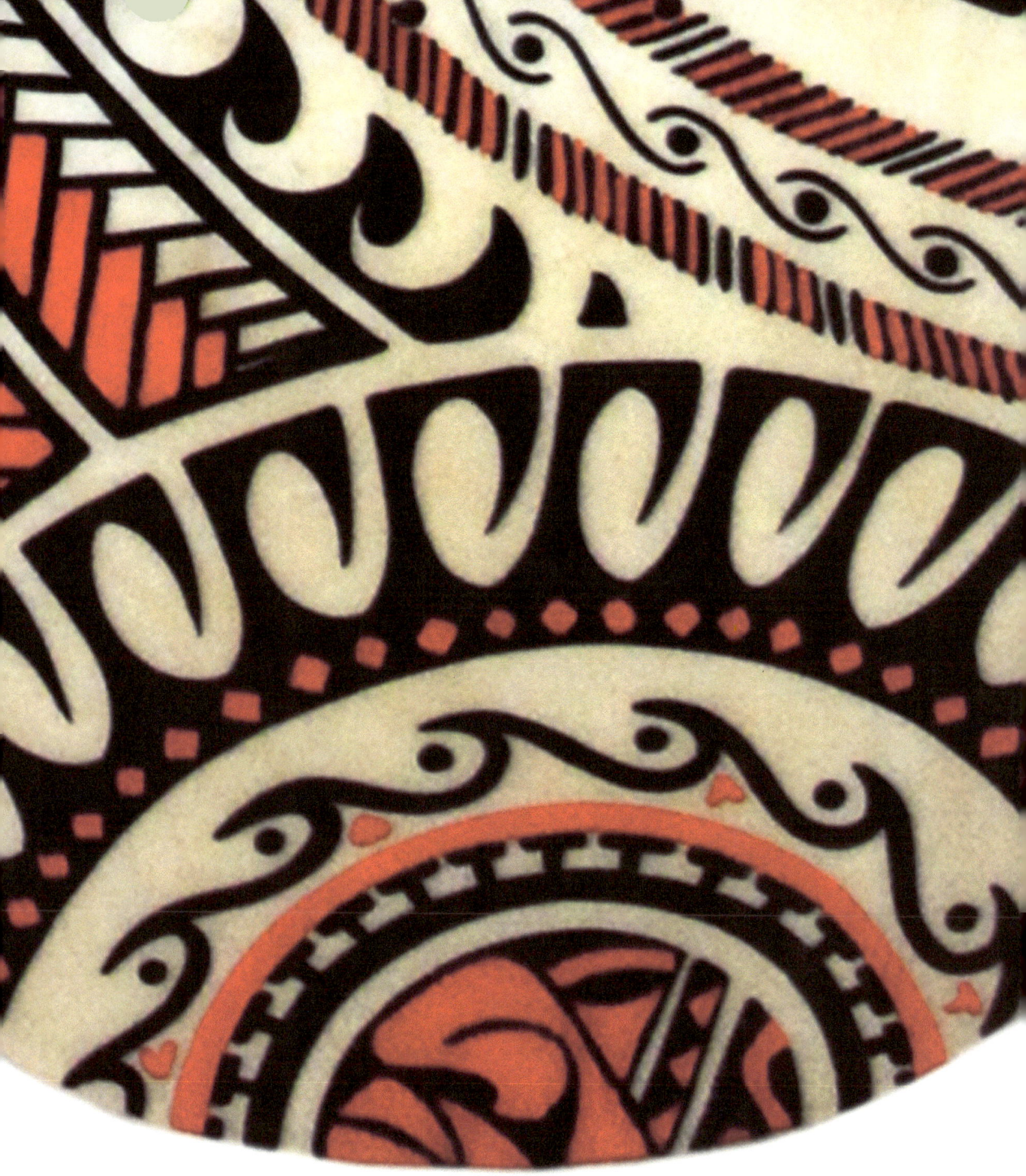

The face on the bottom is keeping a watchful eye on the tuning keys, waves and sun rays give base to the rest of the design.

On the previous page "ducks in a row" is flanked by what may be tall reeds below and the theory of male-female above.

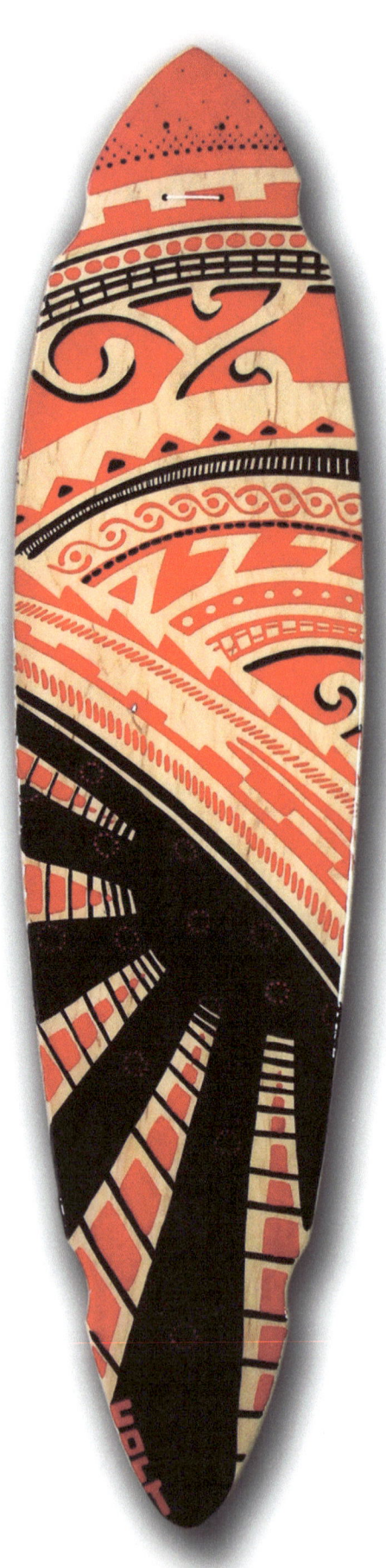

The negative space "Y" at the top was actually a symbol I used to desribe 2 into 1 and 1 into 2.

Above that was the generic symbol for a fence.

By using simple shape in succesion alot of times you create something you didn't even see coming.

The row of long thin triangles reminds me of a mechanical ratchet system.

And then there is the big black sun at the bottom. I got the idea from the red sun on the japanese flag.

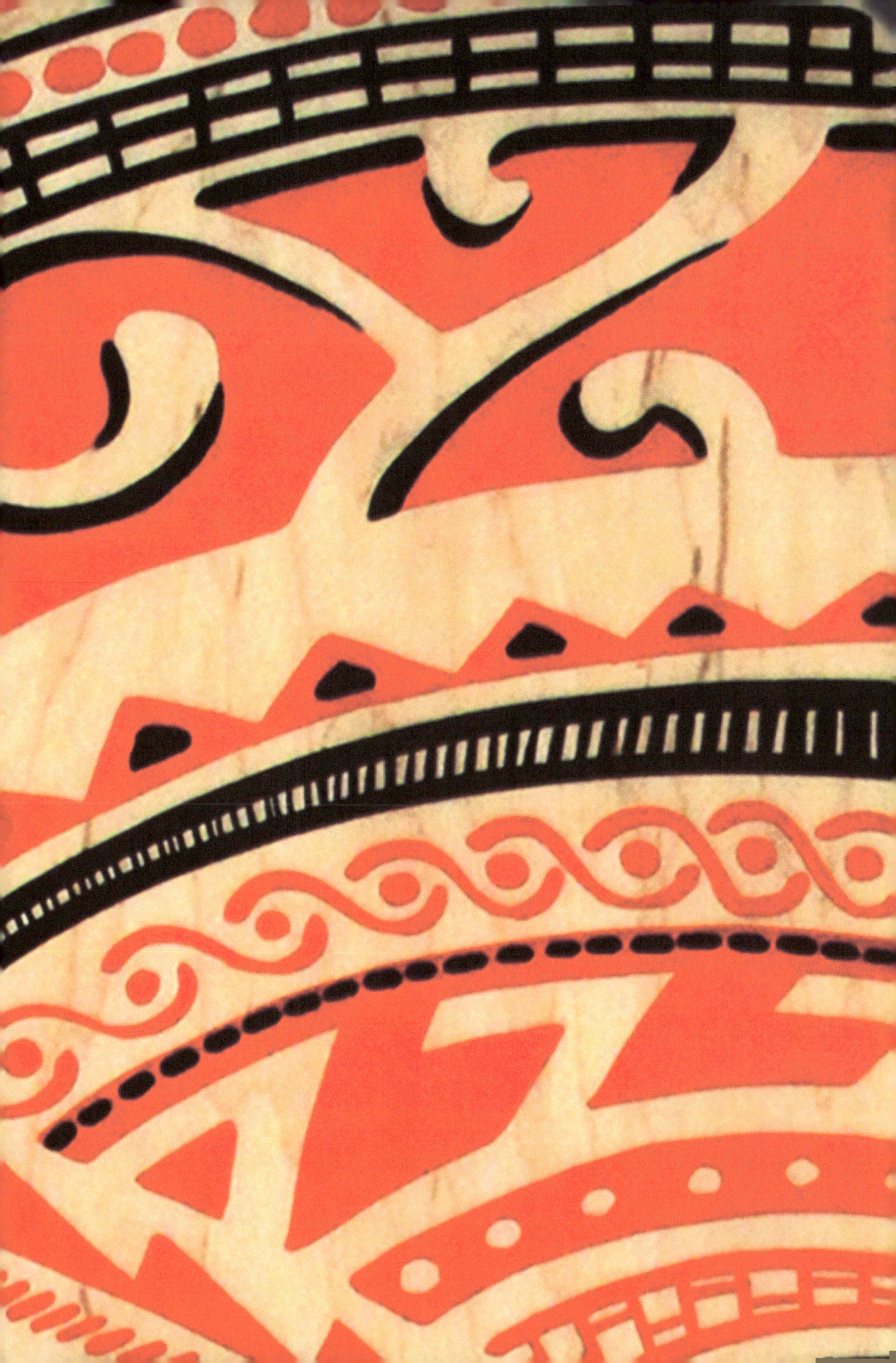

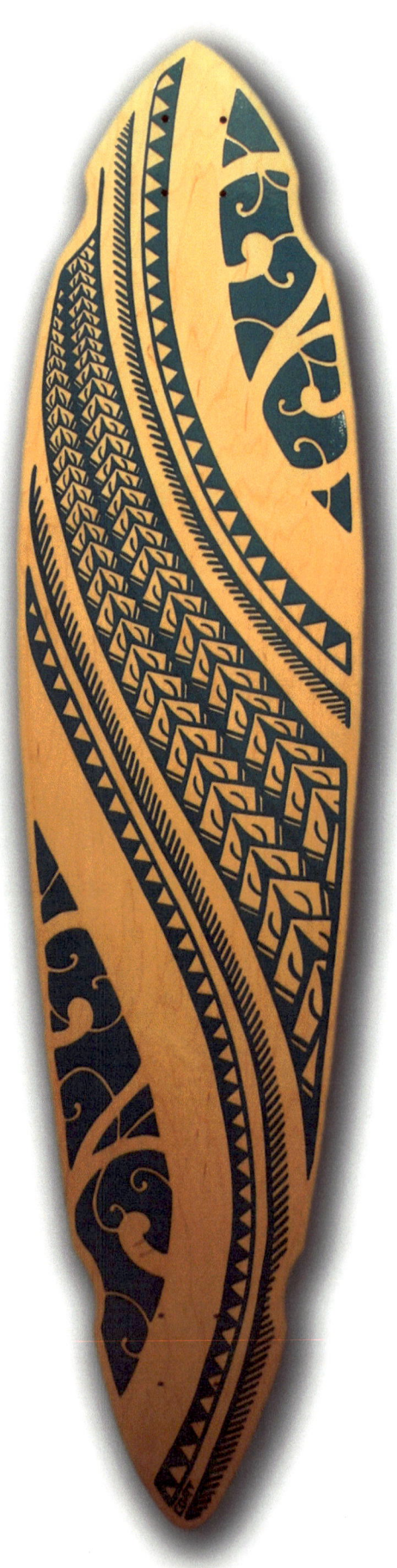

And then there are the shapes in succession. And then there is color. And before you know it you have something someone can make a story out of.
For me it is hard not to think of the water looking at this piece or expierience the perfect jump line at the local race track just looking at the hooks and curves. And if you can tell a story with negative space, That is probably one of the best tattoo lessons you will ever get.

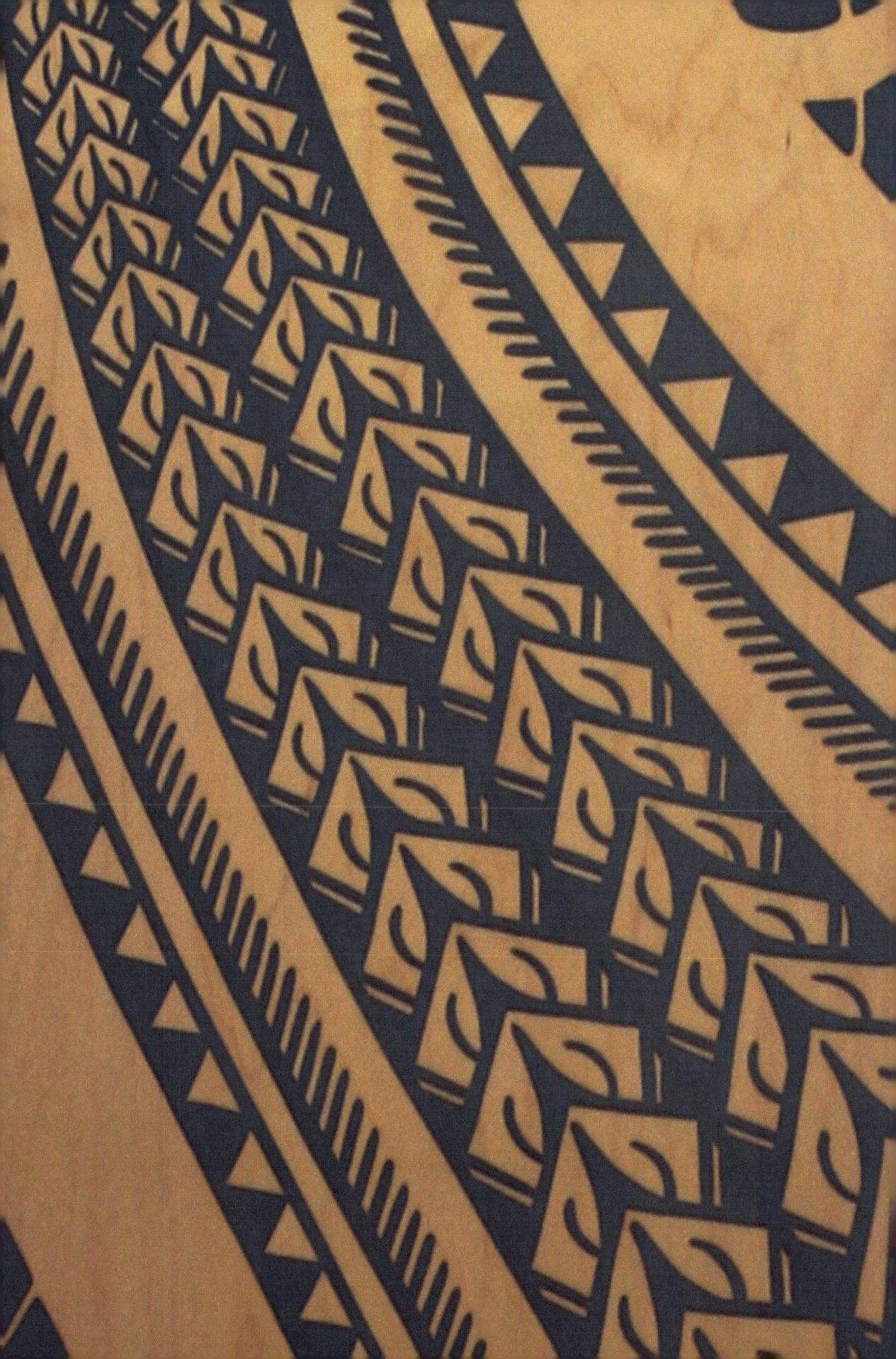

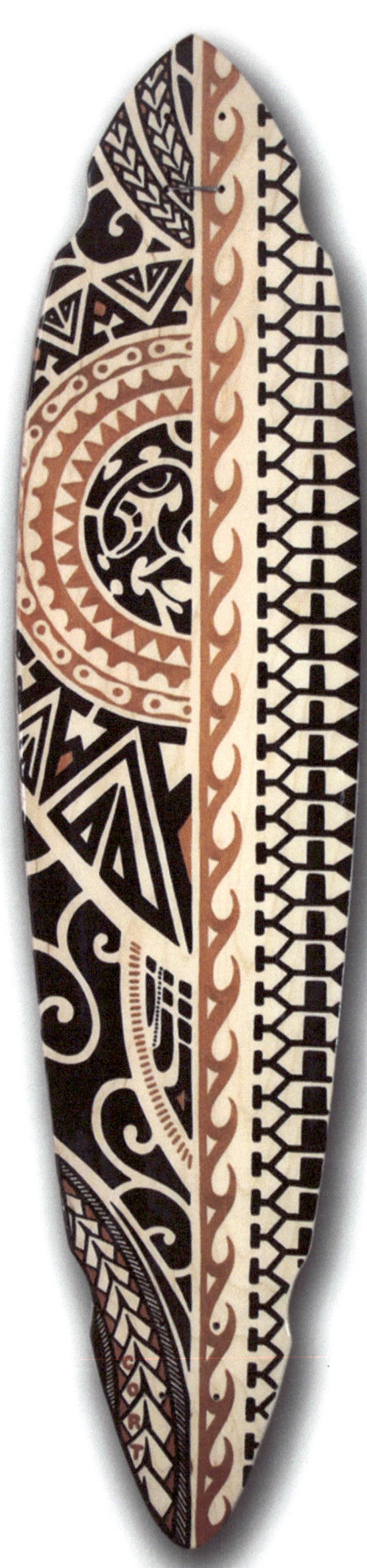

The sun can represent many things to many people.

It has been made to look male, female and even all knowing.

But it always seems to be connected with the giving of life.

Also seen here are the symbols for waves, chains, sprockets, arrows, honey comb and the alpha symbol is repeated around the chain of the sun.

Half of the design going vertical and half radiating out around the face on the left make this piece particularly interesting.

And of course the classic Pintail board lends class and nastalgia to any presentation.

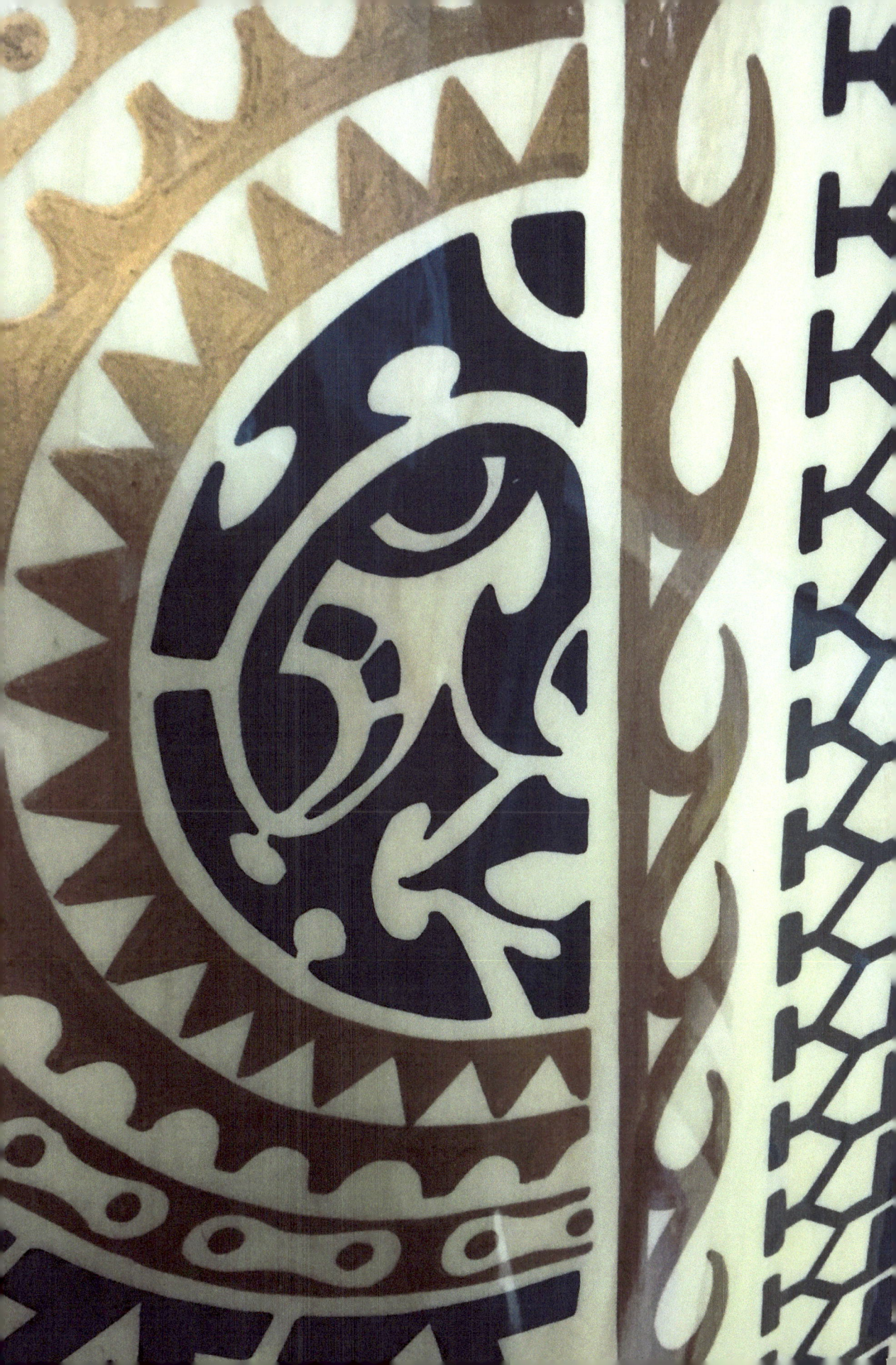

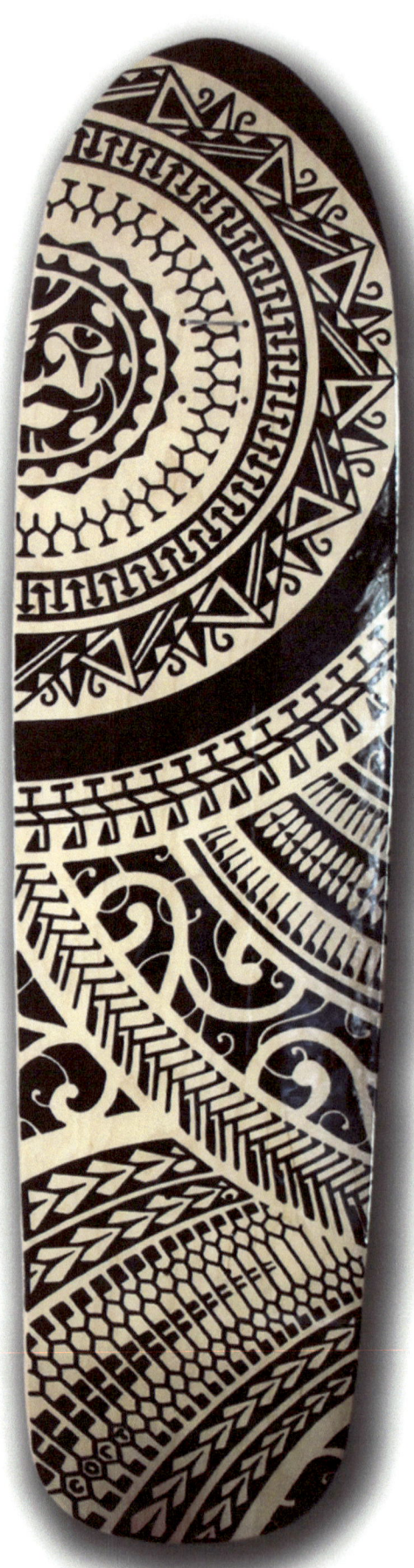

Again the sun takes center stage atop this deck as it's rays almost mimick a crown of structural elements. The alternating direction of arrows implies a transfer of energy between the altered symbol for "enatas" and the face.
  Two thirds of the way down is a marquetry type pattern inlayed with the numerical sequence of whole steps and half steps for the natural scale of music.
  The bottom displays a stretched honey comb design flaked by arrows.with a converging point of view.

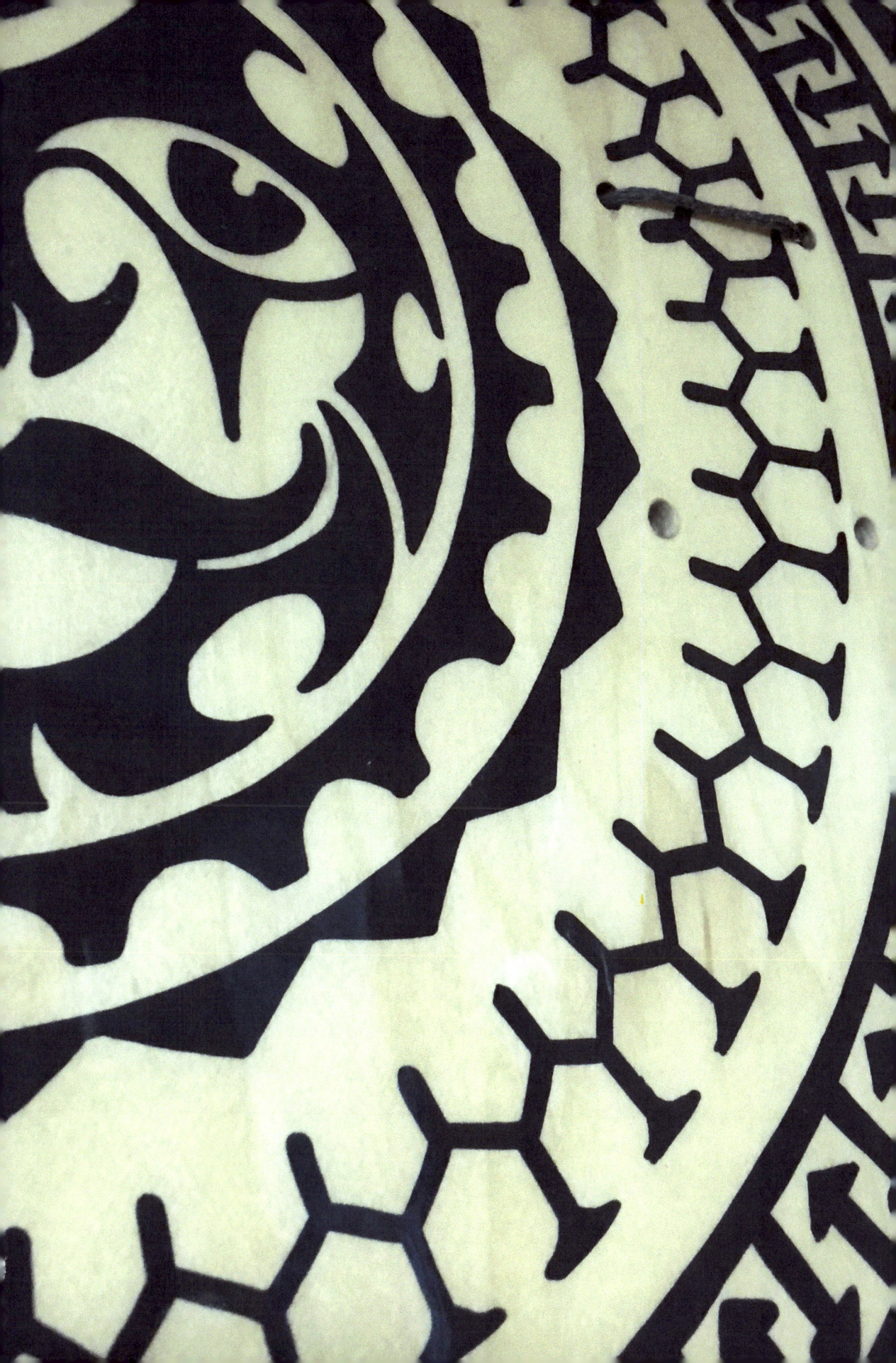

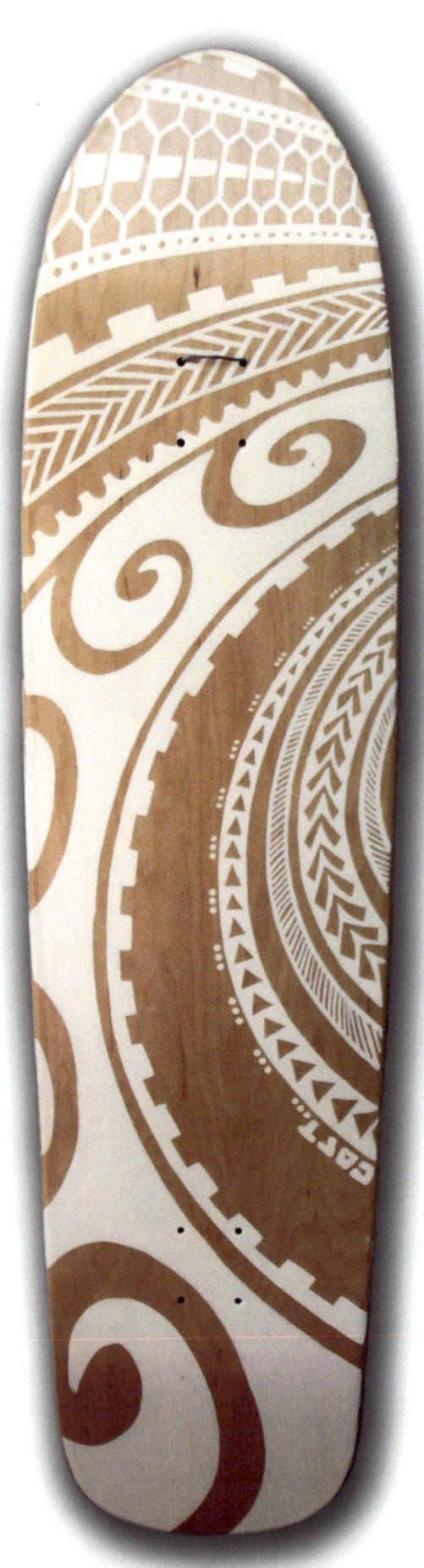

The cluth plate and sprocket motifs are secondary to the giant wave that engulfs the middle of this design.

Here you can see how the positive wave leaves the negative space looking like a upside down version of a wave itself.

The multiple rows of arrows give a definite direction to the overall design.

Converging lines show a sort of foreground to background type of scenario.

This board in particular demonstates how simplicity really allows for instant regognition of shapes.

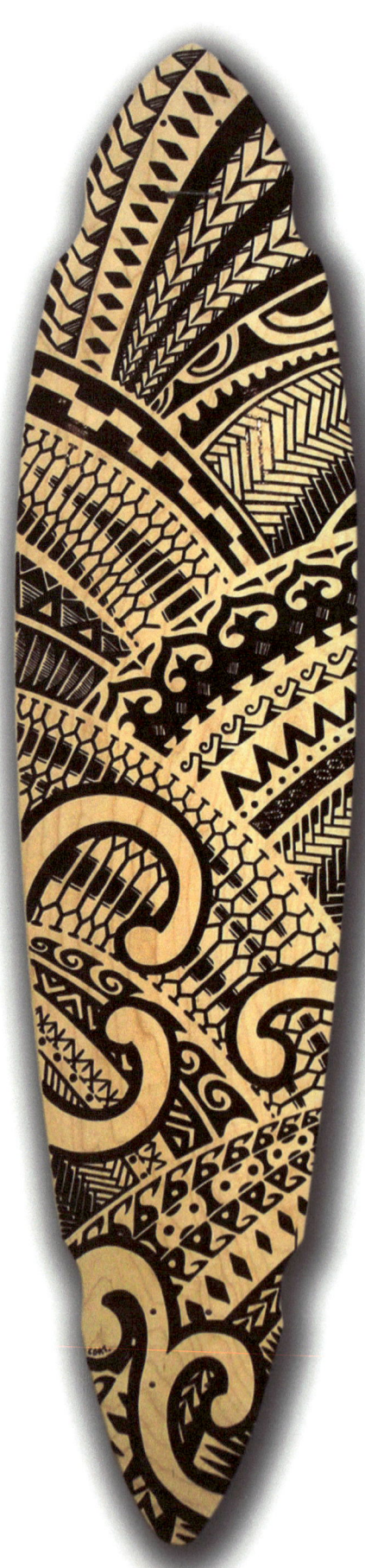

Using alot of complex shapes can tell a fantastic story. The busy nature alone with tons of detail seems to breathe exitement into this piece.

Overlapping rows of different shapes gives a vibe of interlocking as well as front to back perspective.

The are symbols that look like eyes, symbols that look like honey comb, and at the bottom a group of shapes that remind me of a chainsaw blade.

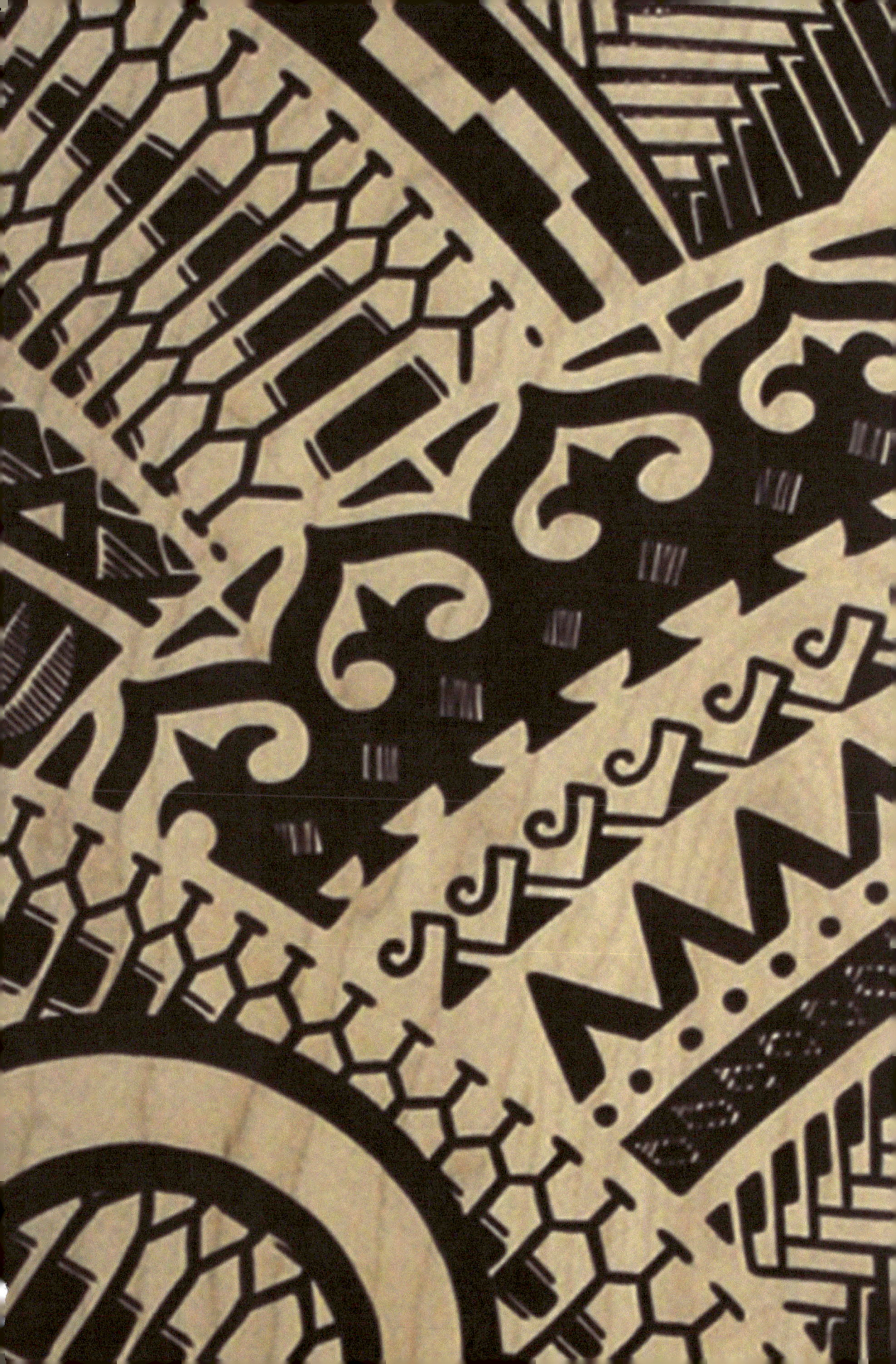

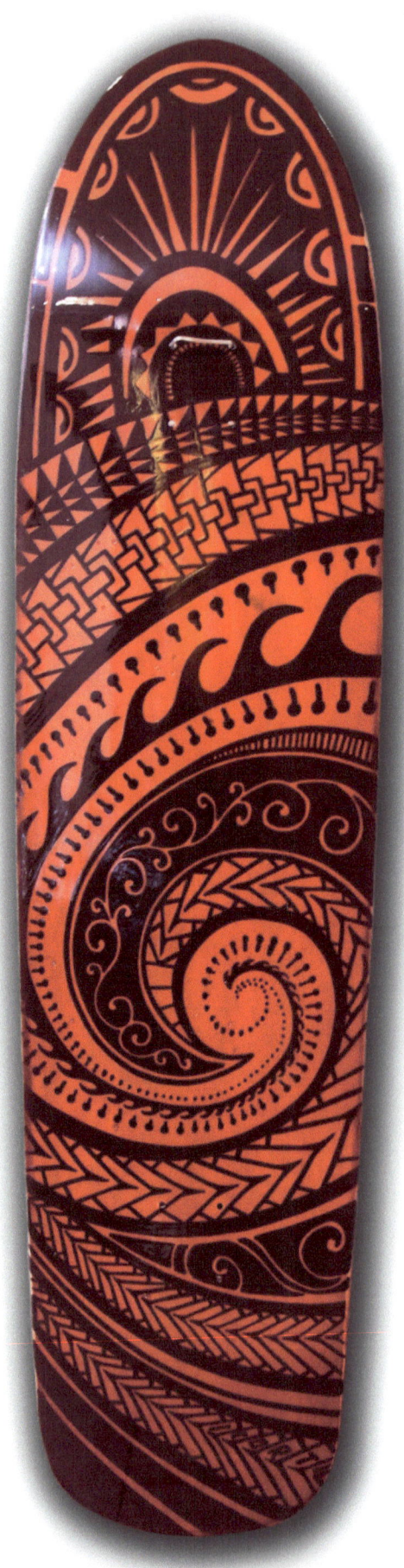

   Here is a good example of how using light to dark and then dark to light contrast each other very well.
   The top shows the images displyed as light against dark. A little lower shows a mixture of both. Then the design is done in just line work. Then there is this big spiral that dominates the middle with a mix of dark and light images.
   Again converging lines adds to the mystery of foreground and background interplay.

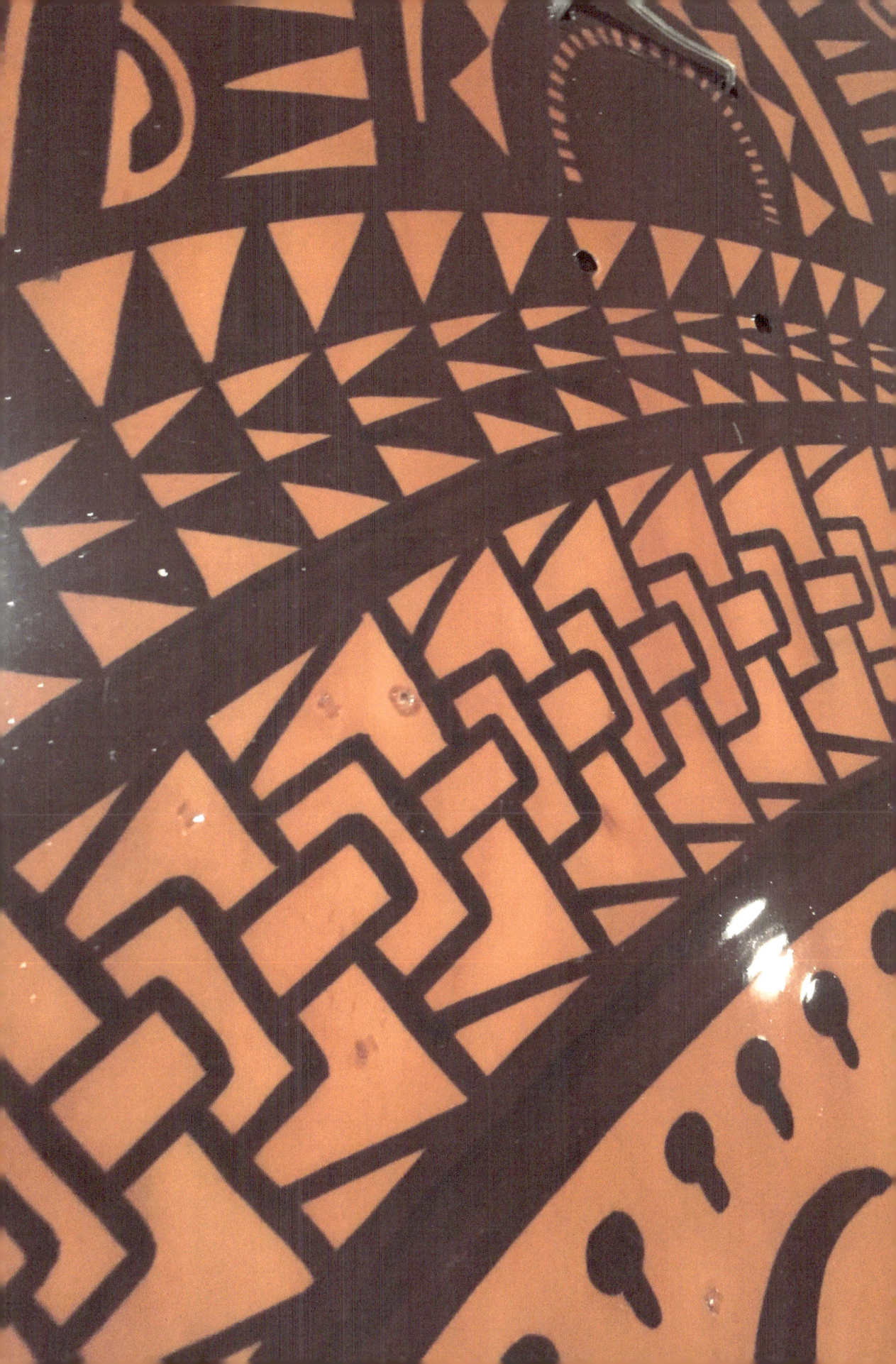

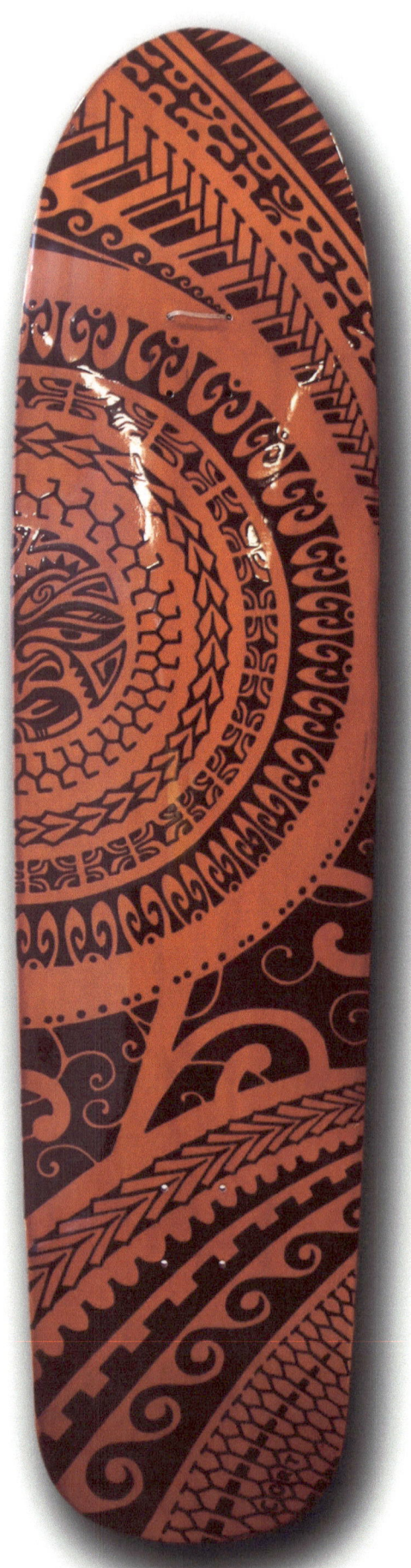

This design is filled with specific images like, tall grass, lizards, and a reference to piano keys.

The sun's face is surrounded by "Enatas" the symbol for humans, arrows, crosses and an ornate style of sun rays.

The two into one symbol done in negative space is flanked by more arrows, sprockets, waves and honeycomb designs.

There is alot going on in this one but somehow remains very legible.

Painted in a dark brown this board was sealed using cheese cloth and light oak alcohol varnish.

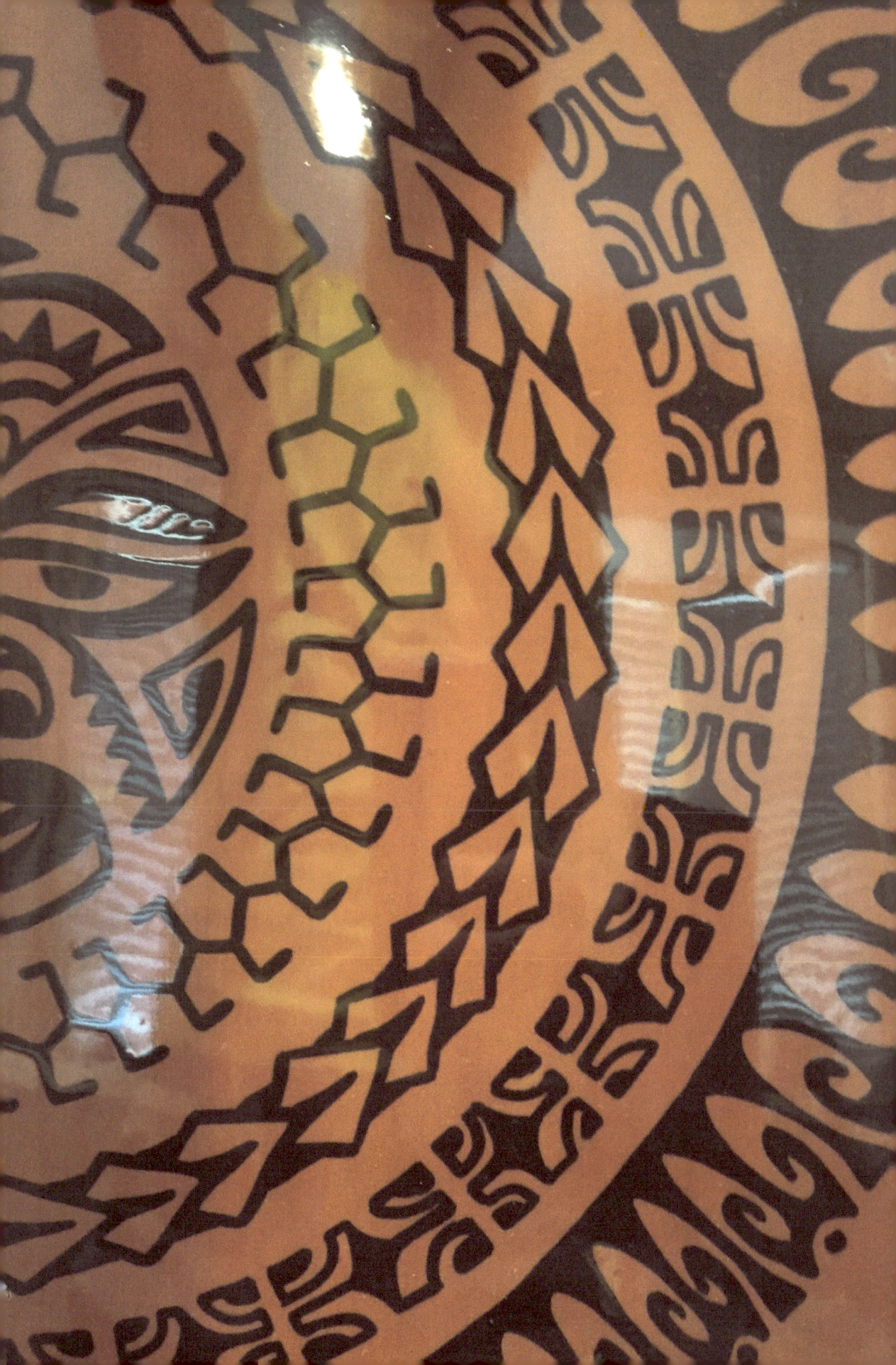

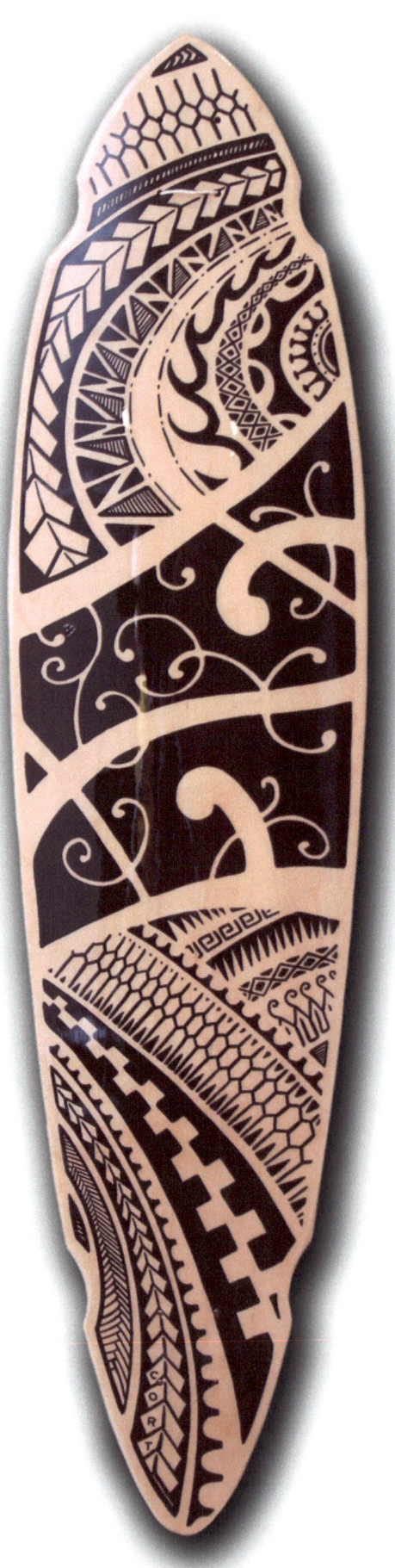

The simpler I block things out in the beginning the better the success of the design.

Here I decided the middle third will be dark with light detail and the two ends will be light with a collection of dark symbols.

There really is nothing like simplicity to create legibility.

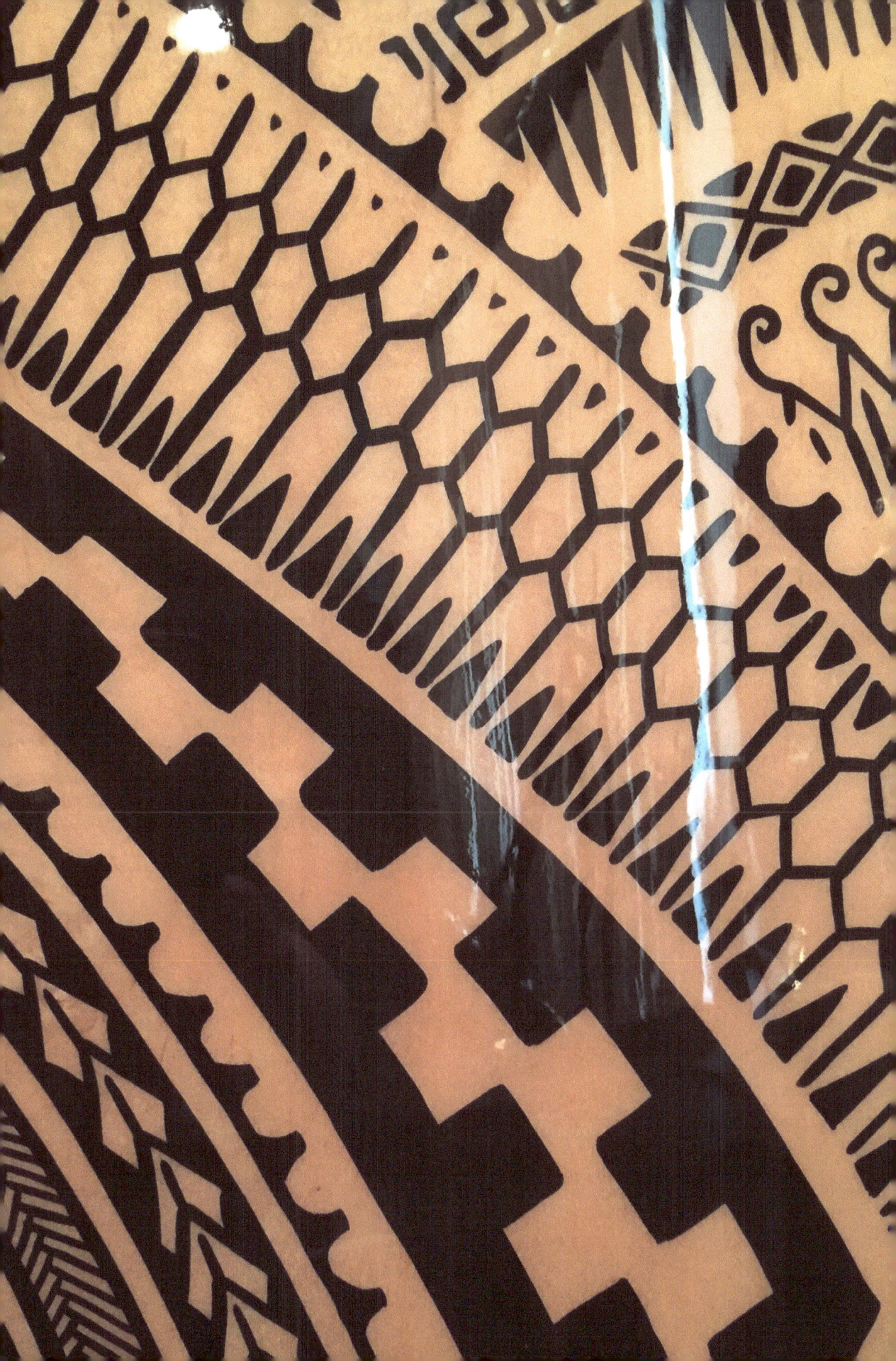

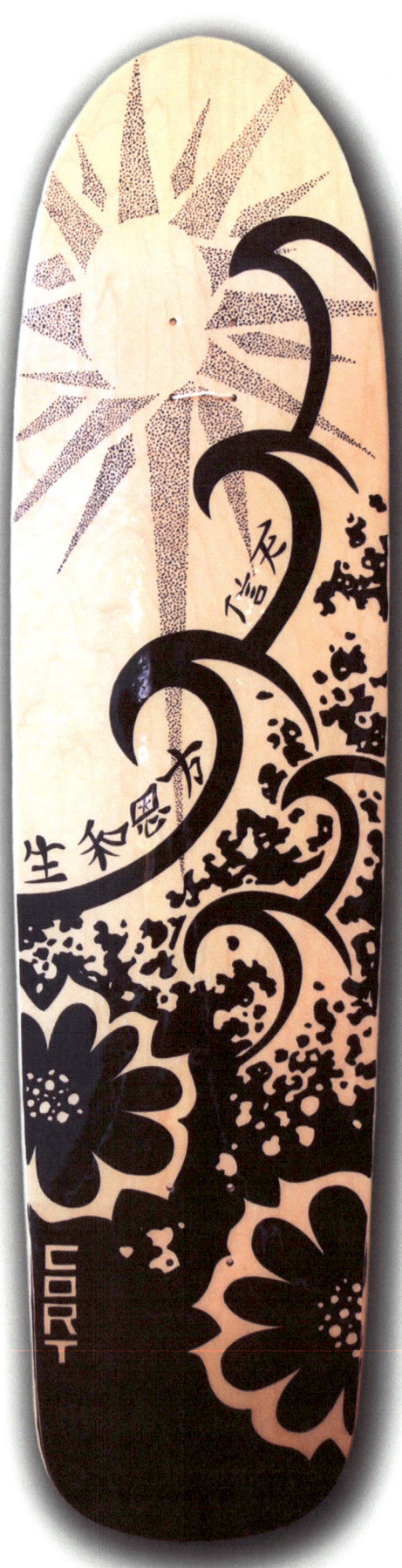

Three simple elements for this one. The sun, waves and cherry blossoms with a little message in Kanji's.

Look at how all of the negative untouched space lets the sun and waves stand out. The wood grain showing through gives such a natural feel as well.

Turning the dark of the water into the negative space of the flowers is a great example of how positive and negative space can define one another.

Using a stippled texture of the sun helps it stand out from the crowd and adds to the overall character of the design.

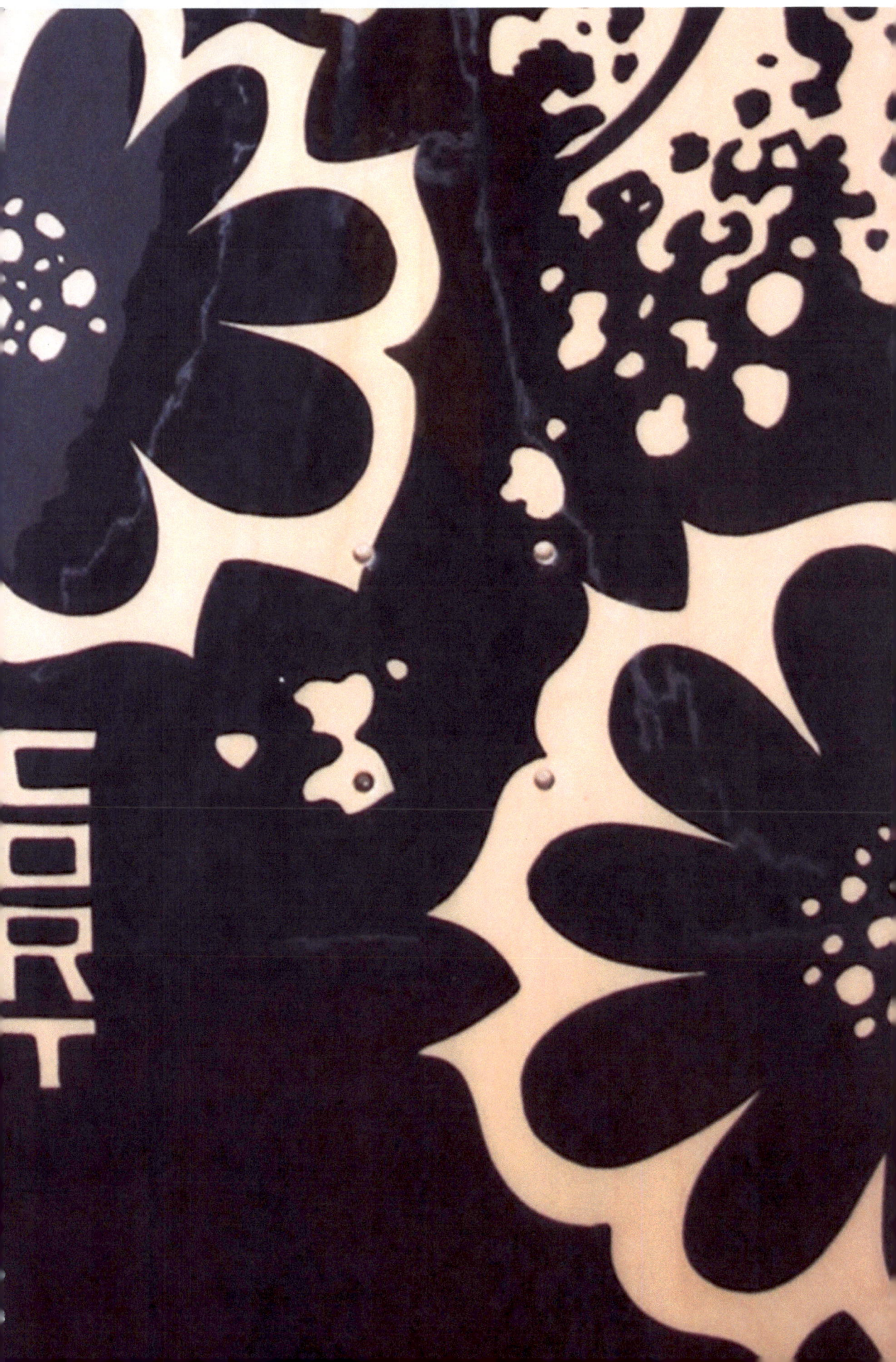

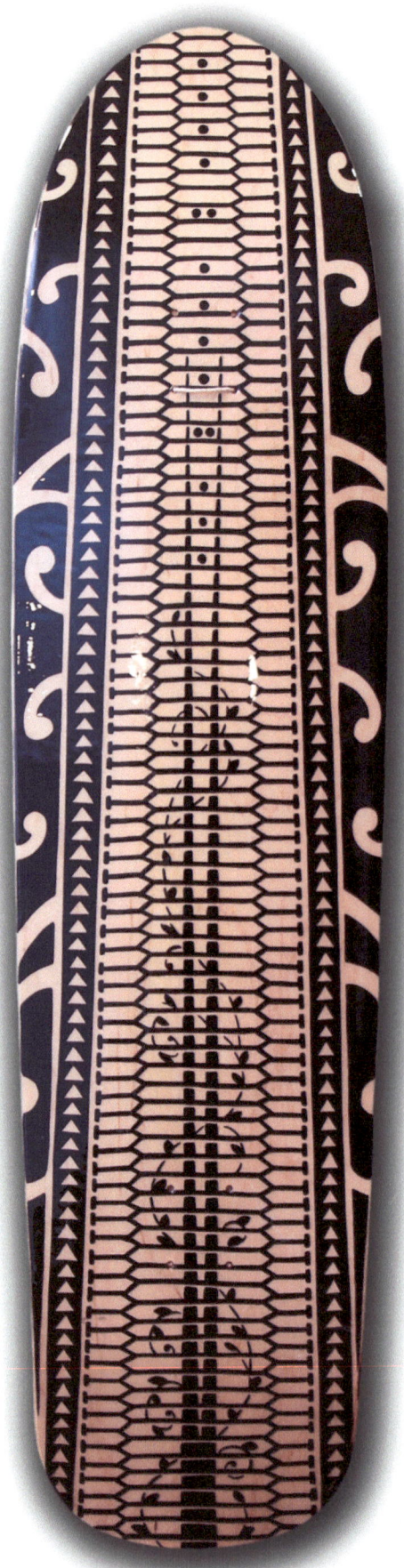

By letting the honey comb desig take up most of the board, I was able to incorporate musical elements to it like the dot formations that represent placement on most guitar fretboards. And then there is the interwoven vine design made famous by one of todays most influential guitar players of my time.

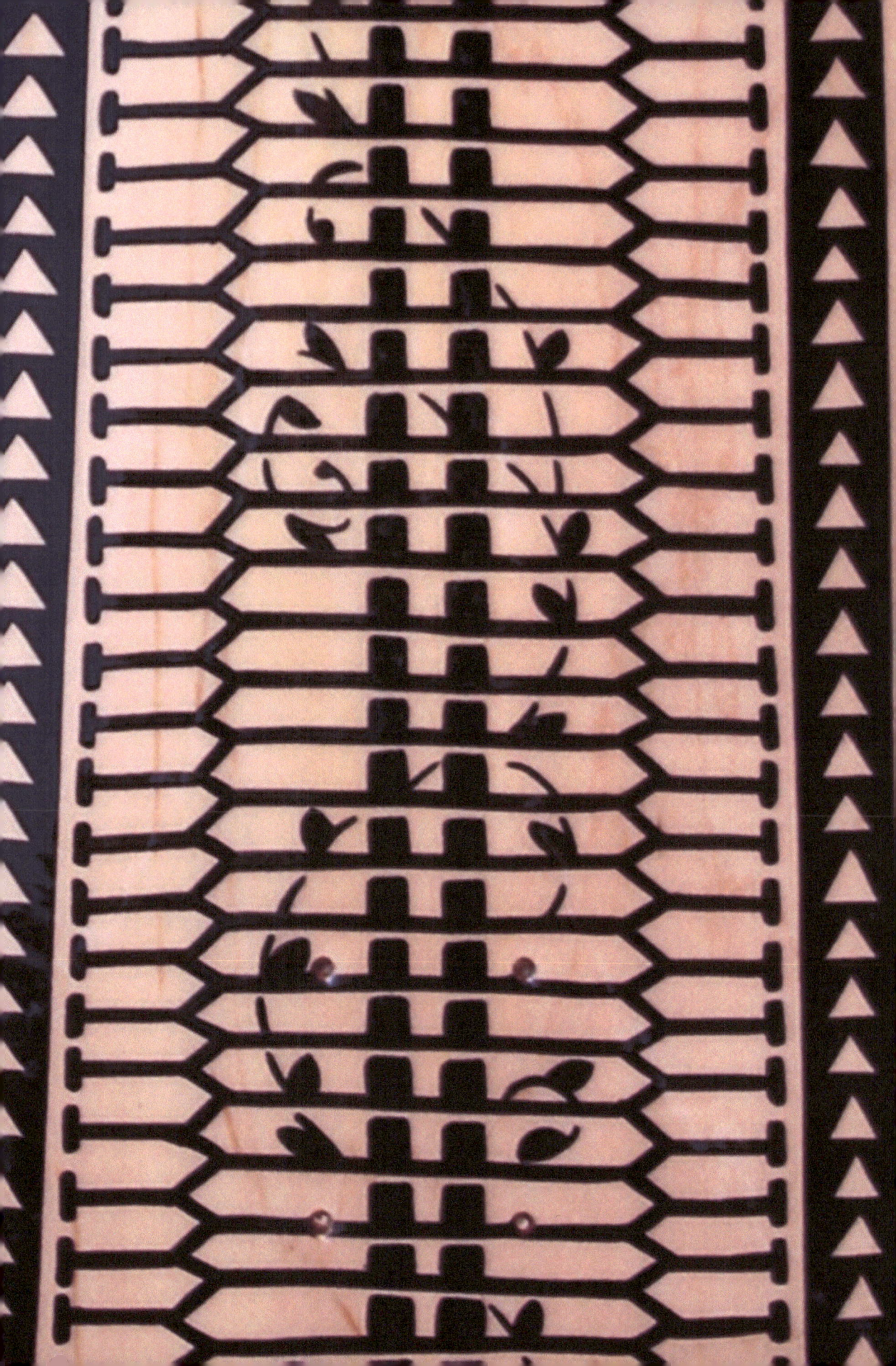

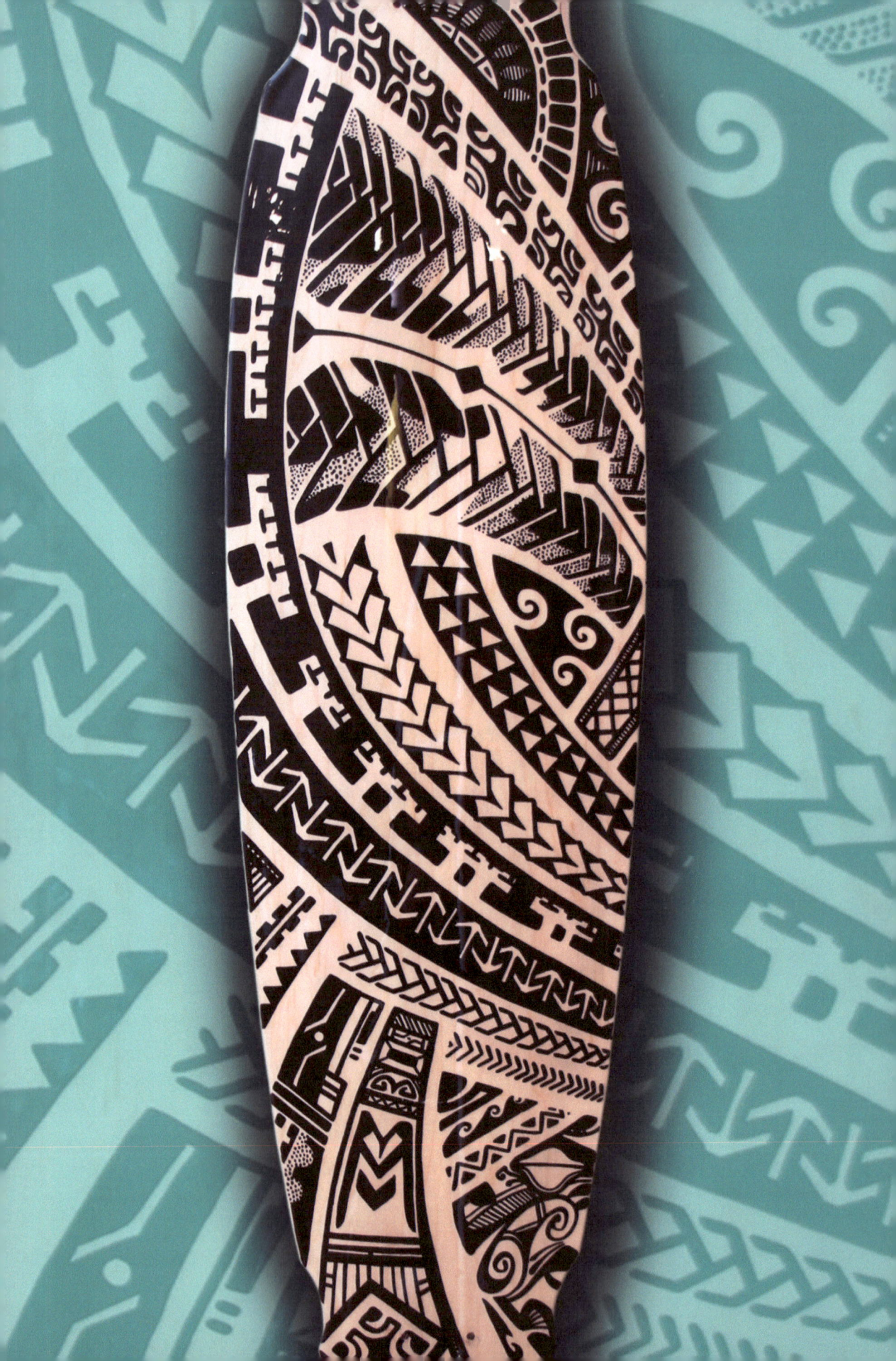

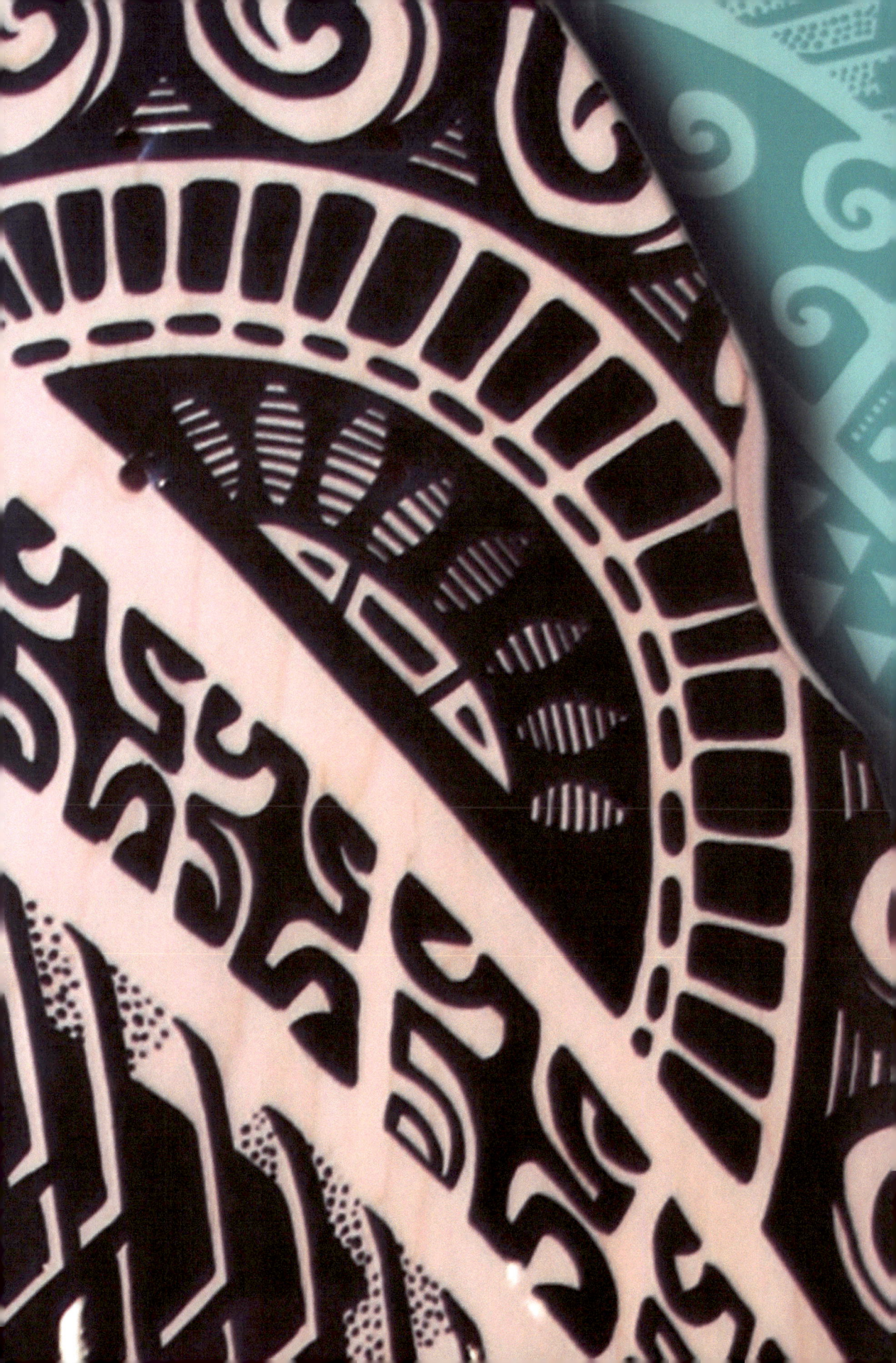

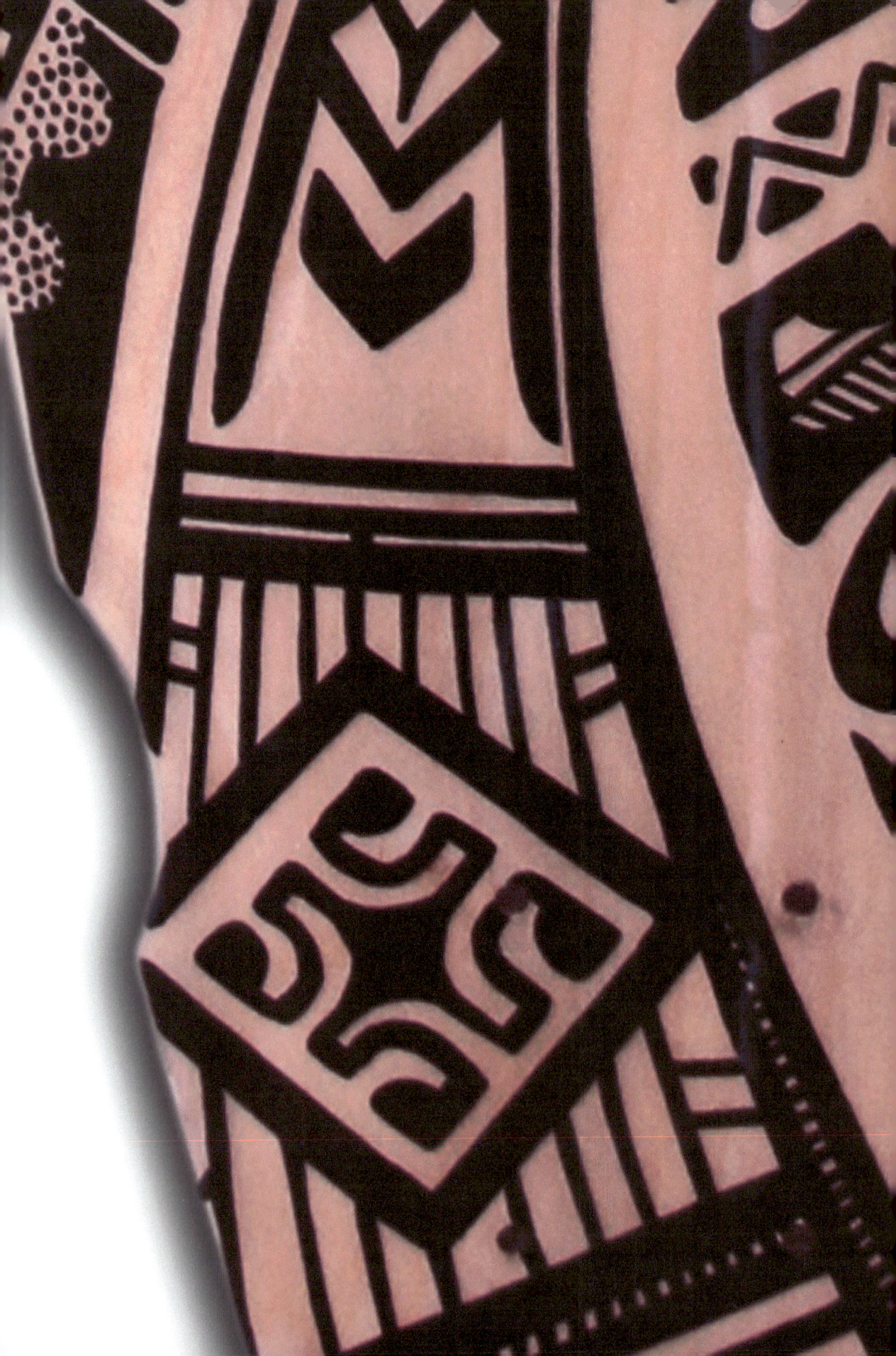

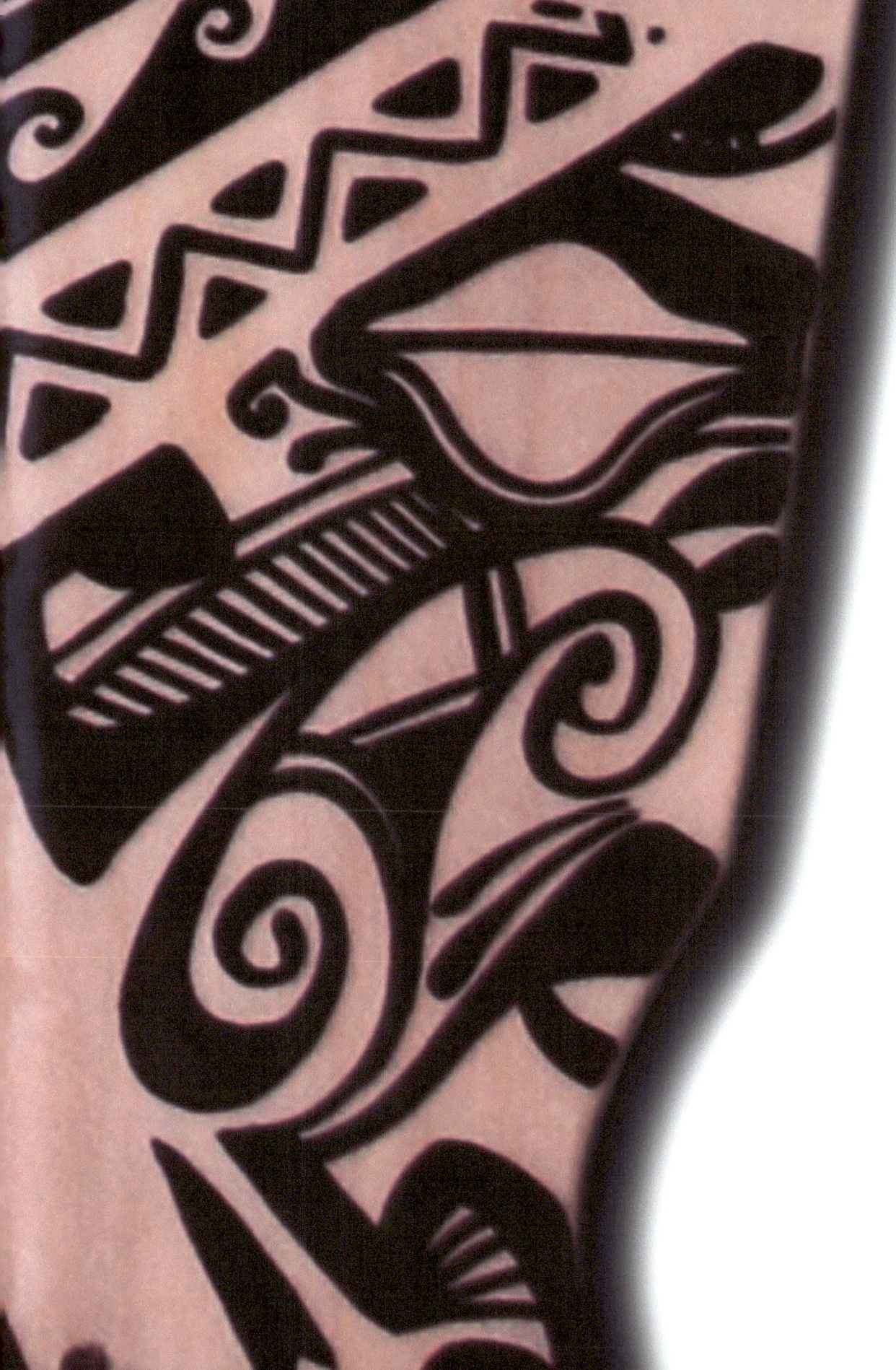

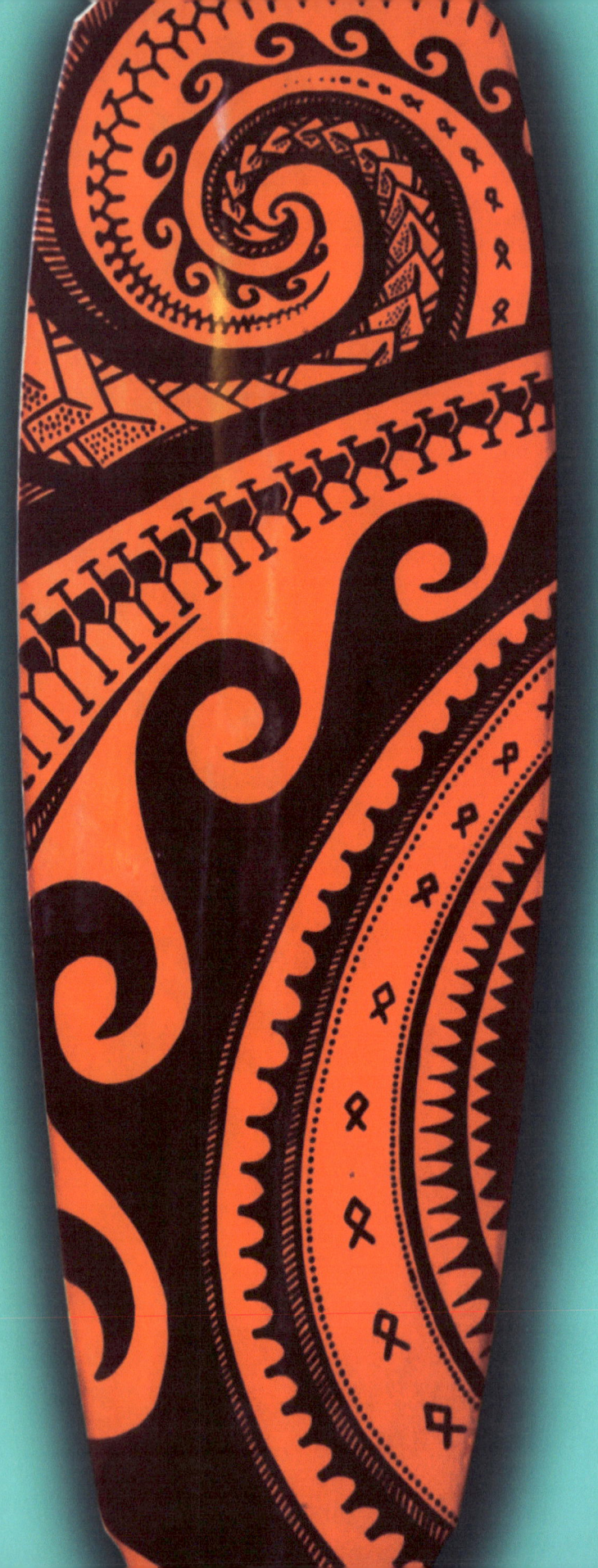

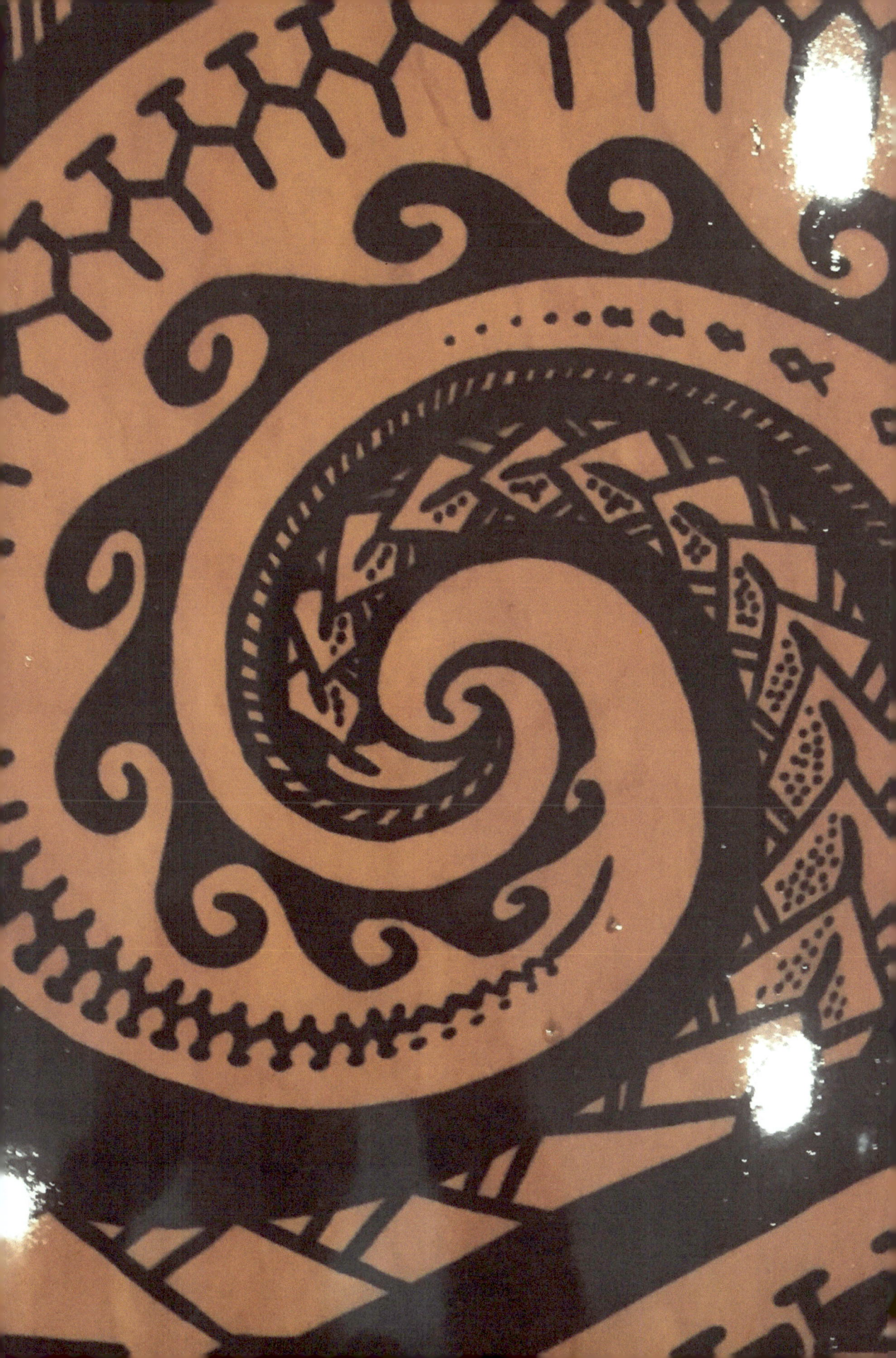

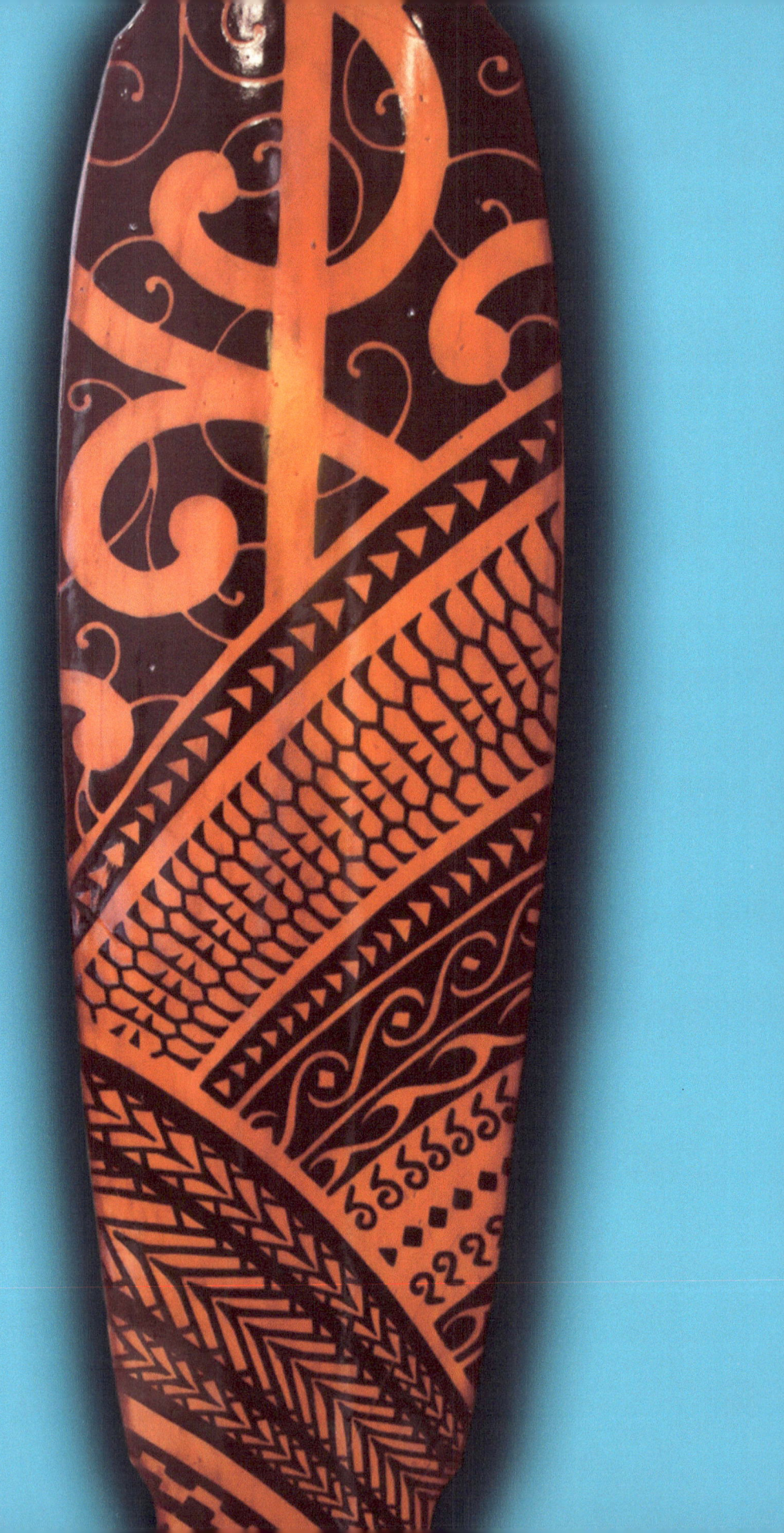

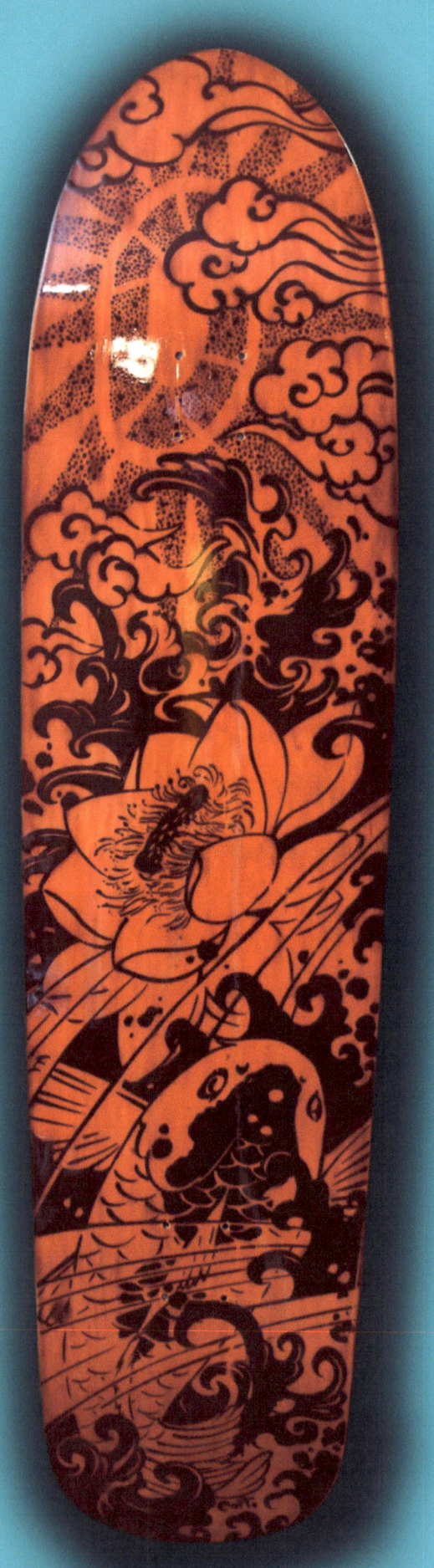

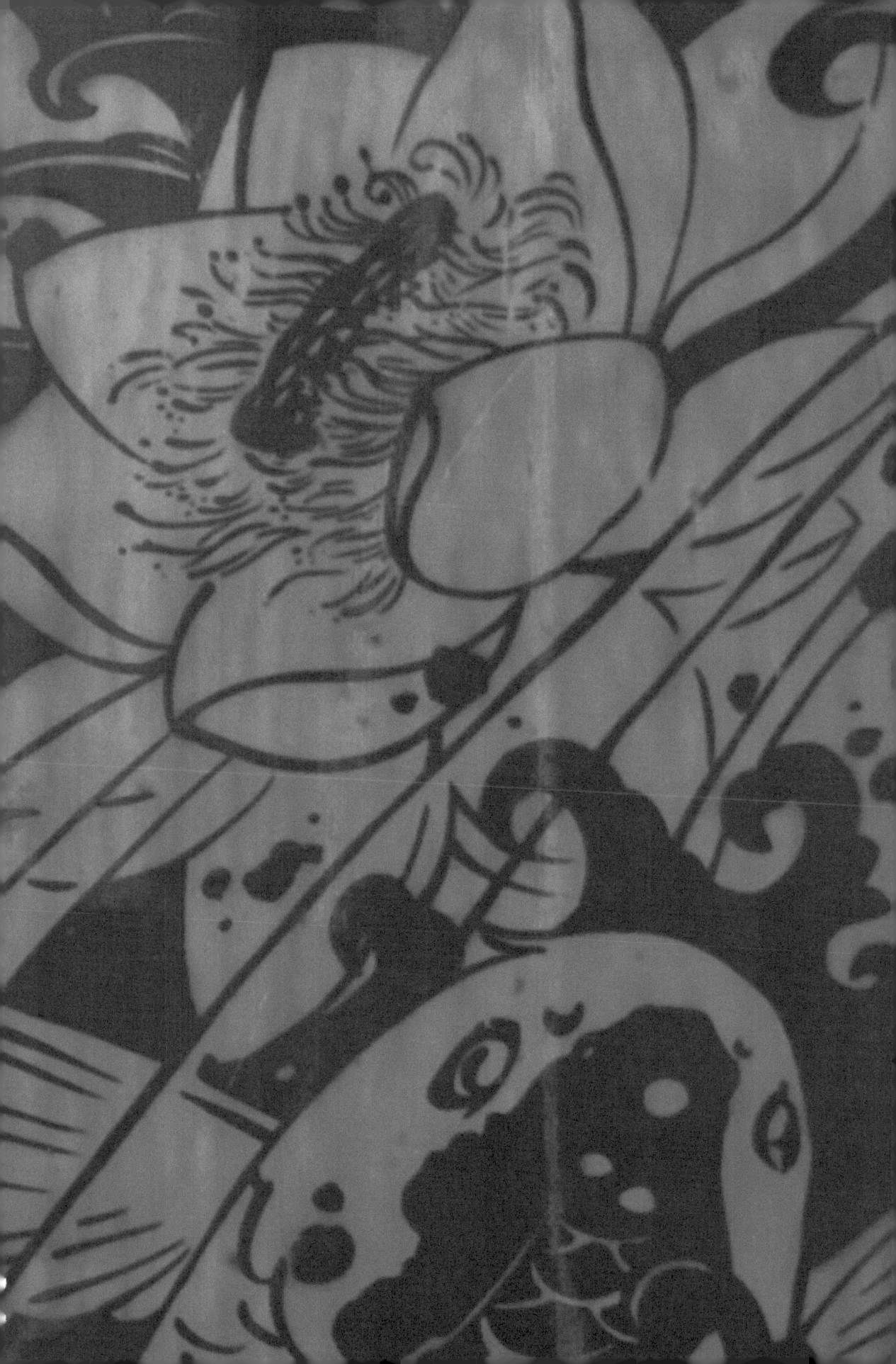

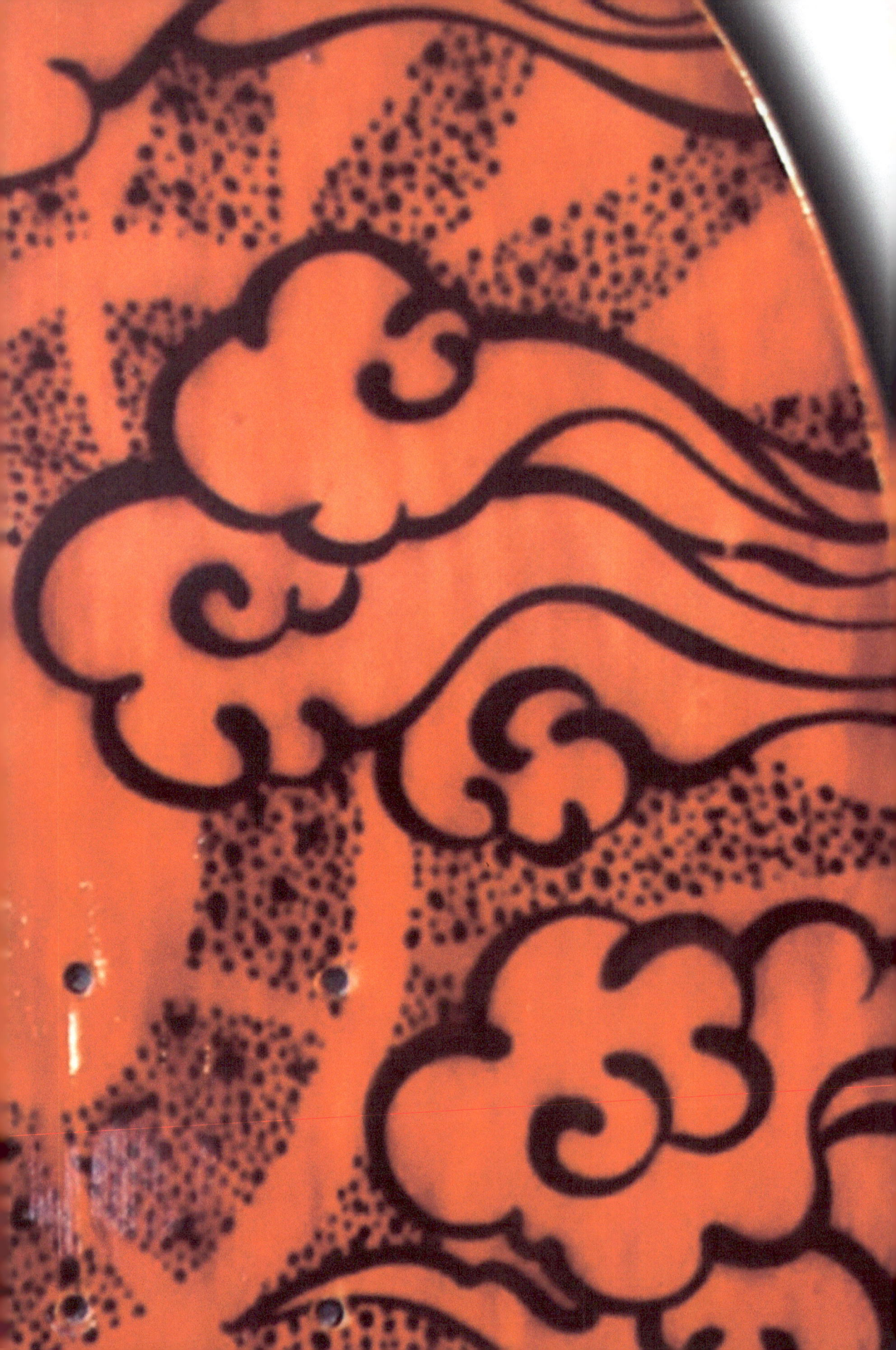

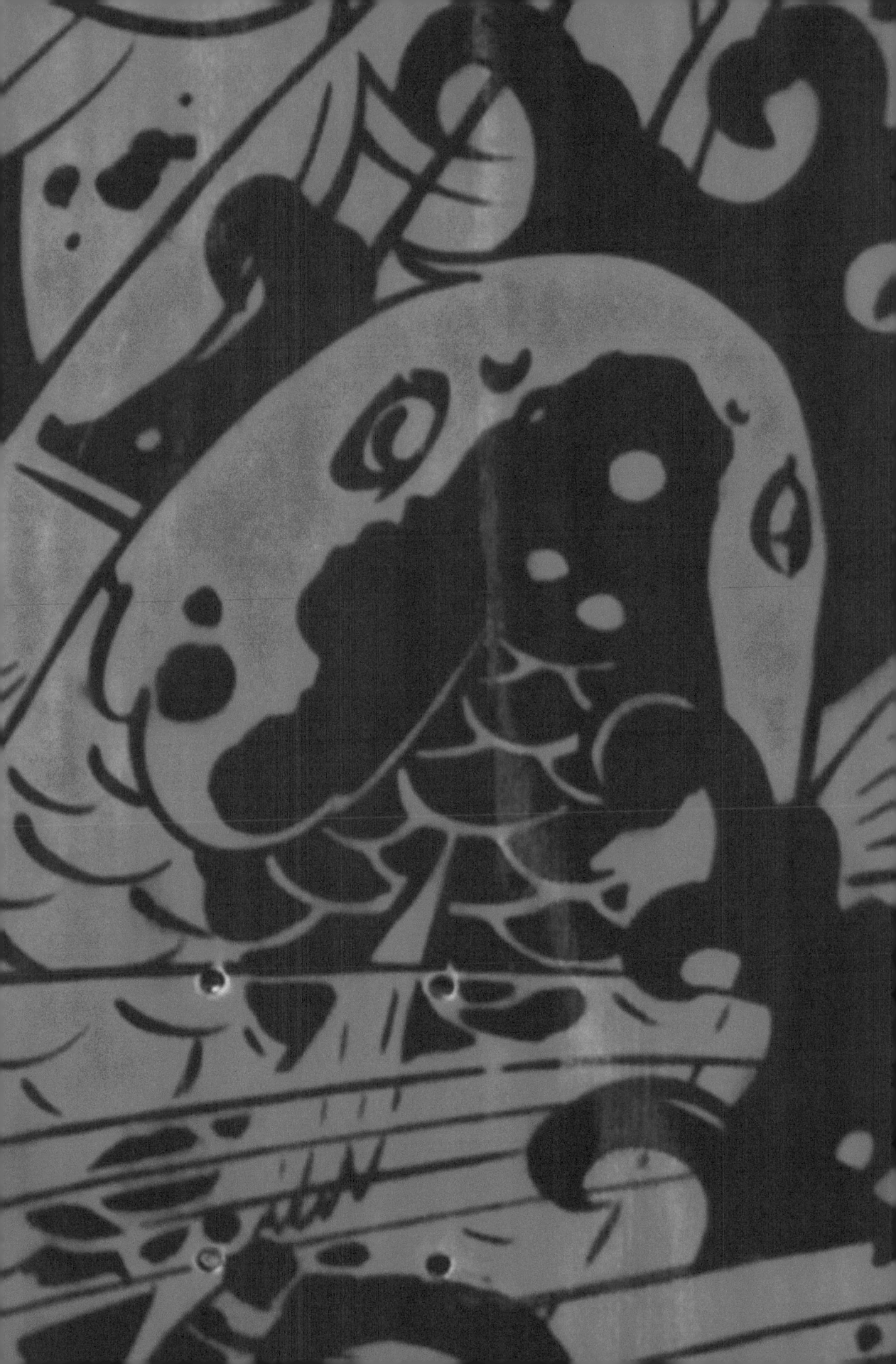

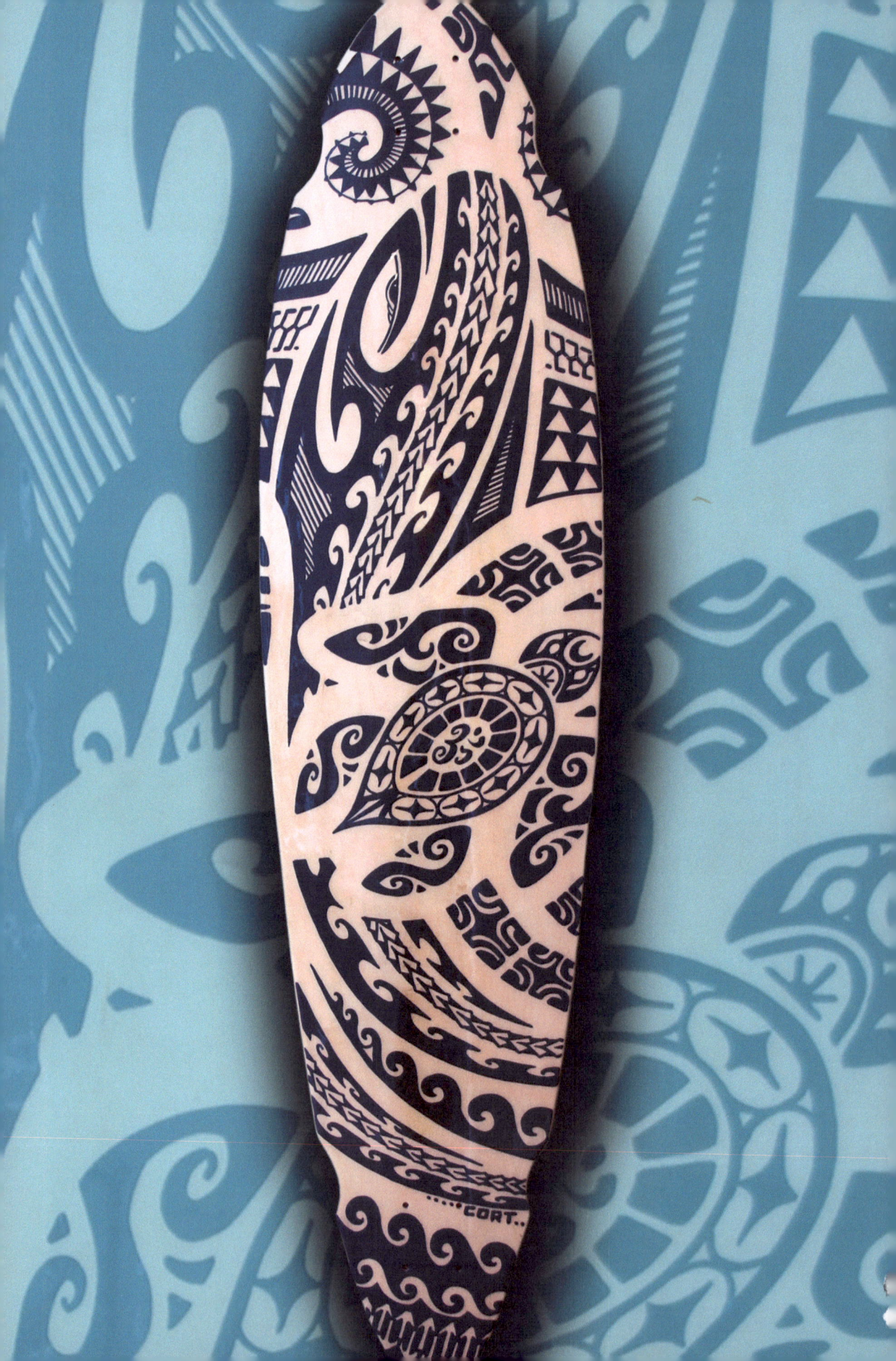

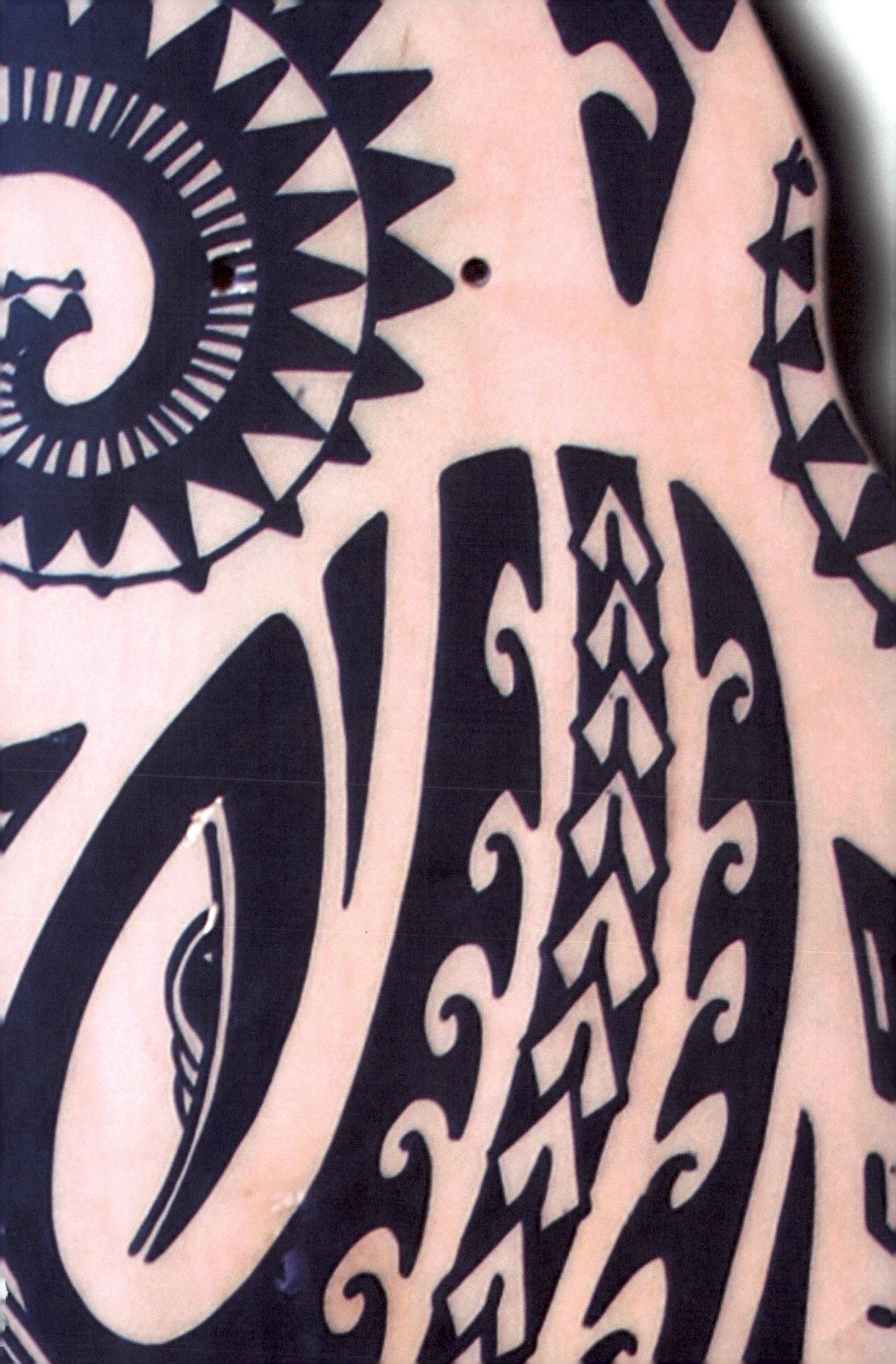

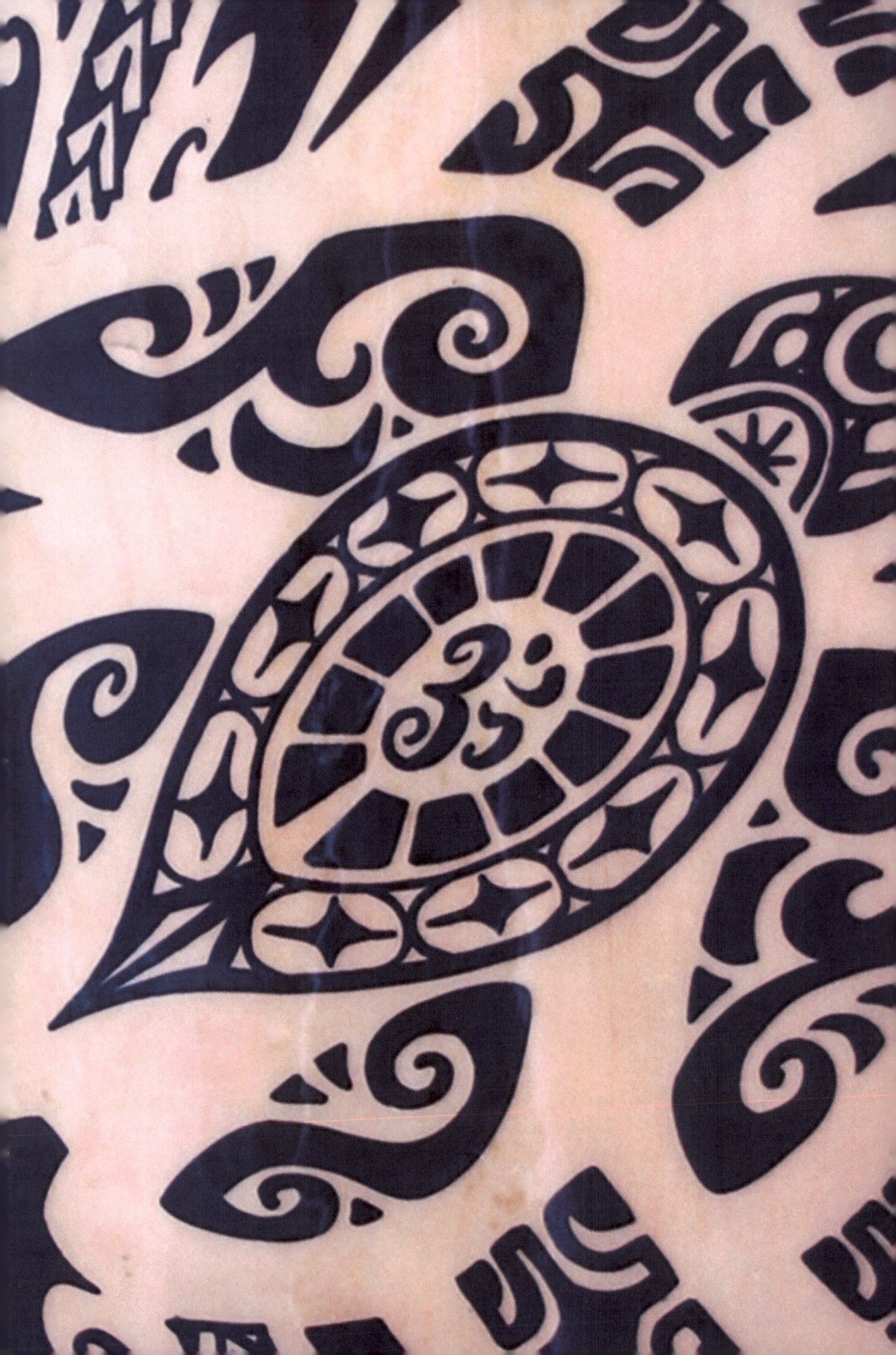

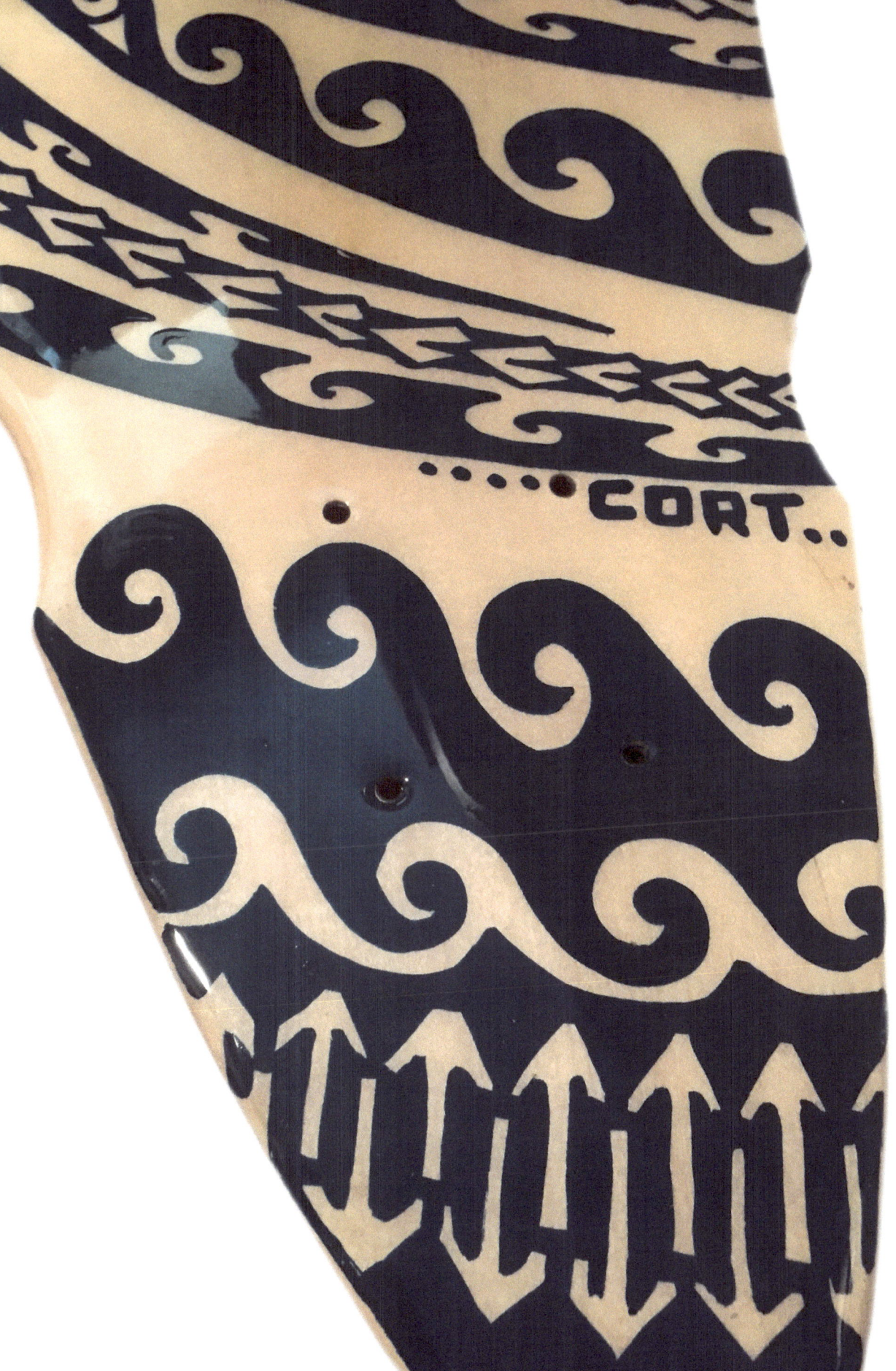

The sun is probably one of the most visually communicated symbols the world has ever known. Done in metallic copper this deck has been split right down the middle. One half depicts the sun, the other honeycomb for nature. In between the two is a single row of opposing arrows which add to the story of the tranfering of energy between the sun and nature.

The outer parts of the face reference both sprocket and chain link as well as arrows from outside towards inside pointing at what is commonly refered to as the third eye position. The all knowing intuitive sense.

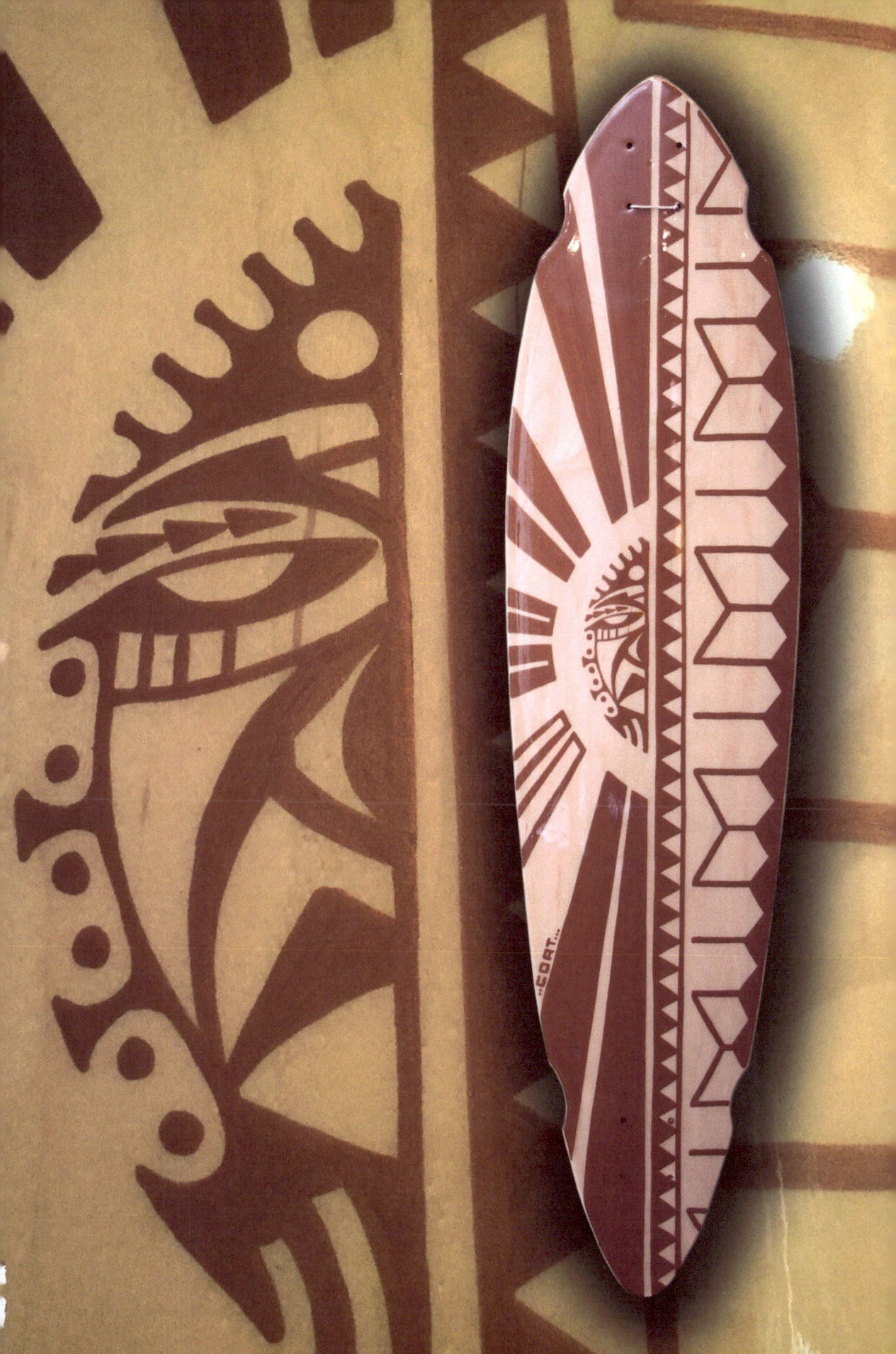

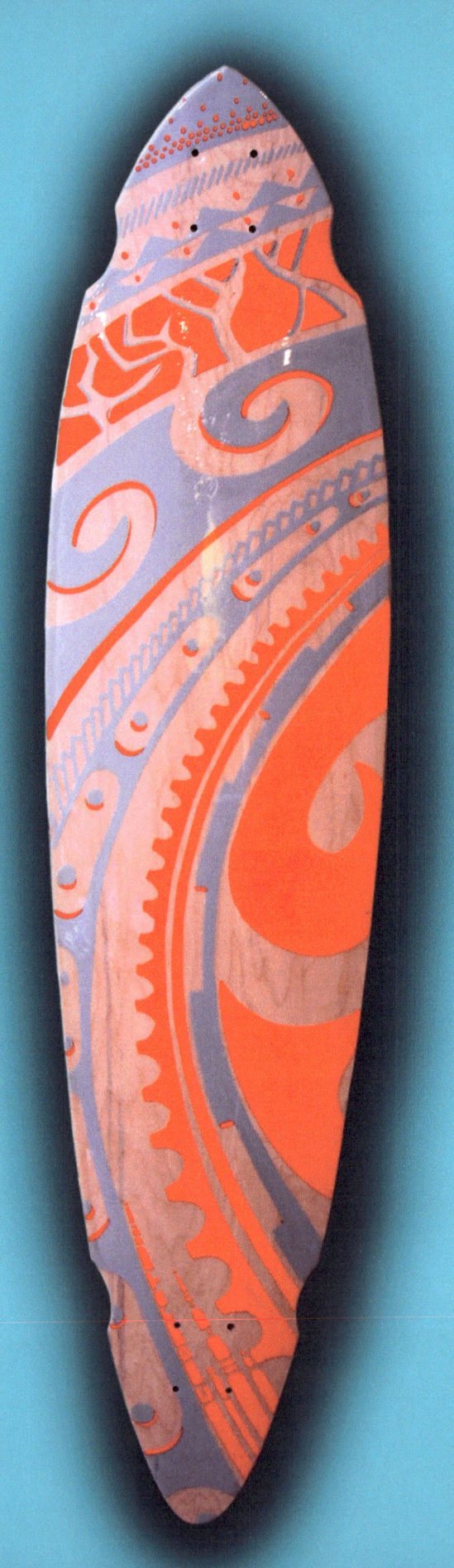

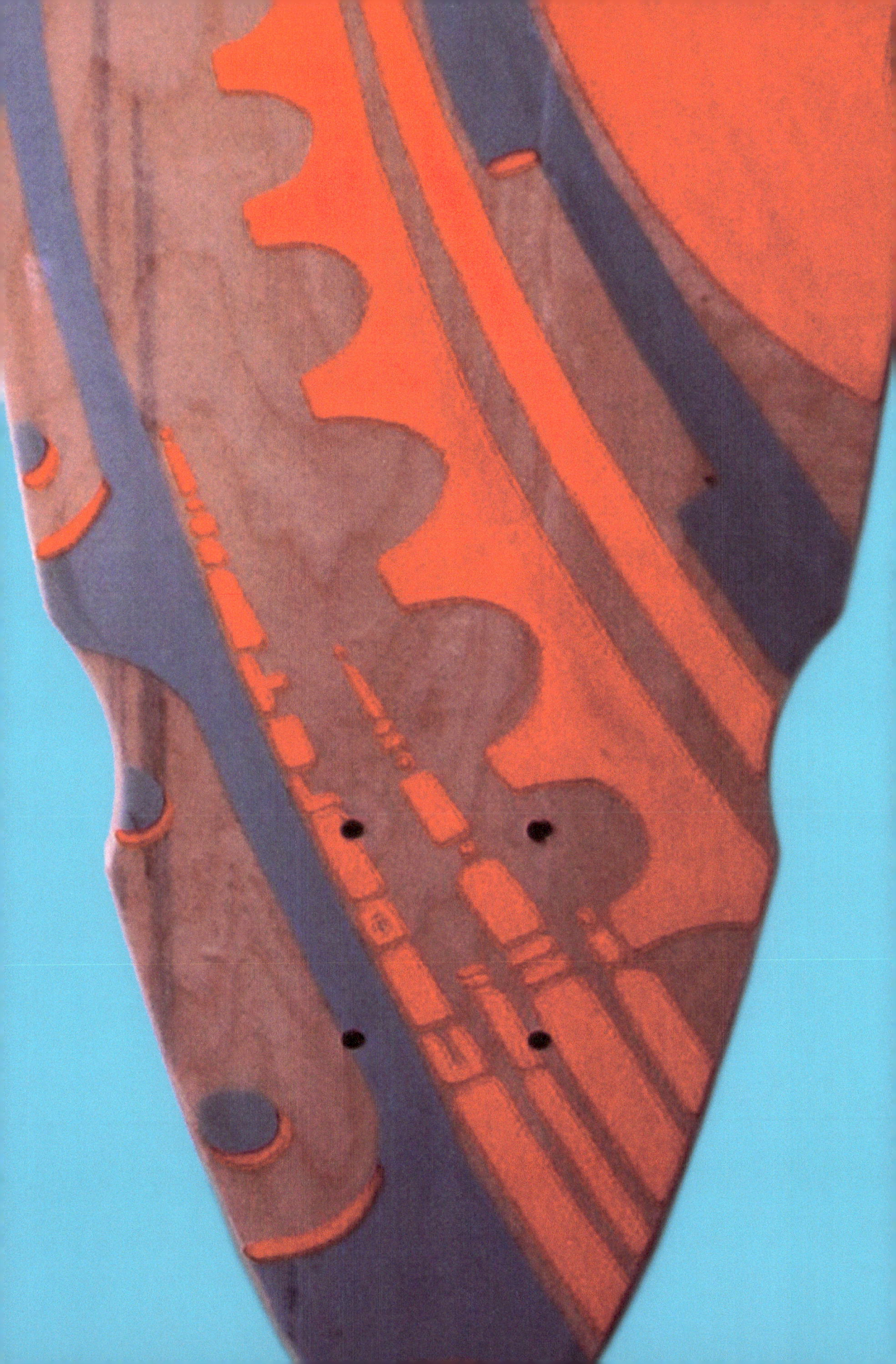

Tribal art has it's beginnings from a time when tools were very simple and could only accomplish simple renderings. Kinda funny how only the simplest of design will stand the test of time.

The simple things in life were other humans, enviorment,food source,landscape,and water.

The ocean has always played such a huge part in this art. Some of the reasons for this are the ocean meant the ability to travel, hence shipping and trade and the abundance of food from fishing.

No wonder why so many of the communities where this type of art is found tend to be near water.

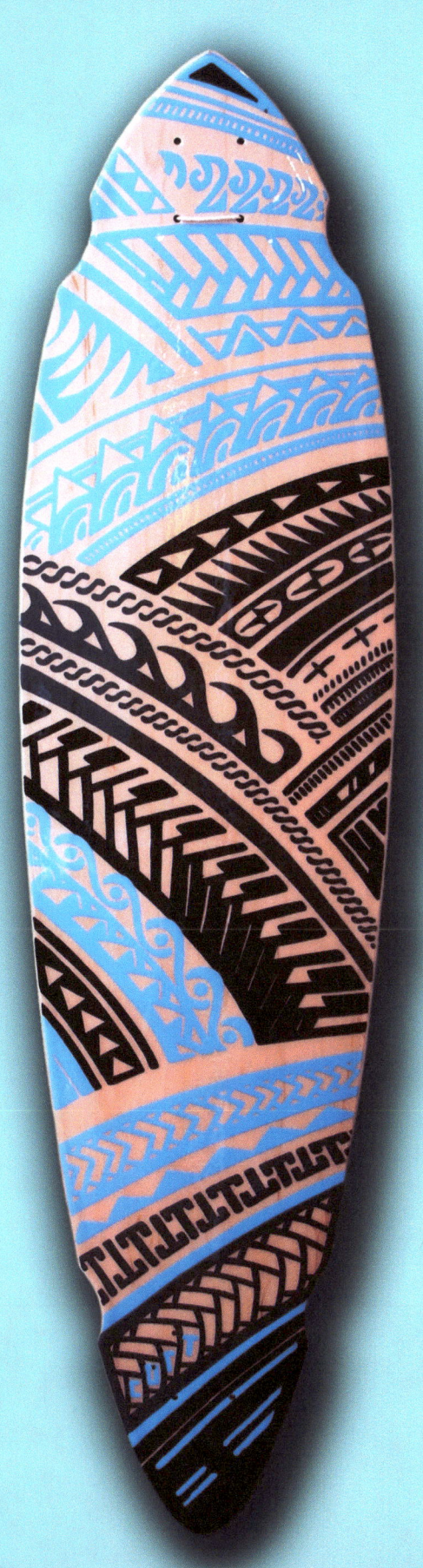

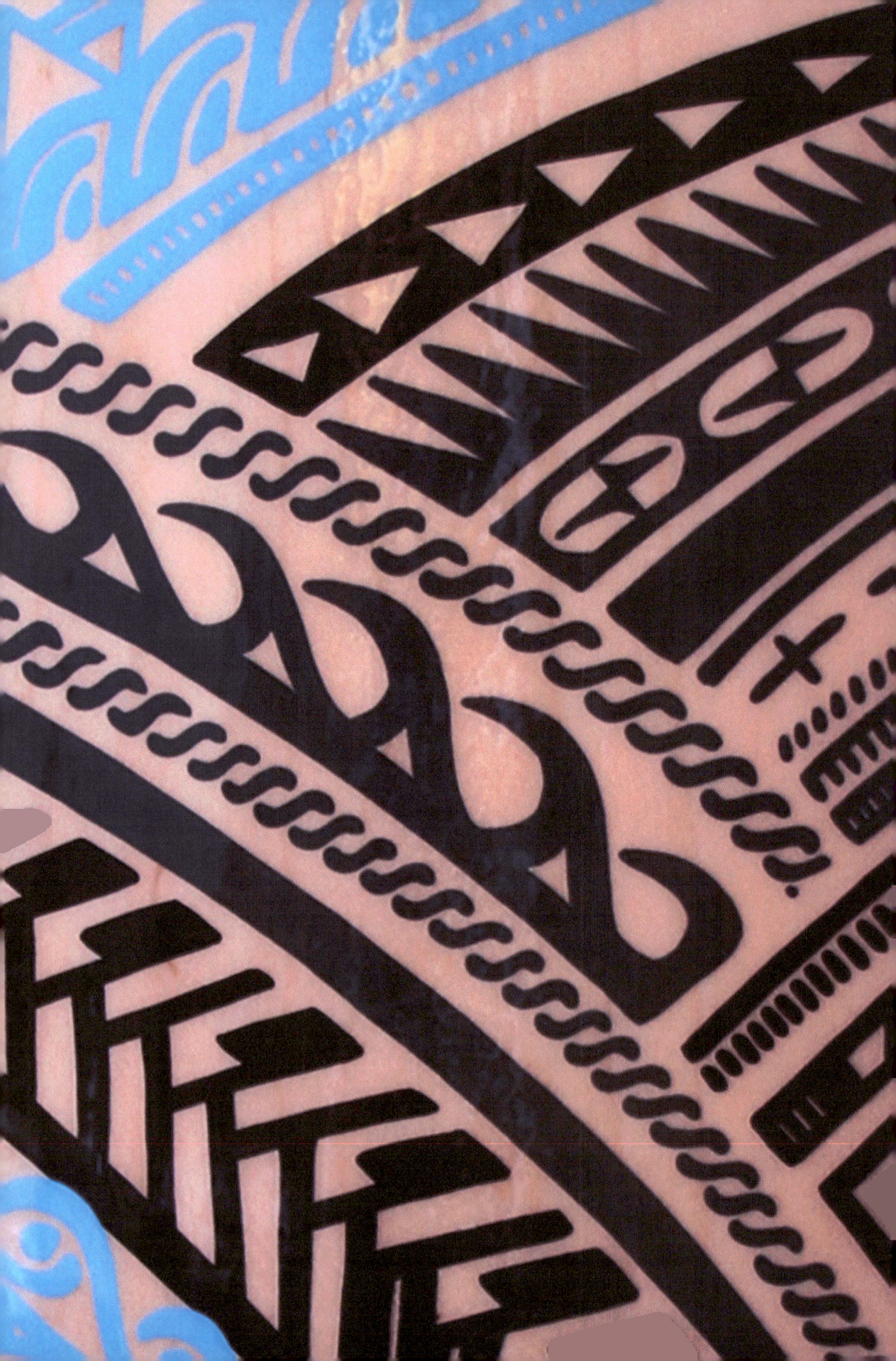

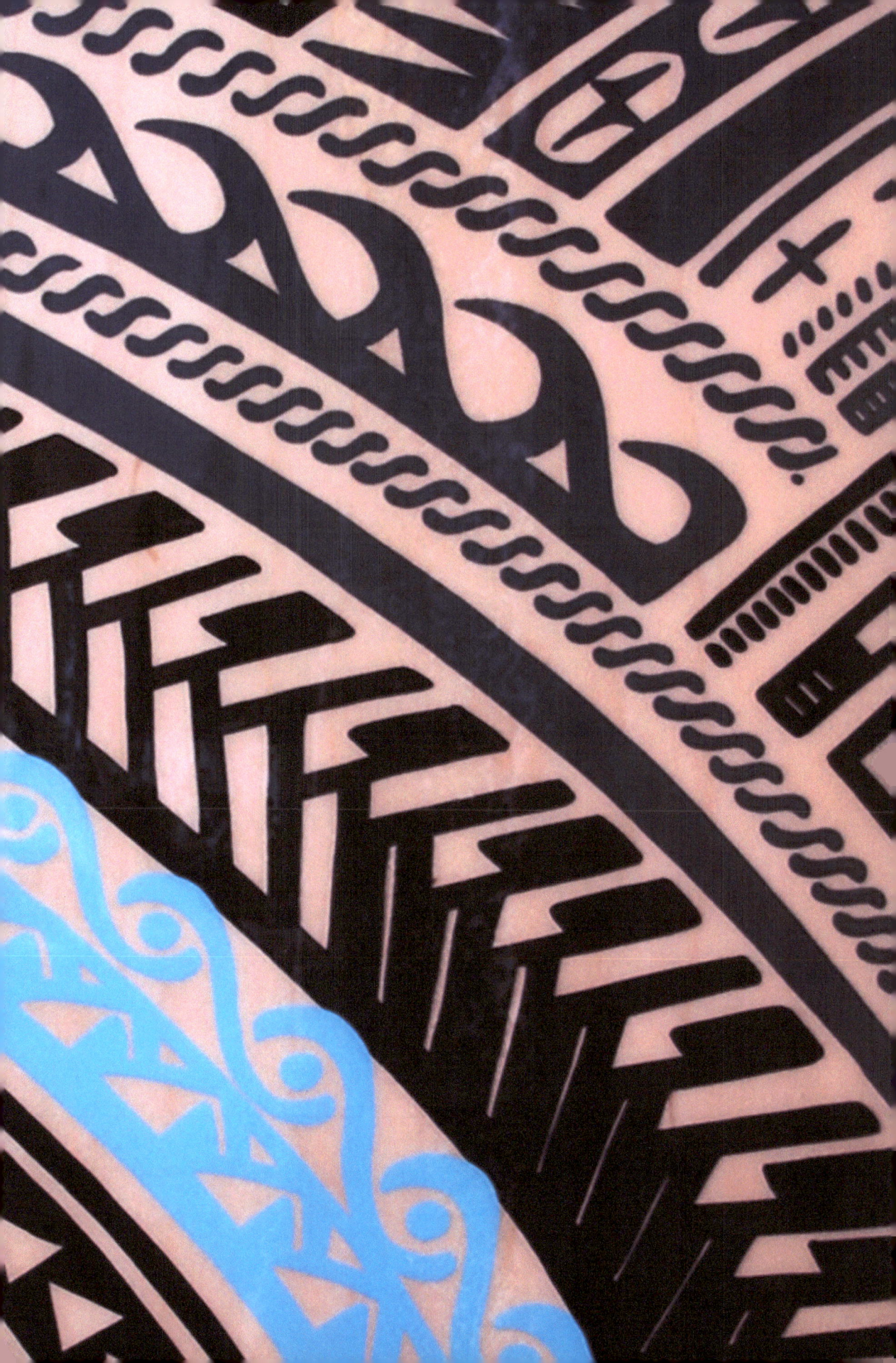

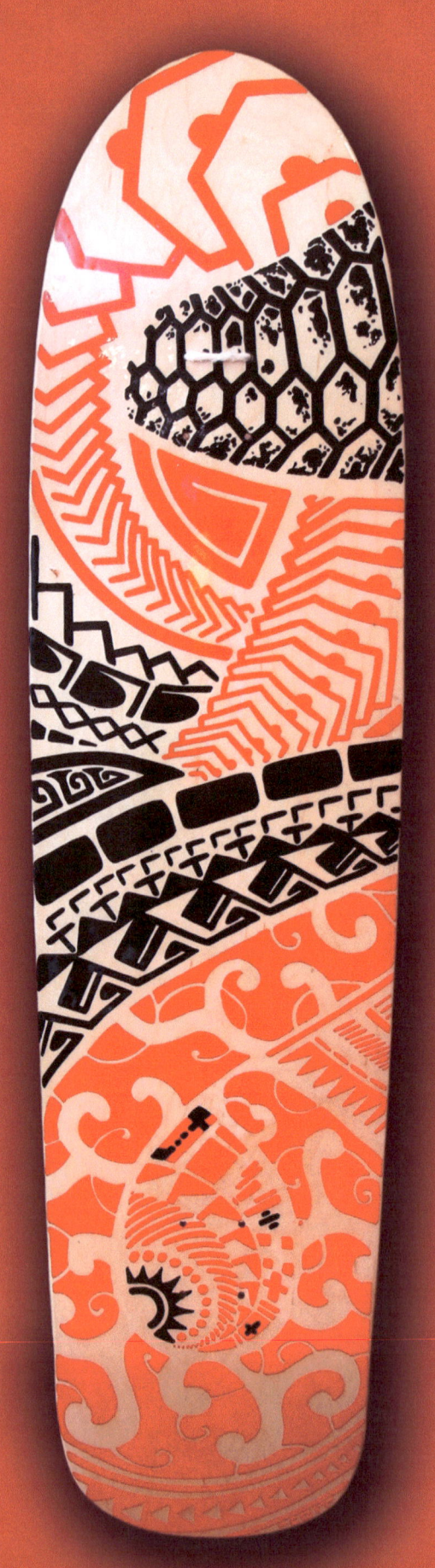

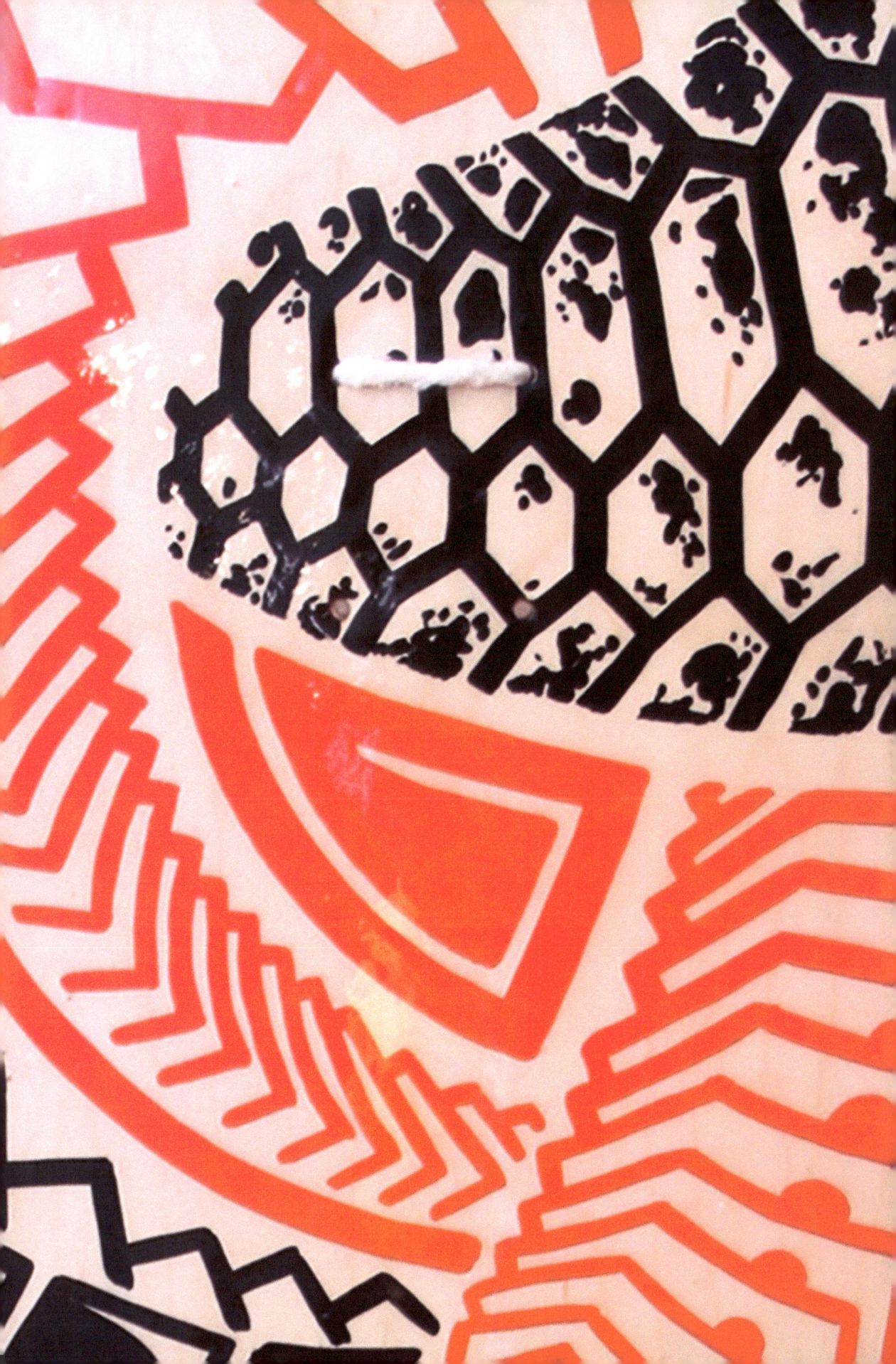

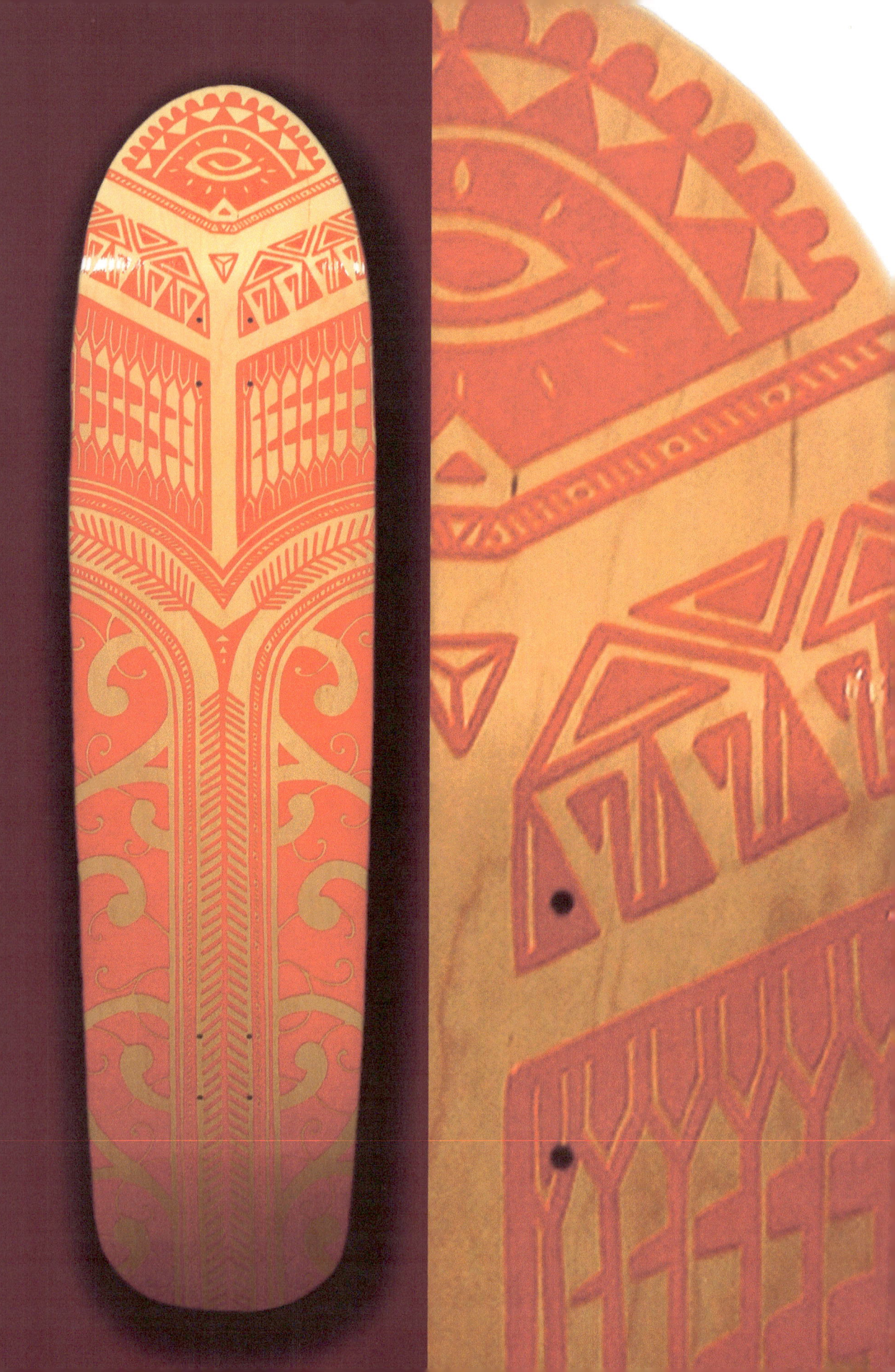

The use of simple designs like triangles and short lines when pointed in the same direction can really help give the impression of movement and direction.

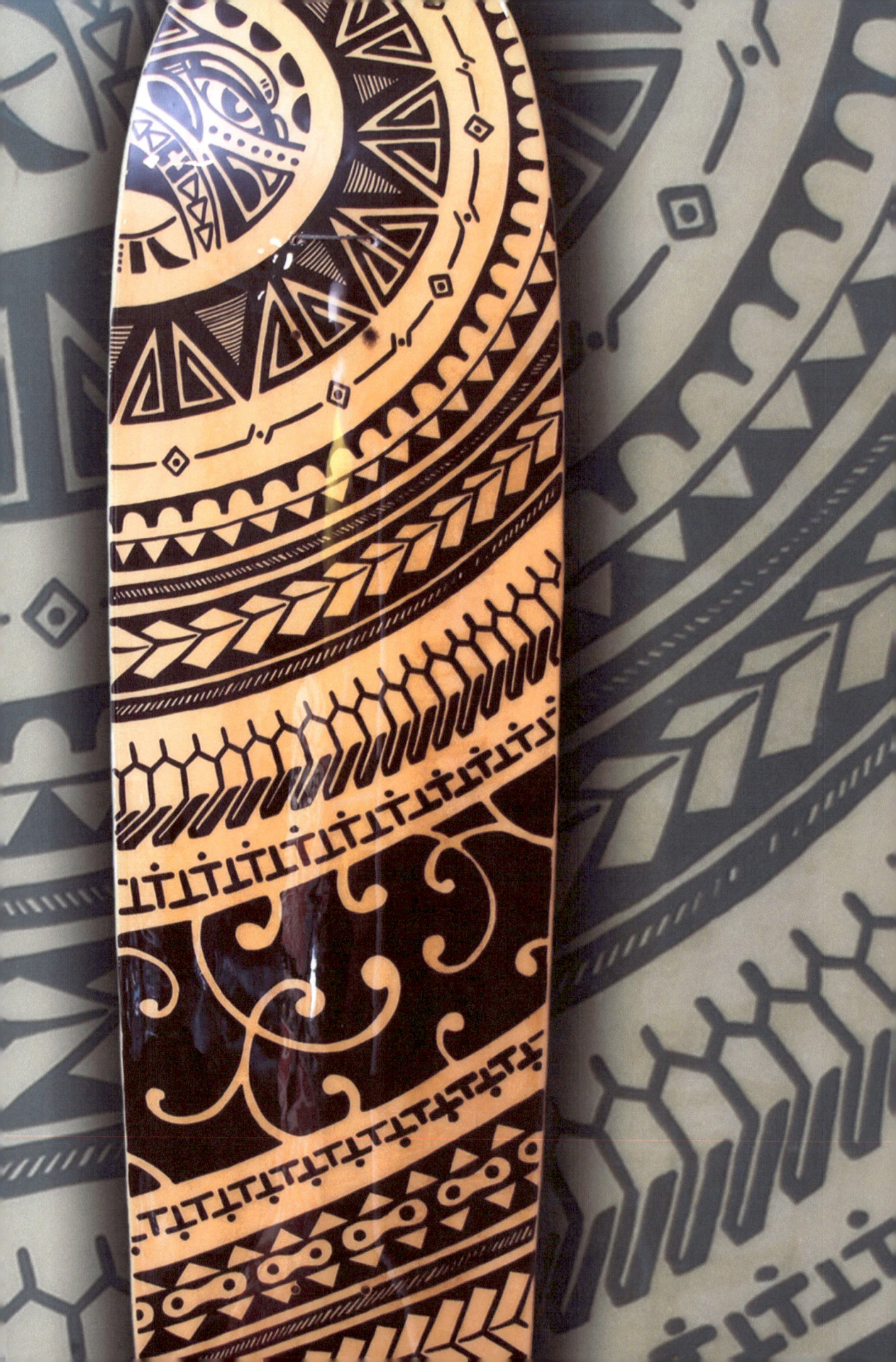

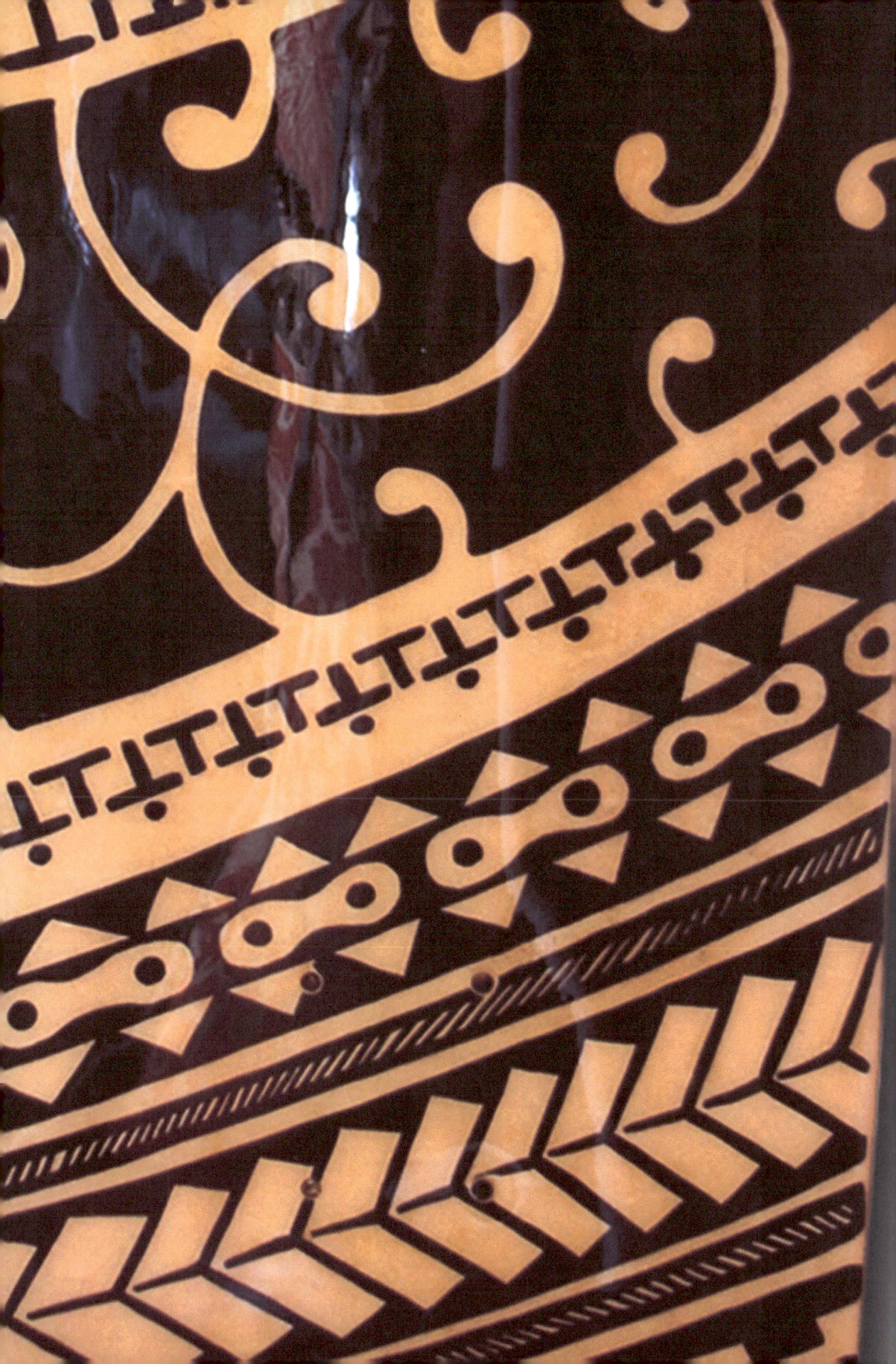

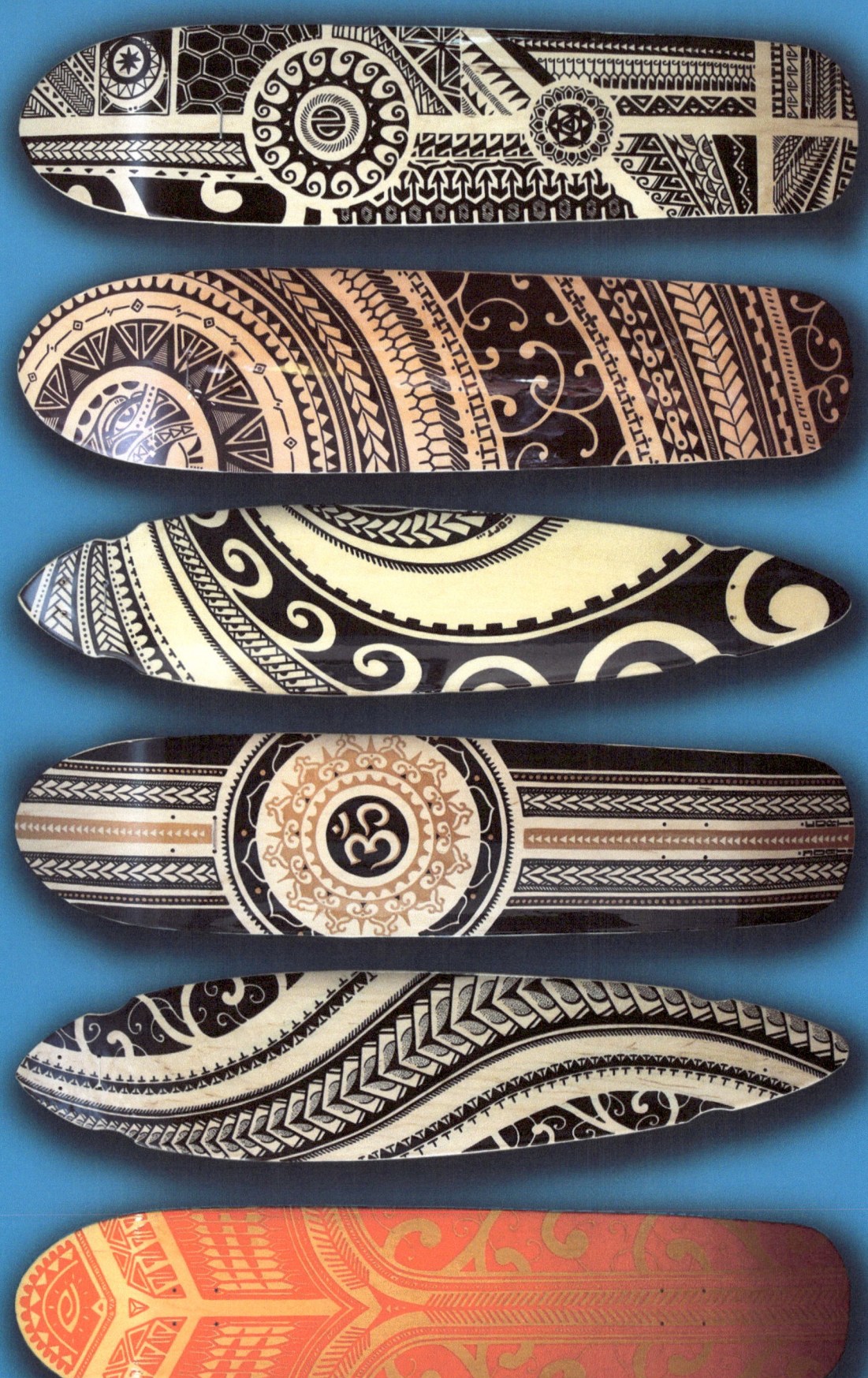

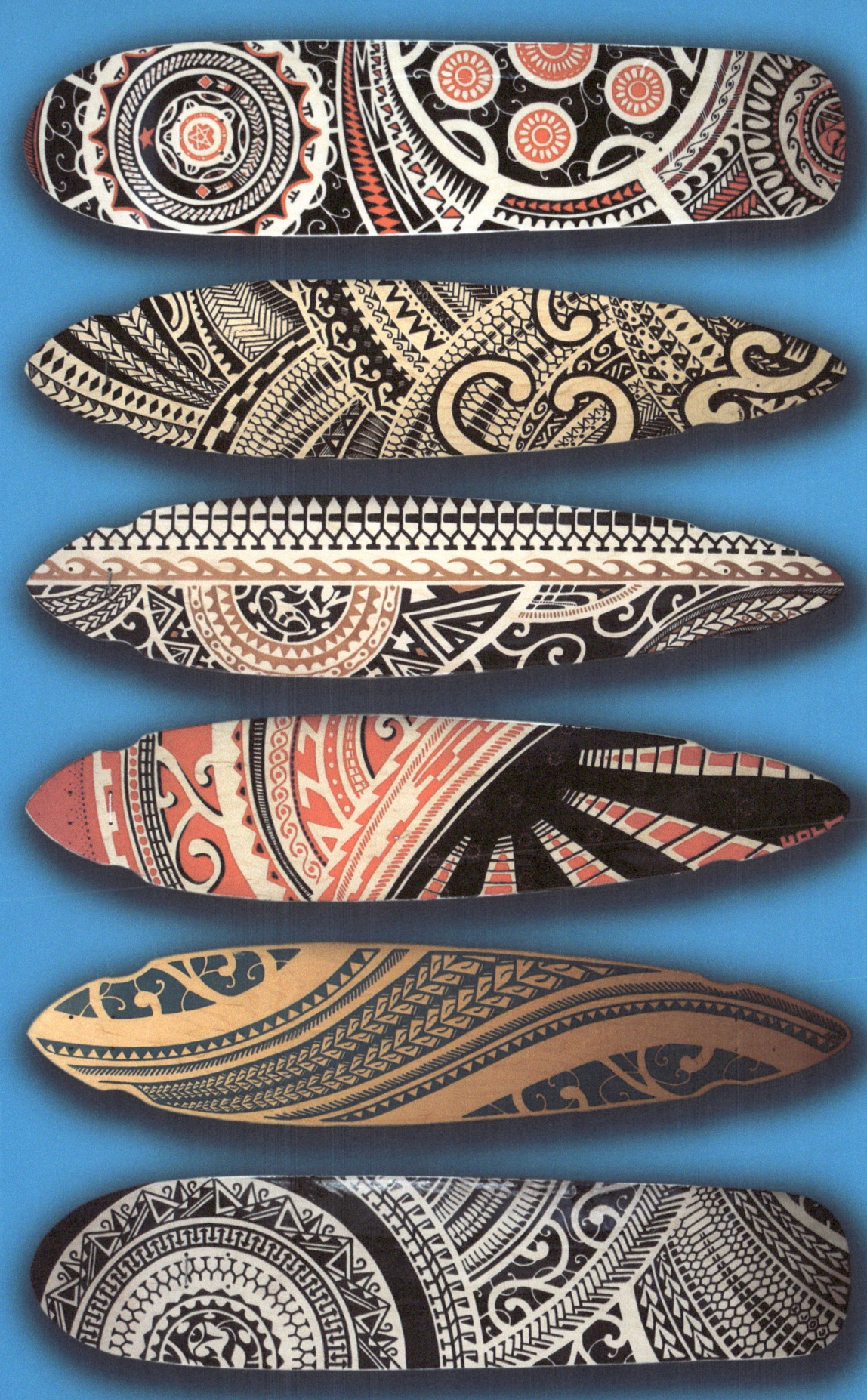

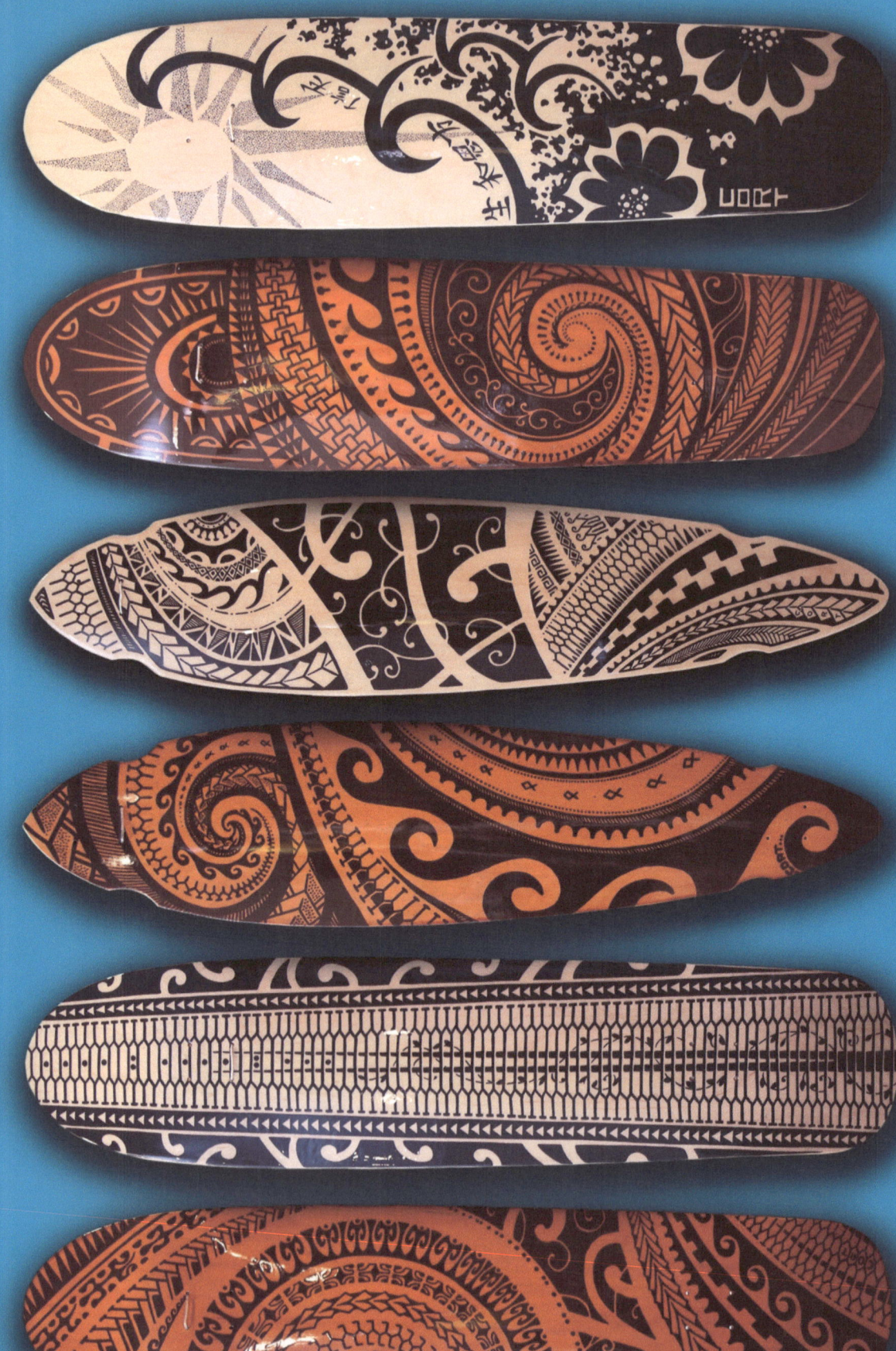

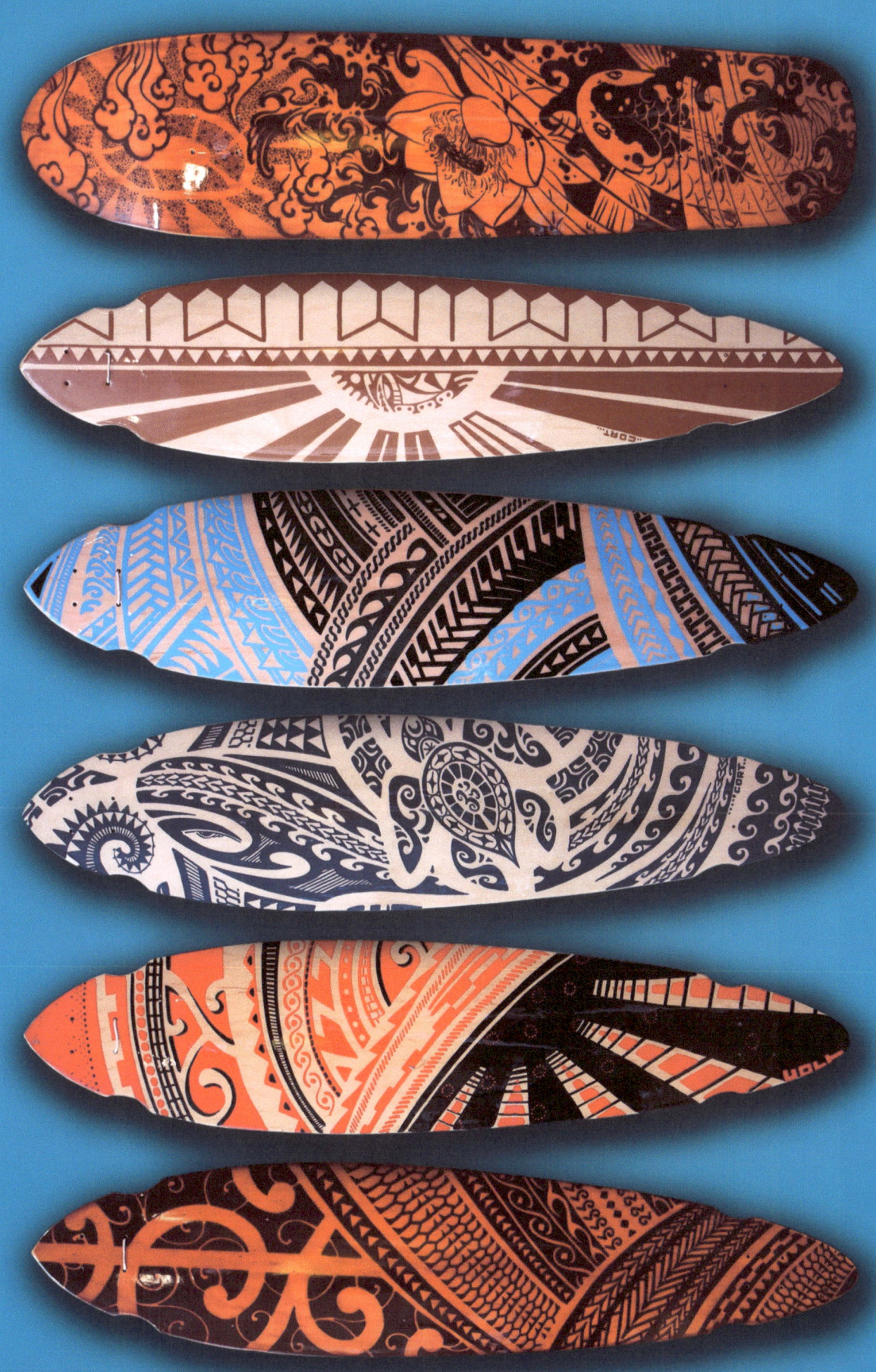

Murals and Sketches

Most of these drawings are done with black markers on 100-300 wieght bond paper or watercolor paper and done over a 4-5 year period. Some of them were sketched first some went marker right to paper.

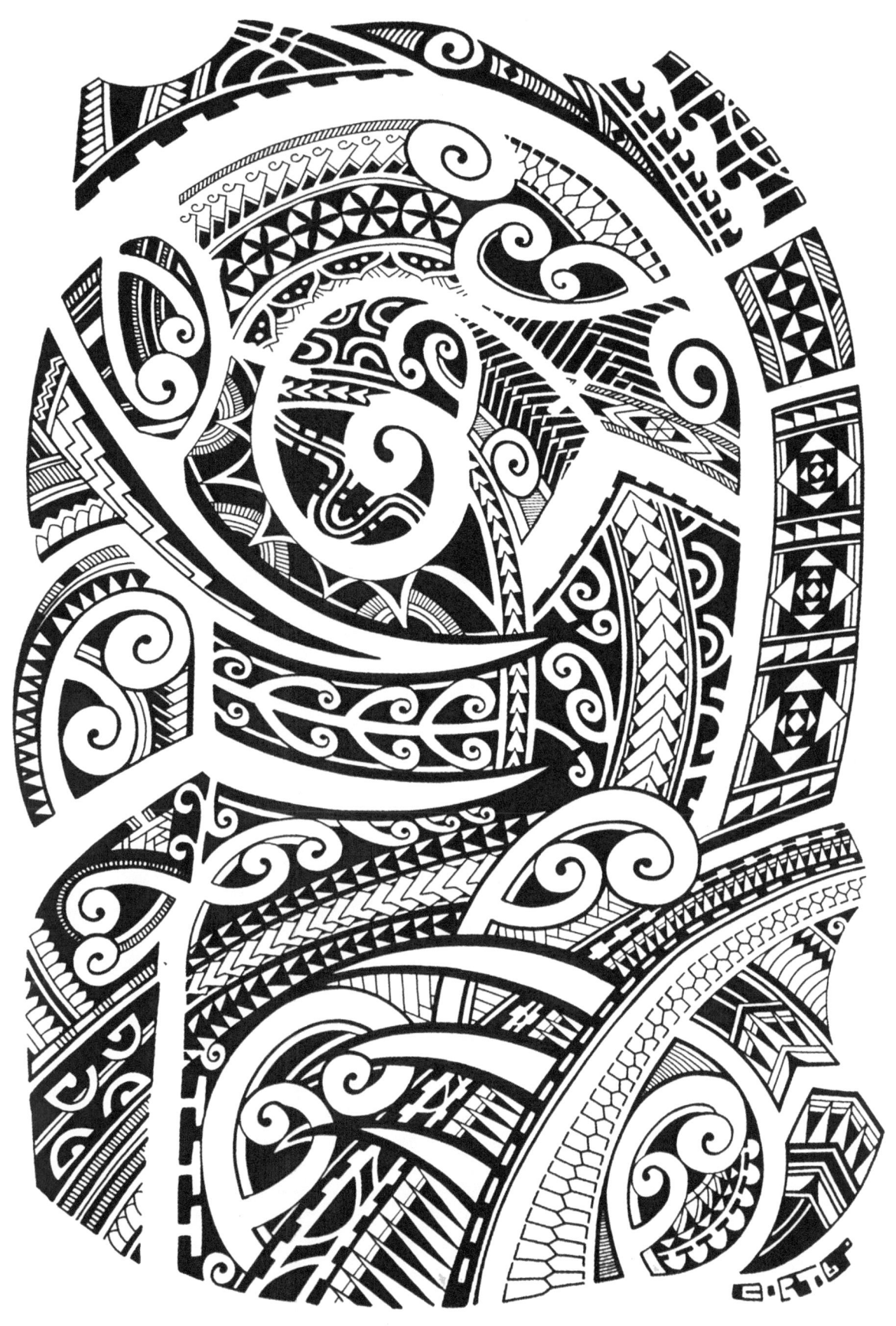

Marker on 160 lb hot press   27" x 40"

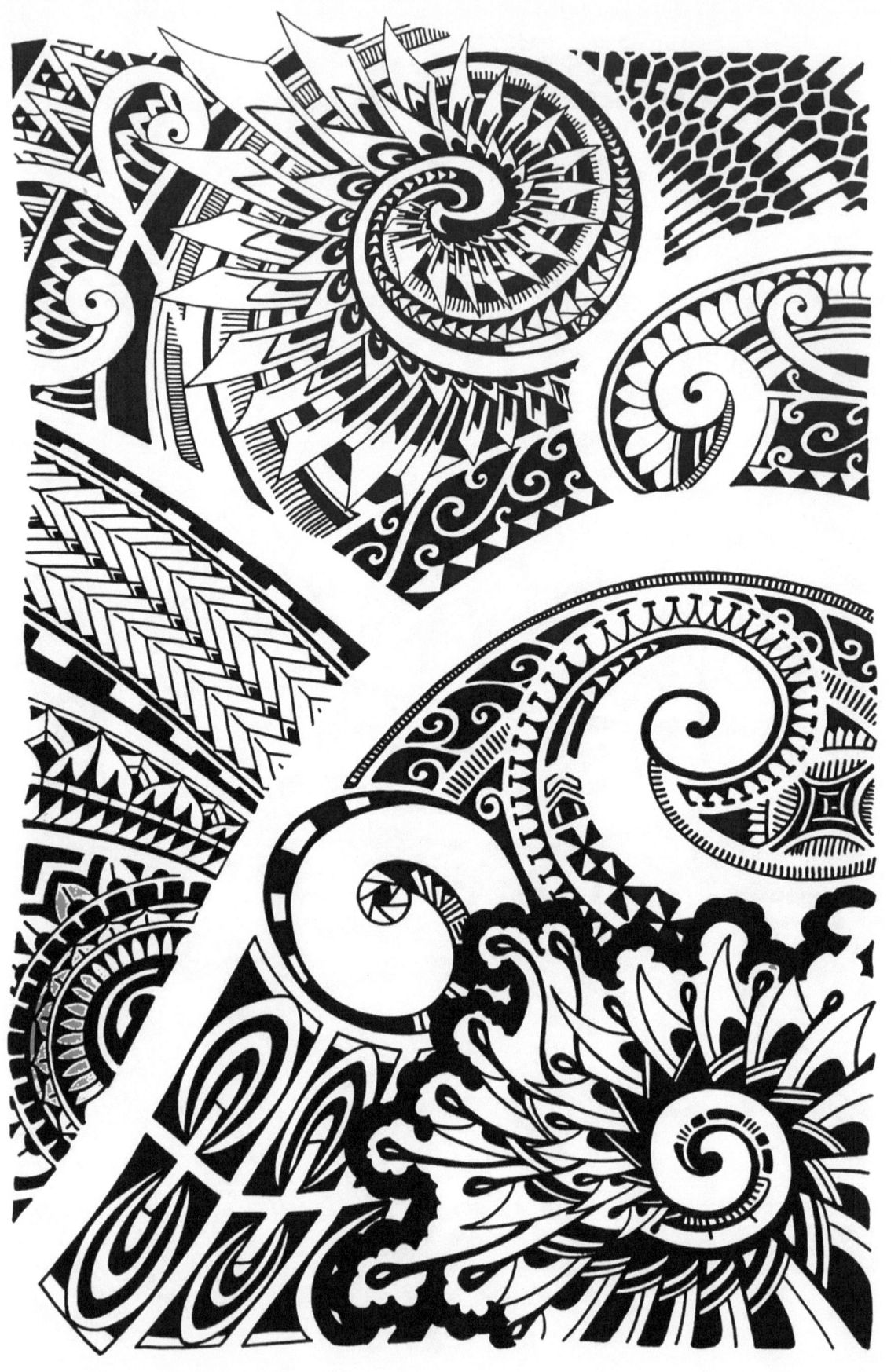

Marker on 160 lb hot press bond   27" x 40"

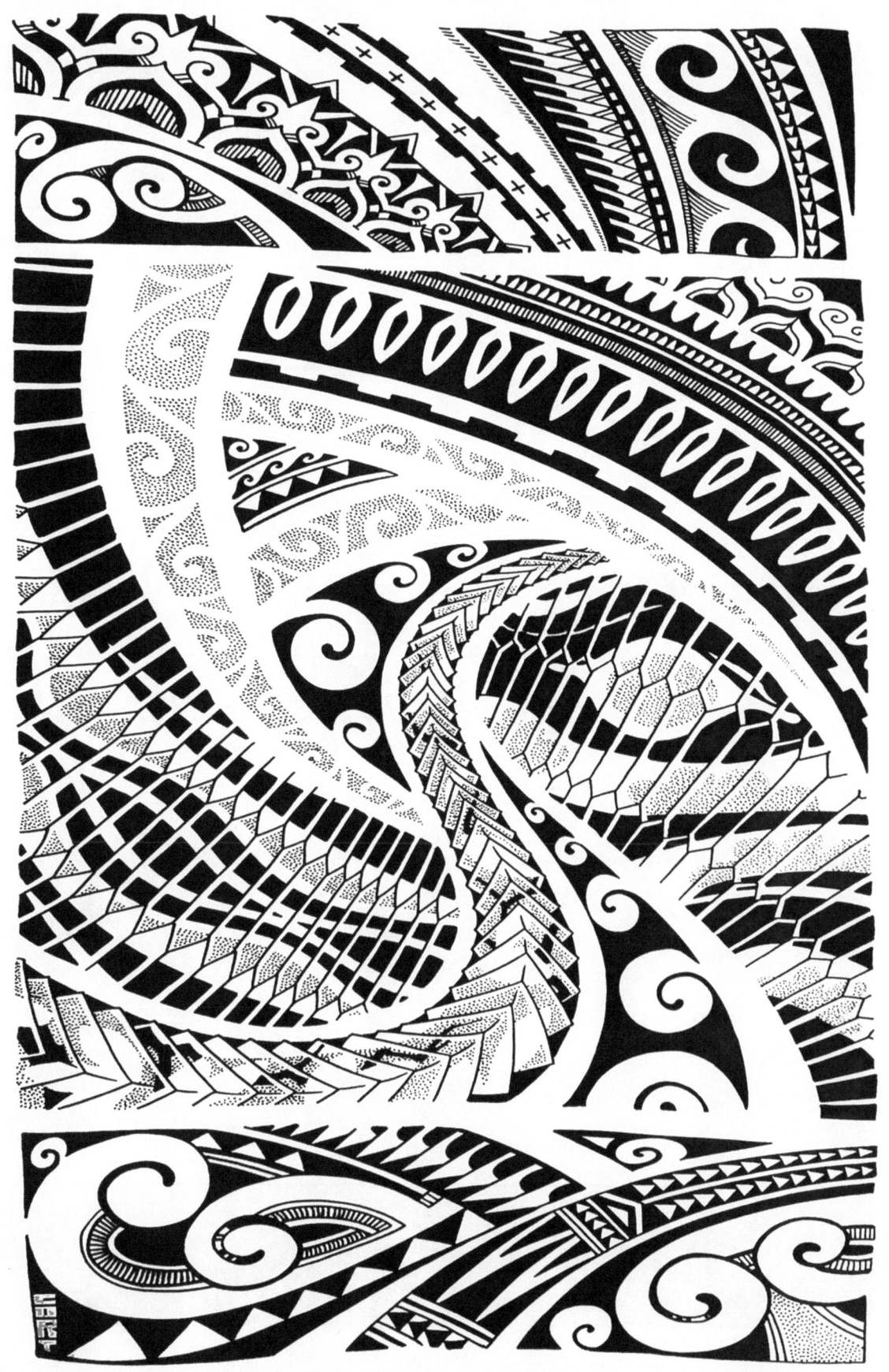

Marker on 160lb hot press bond   27" x 40"

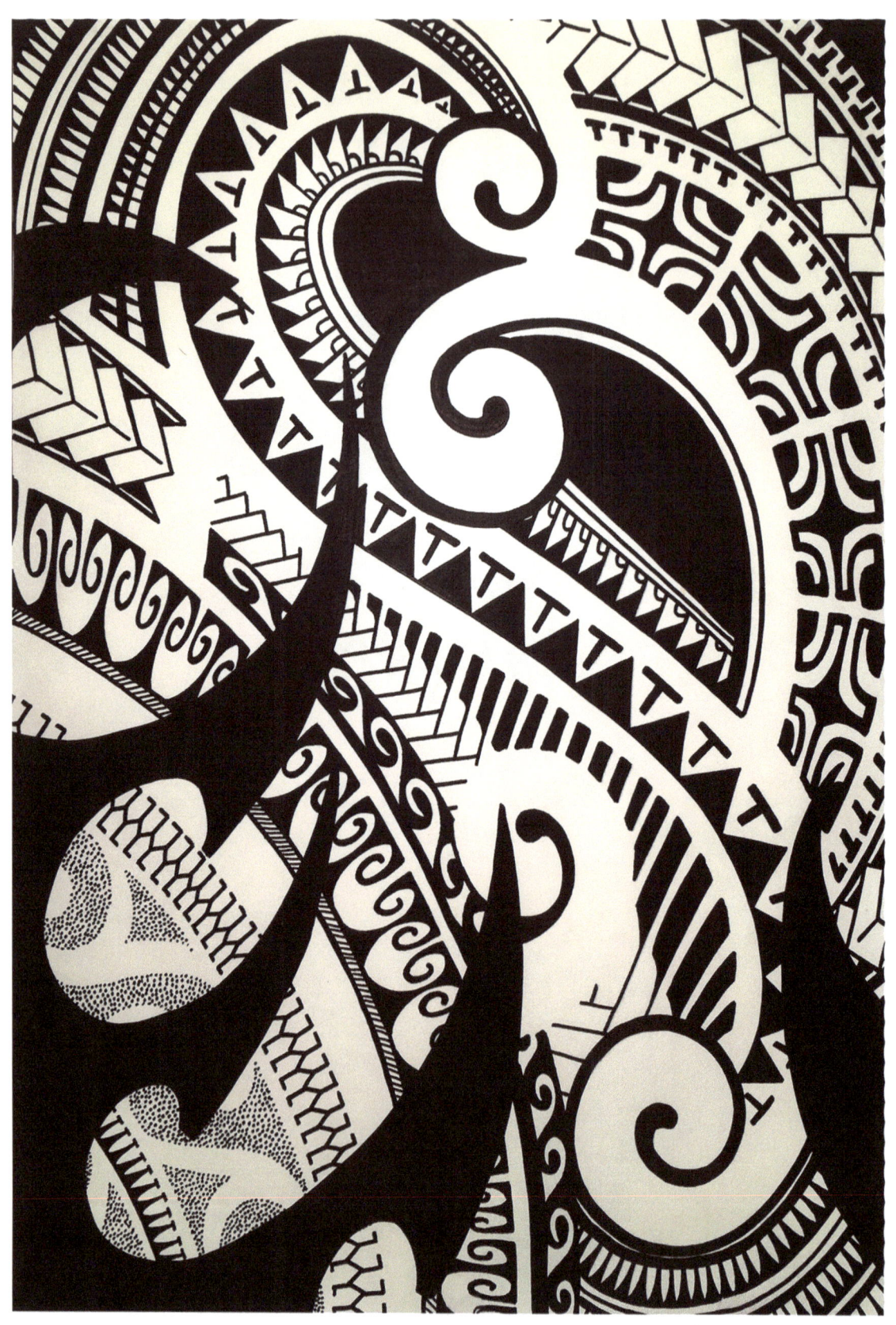
18" x 24"

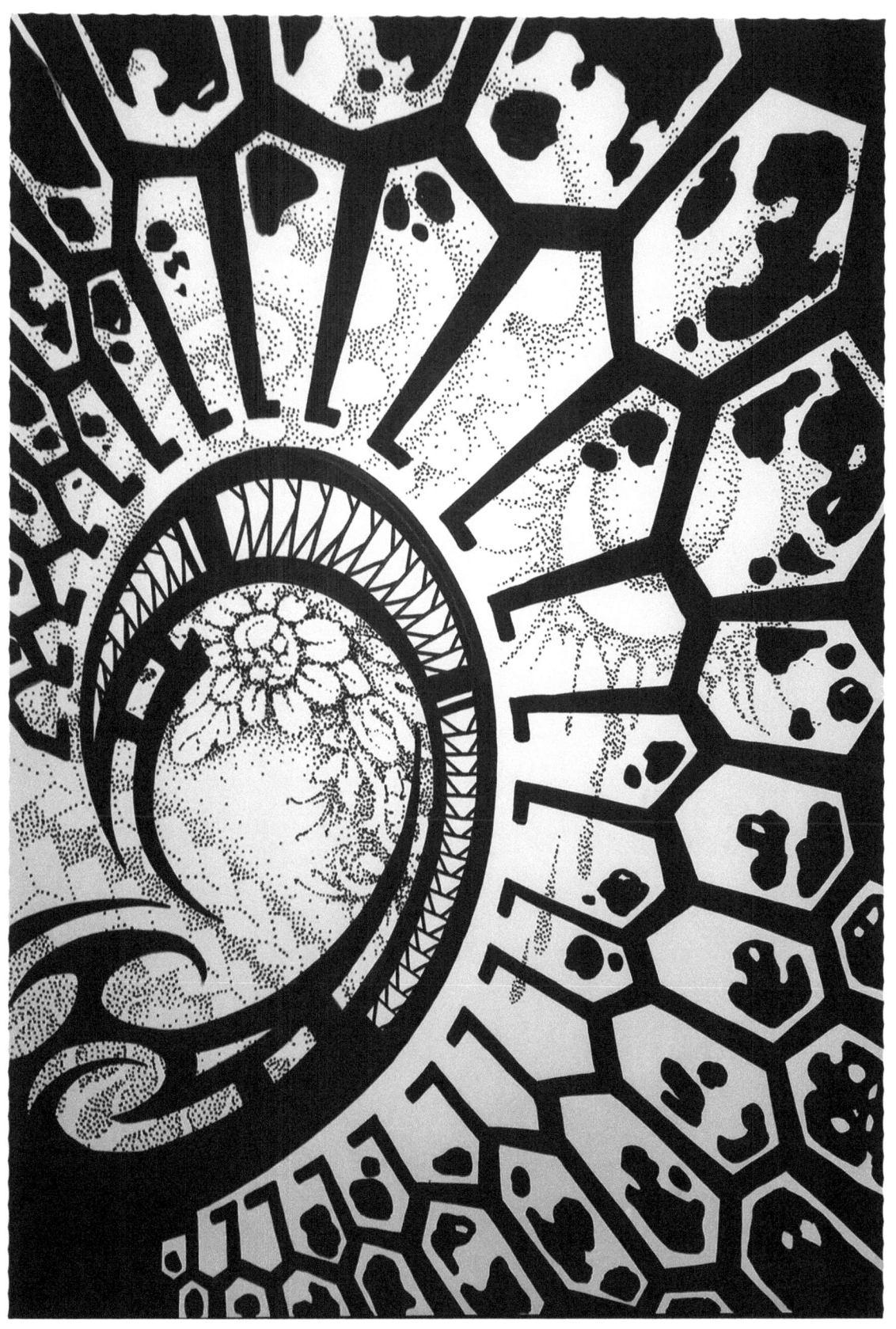

18" x 24"

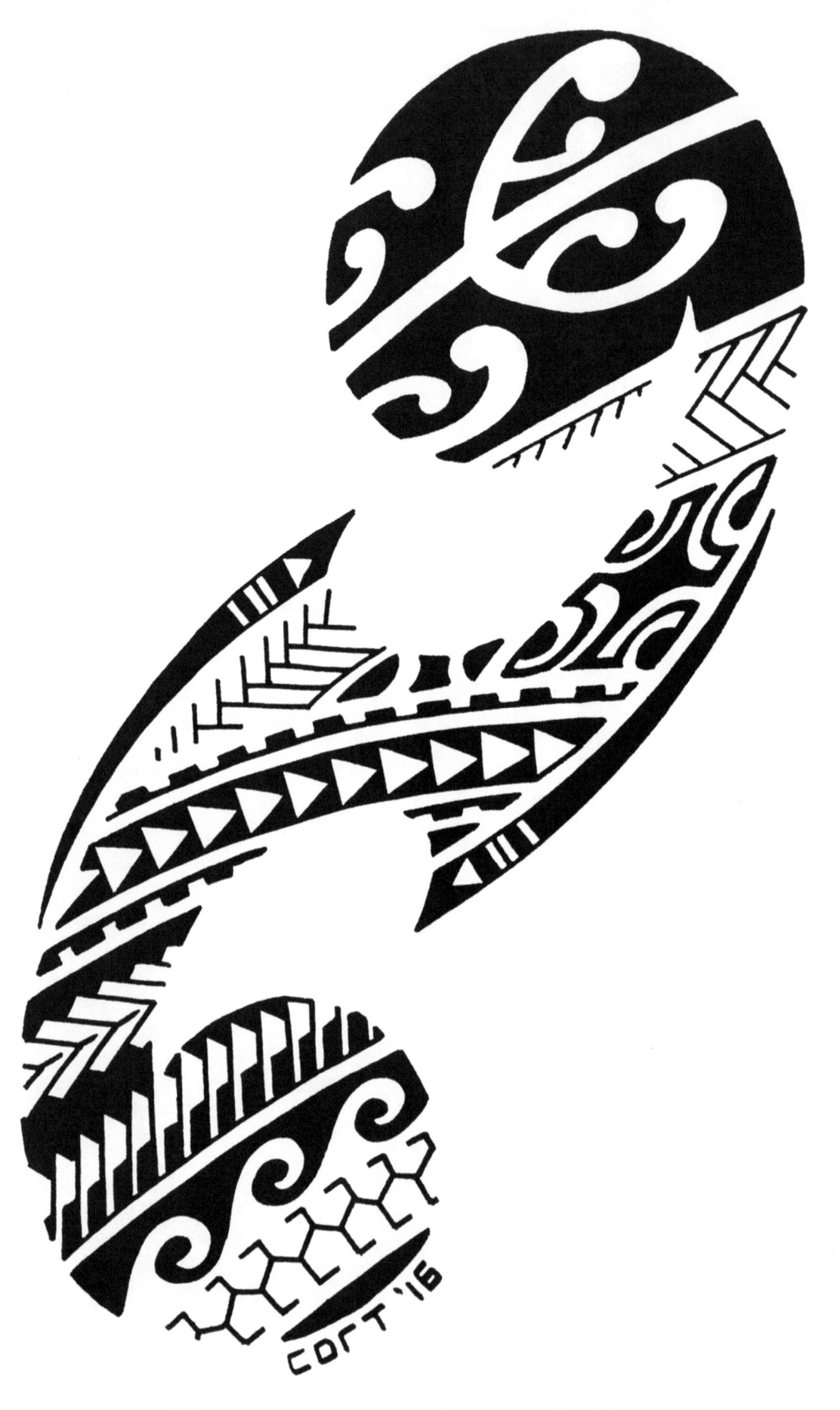

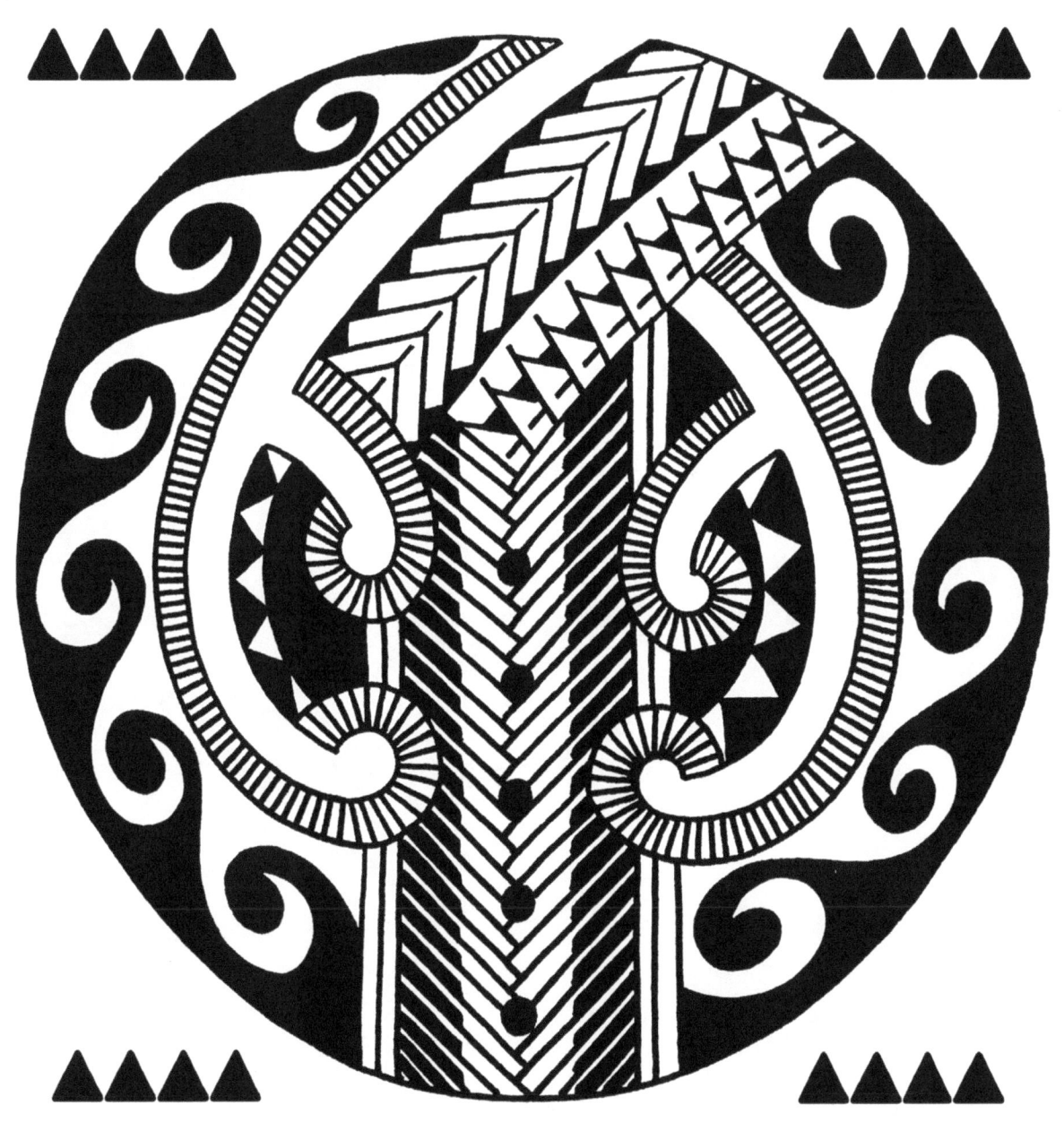

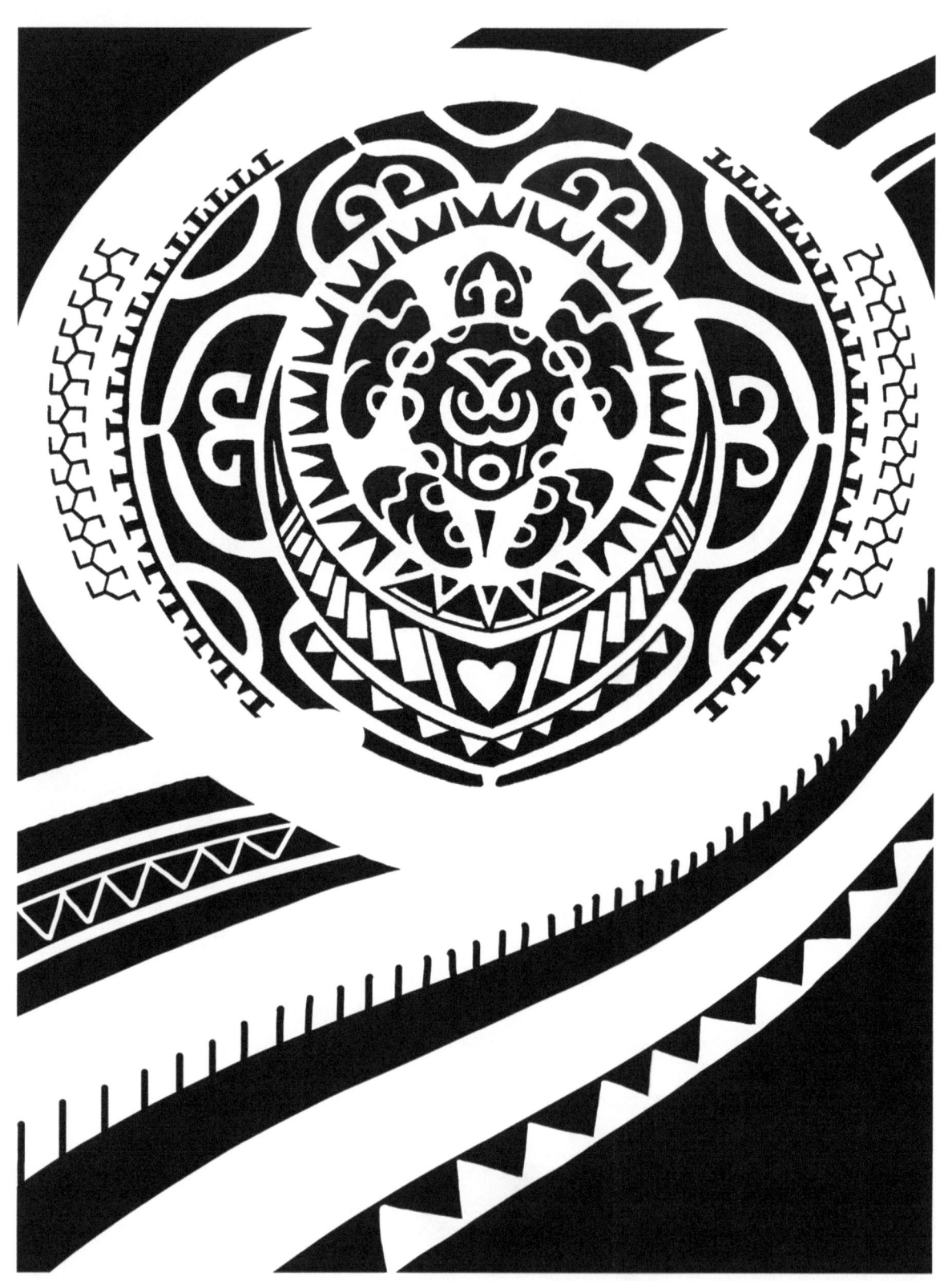

18" x 24"

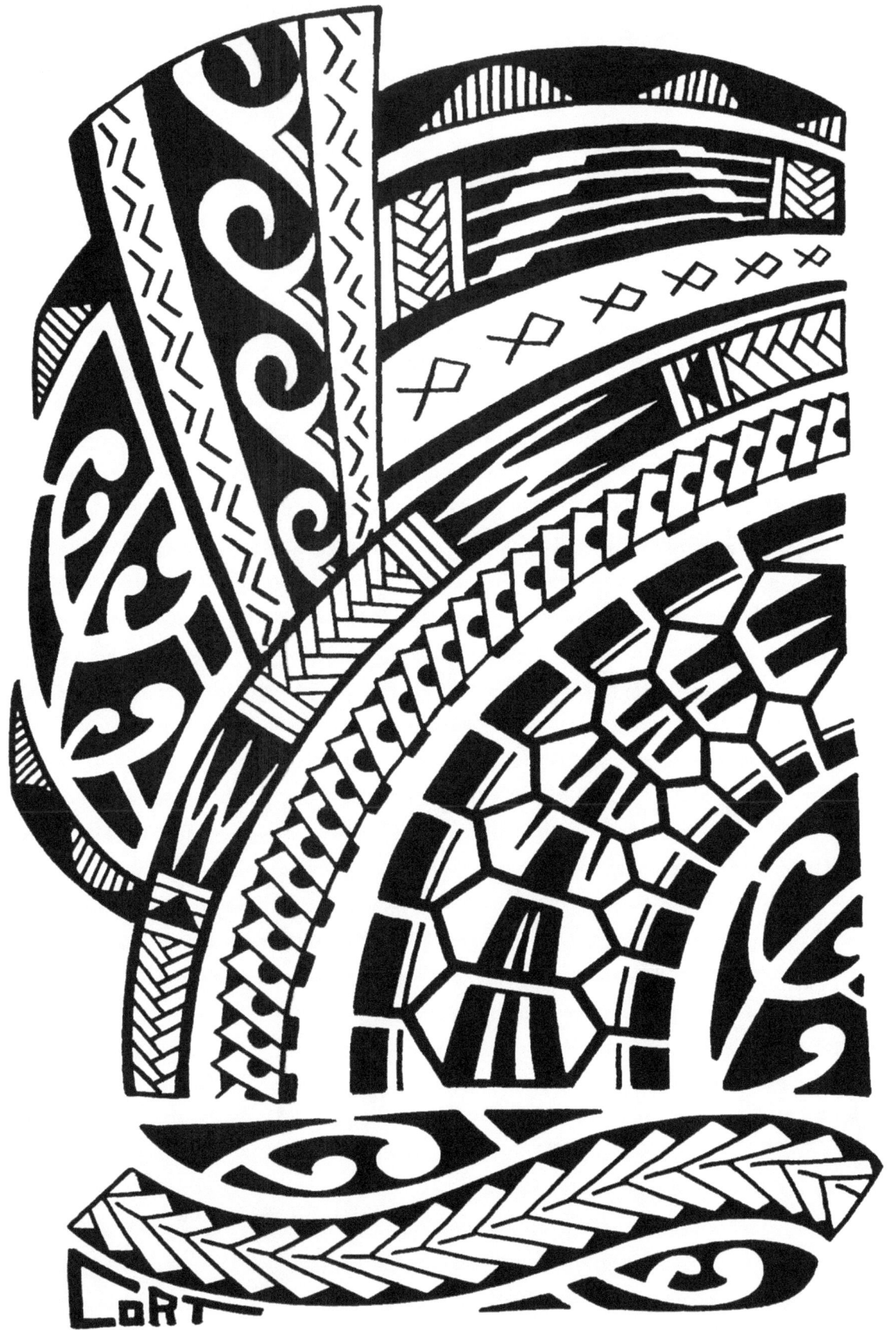

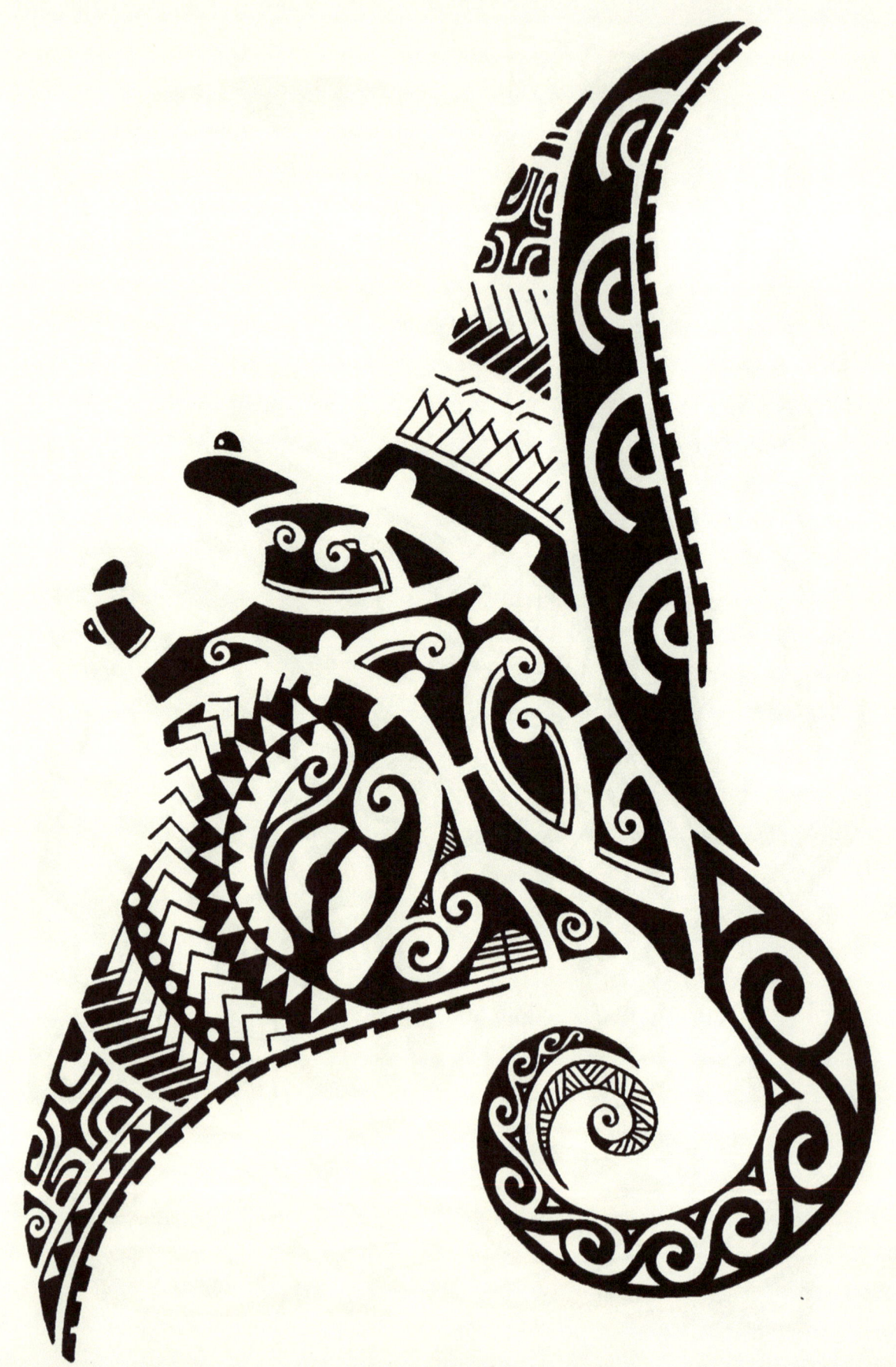

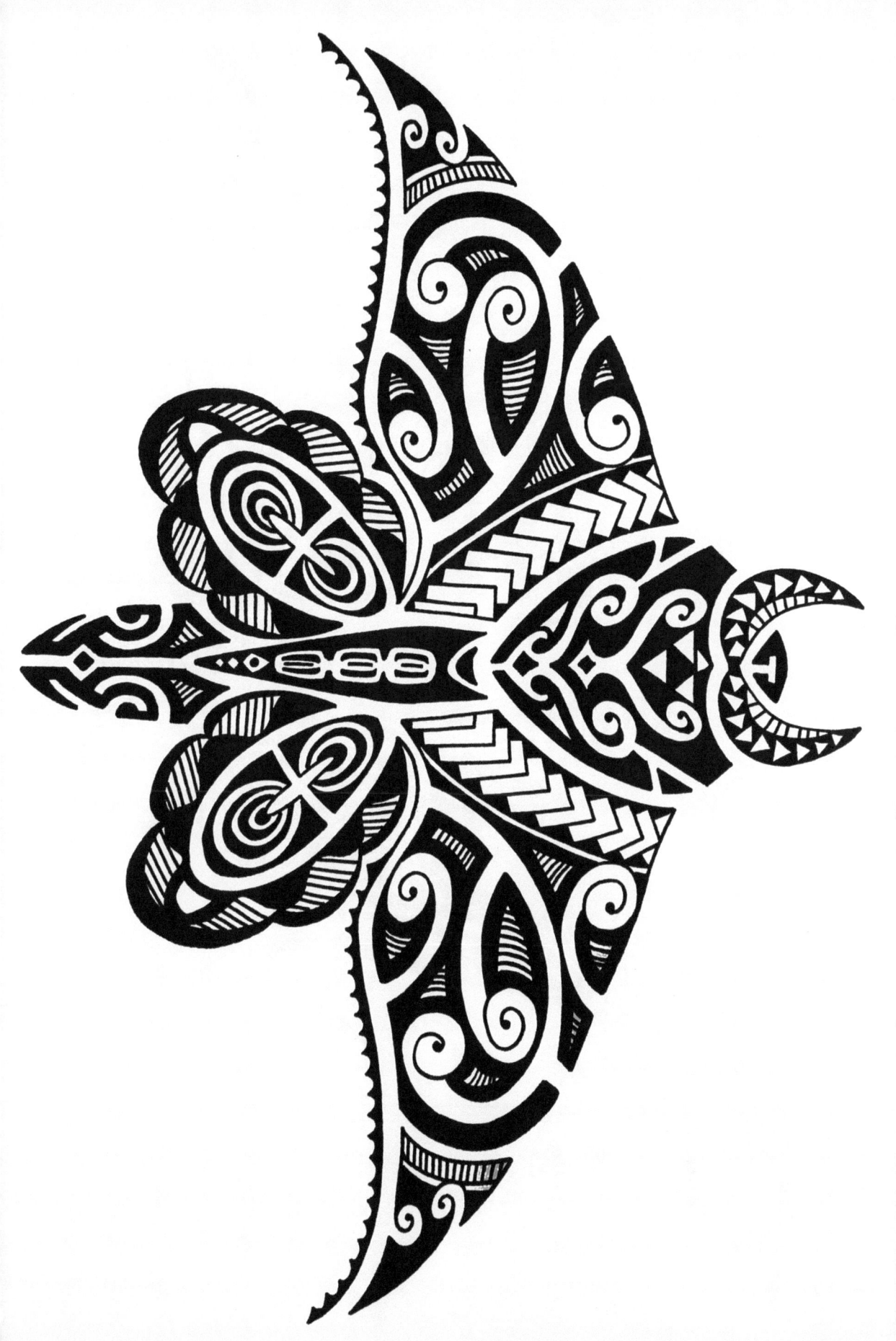

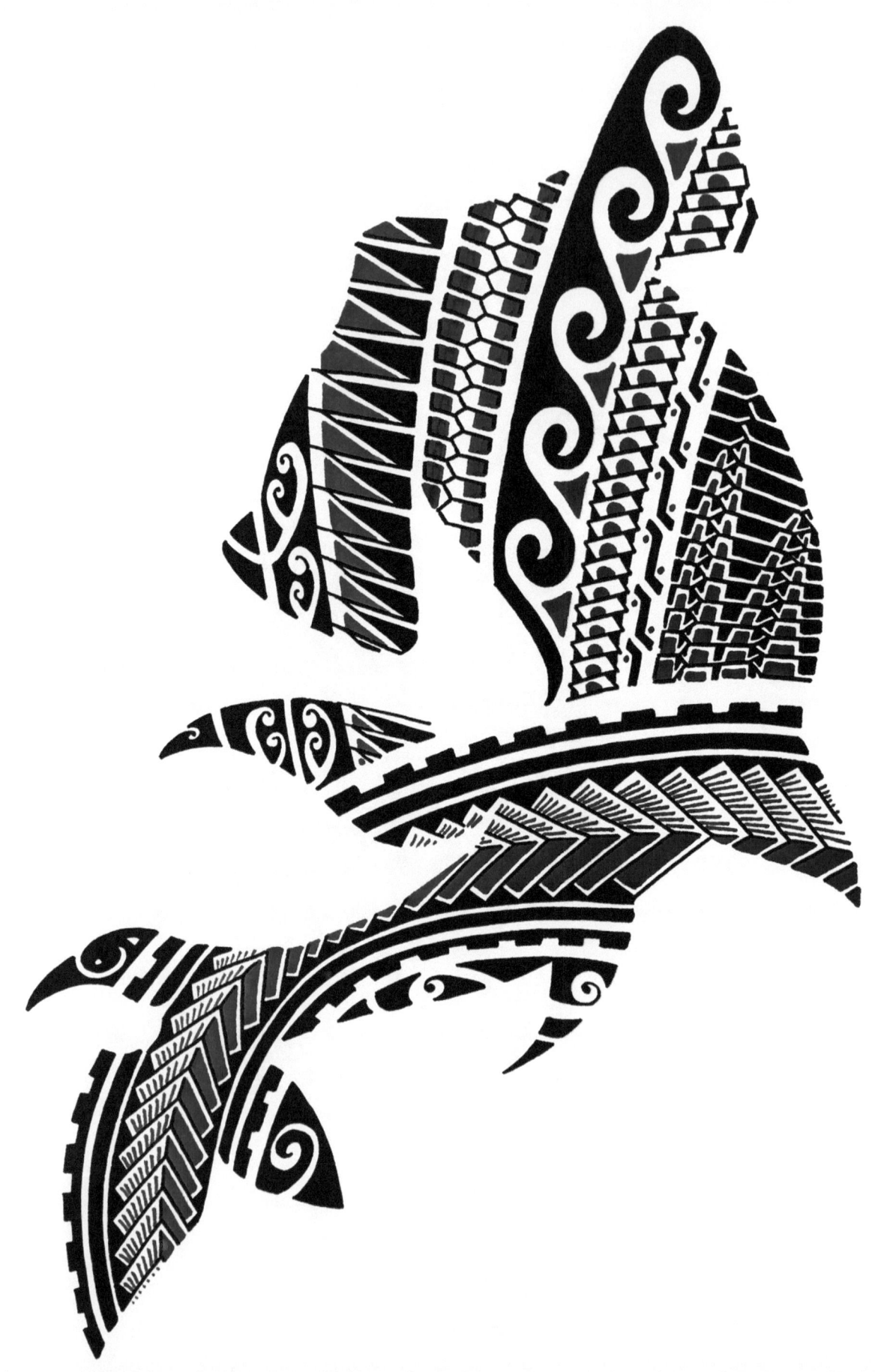

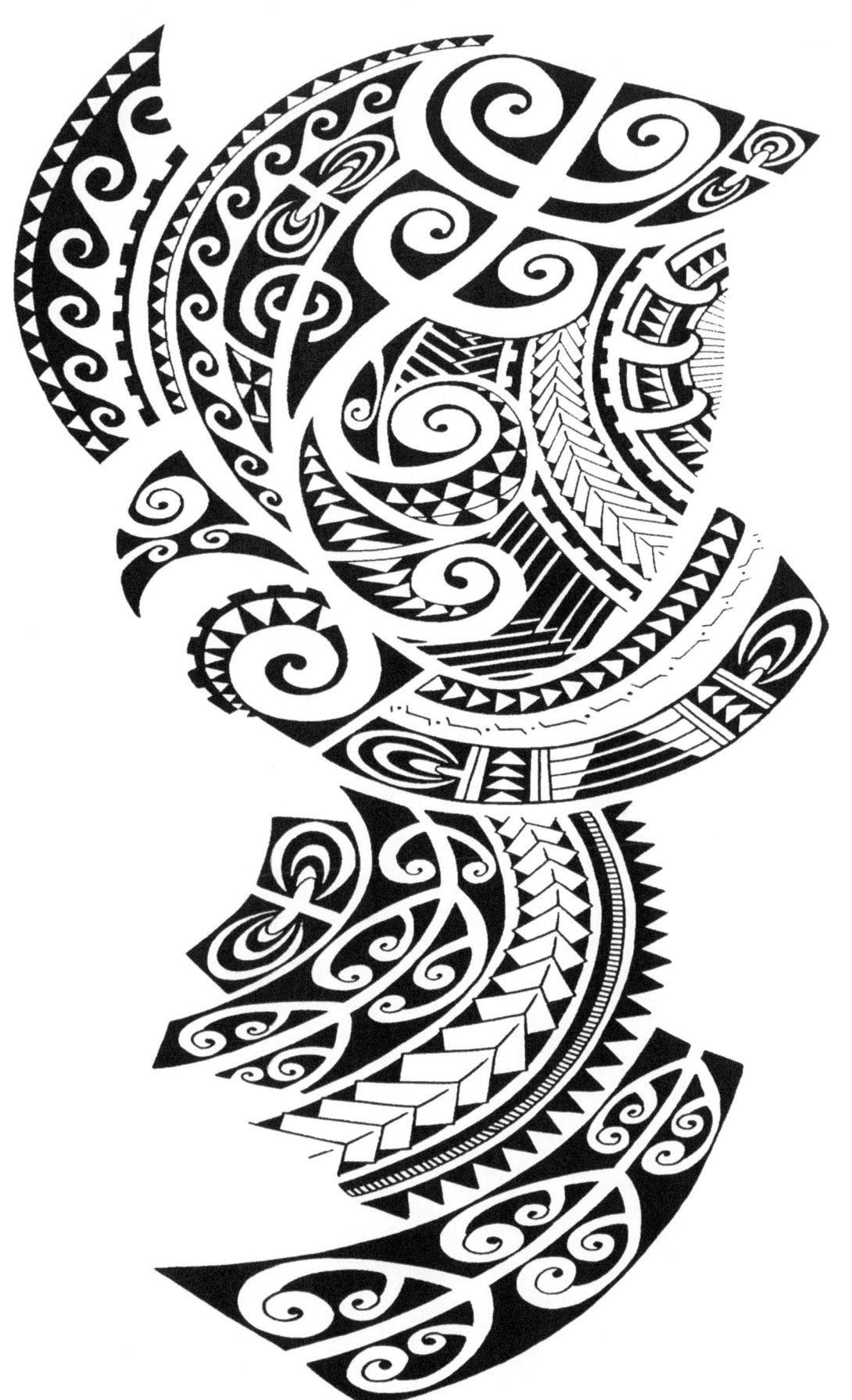

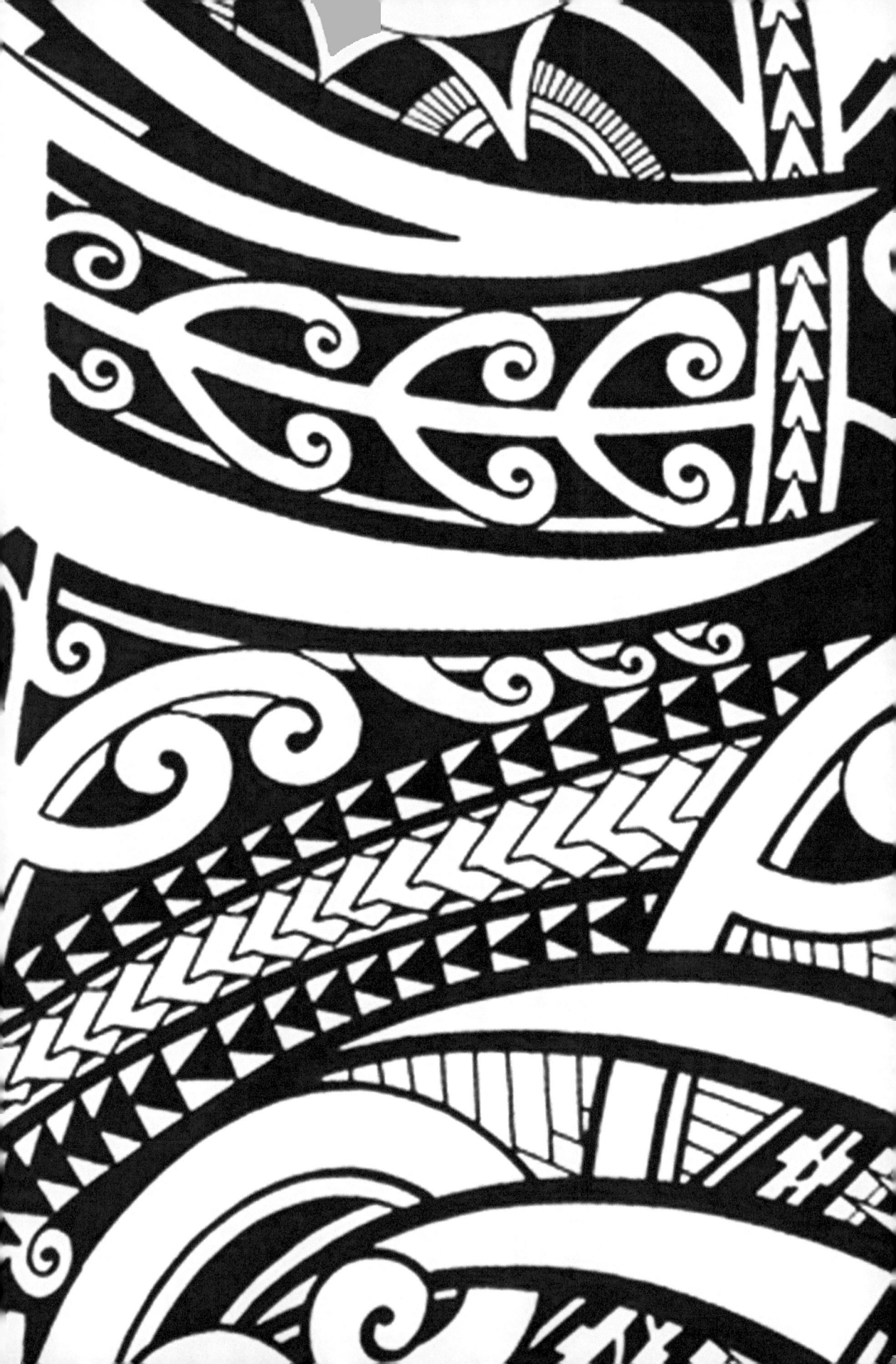

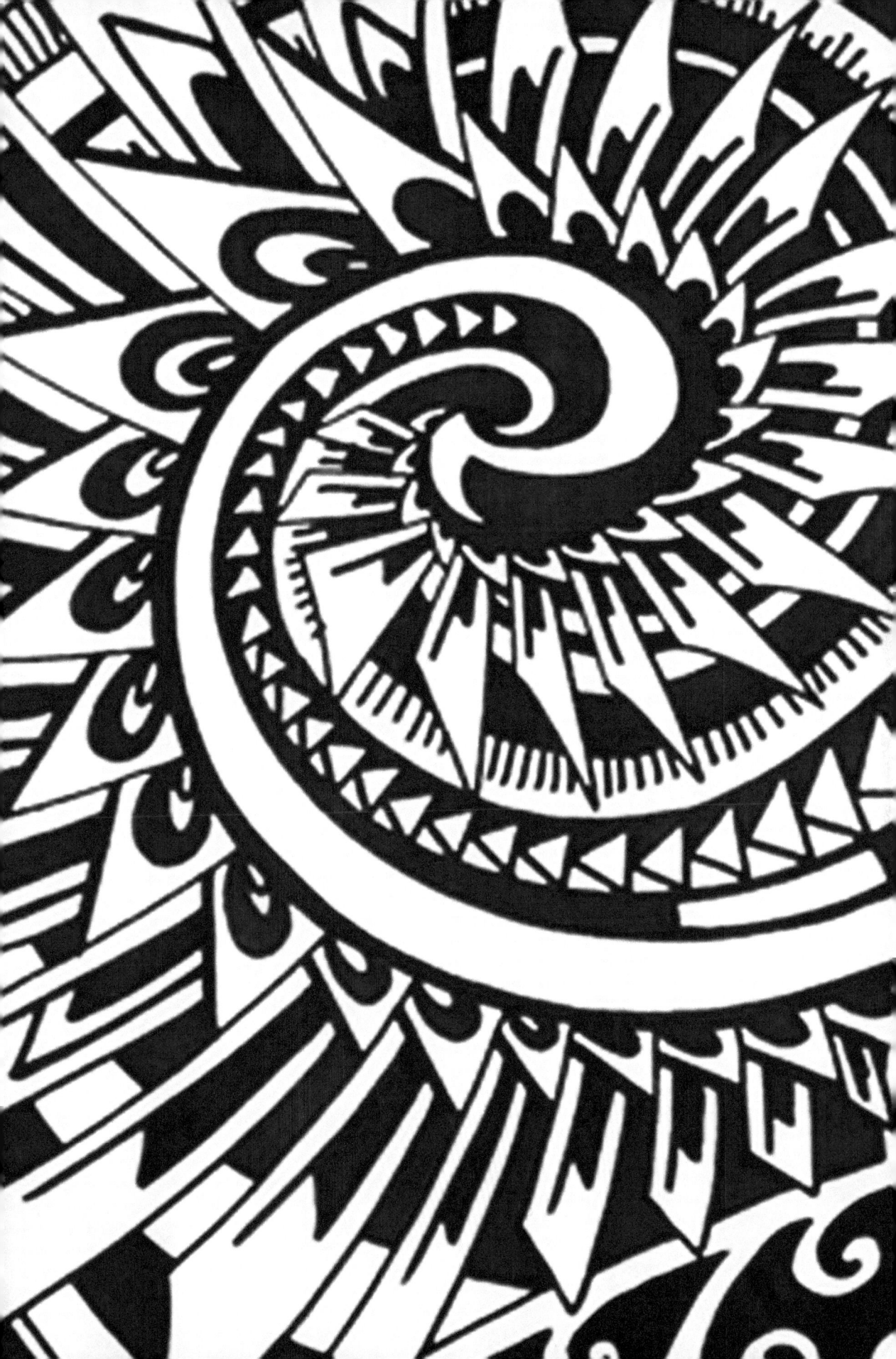

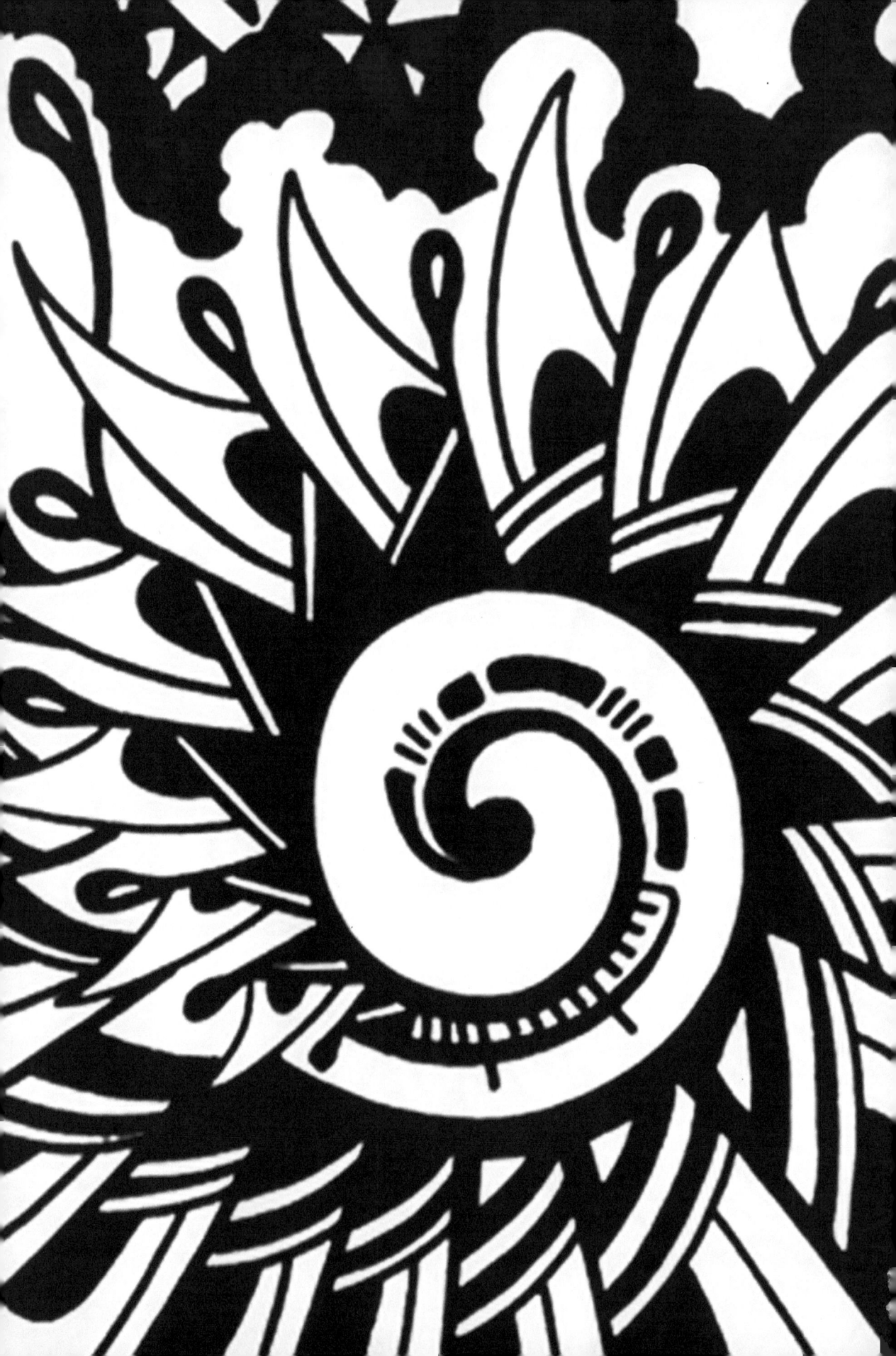

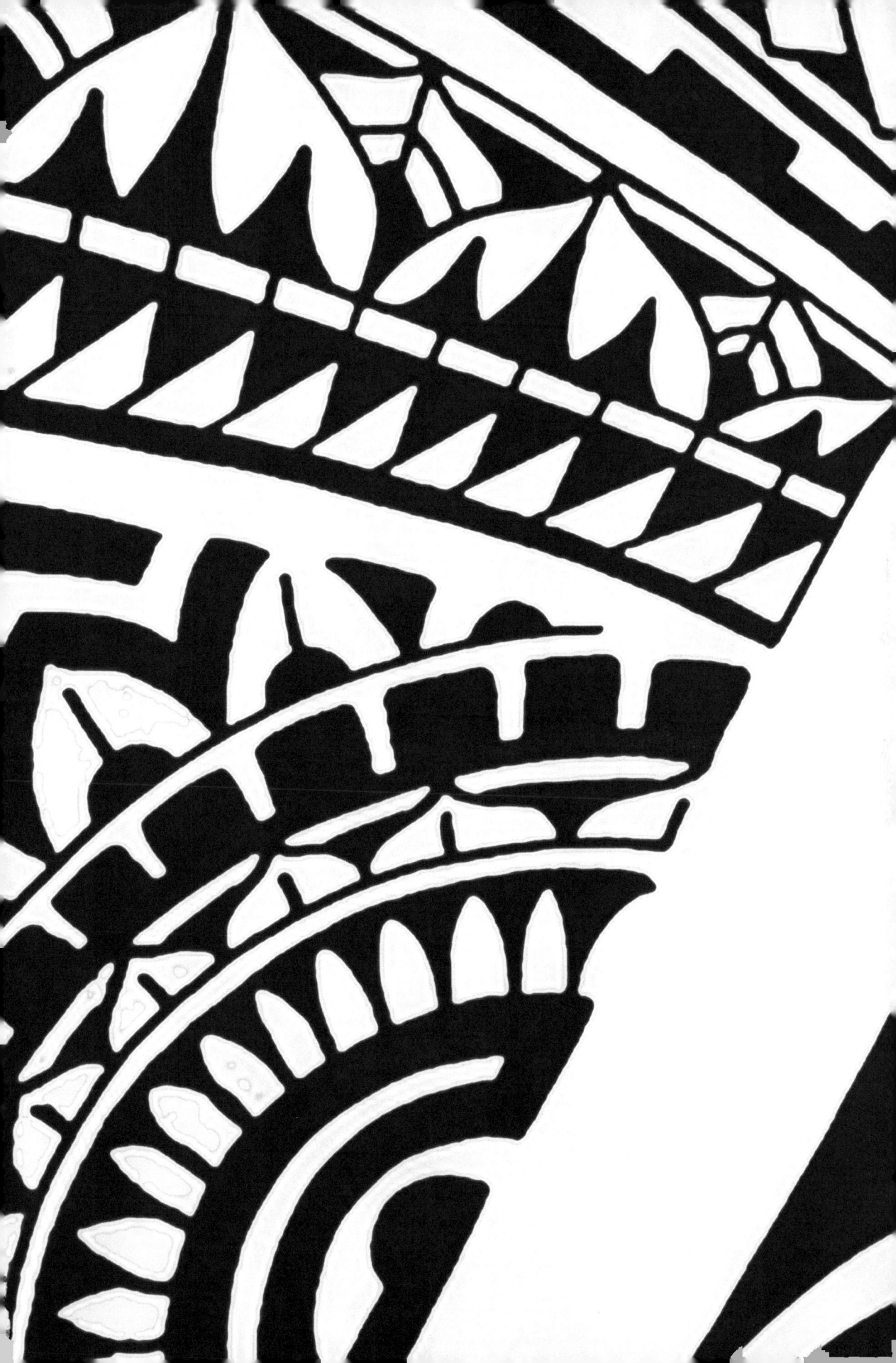

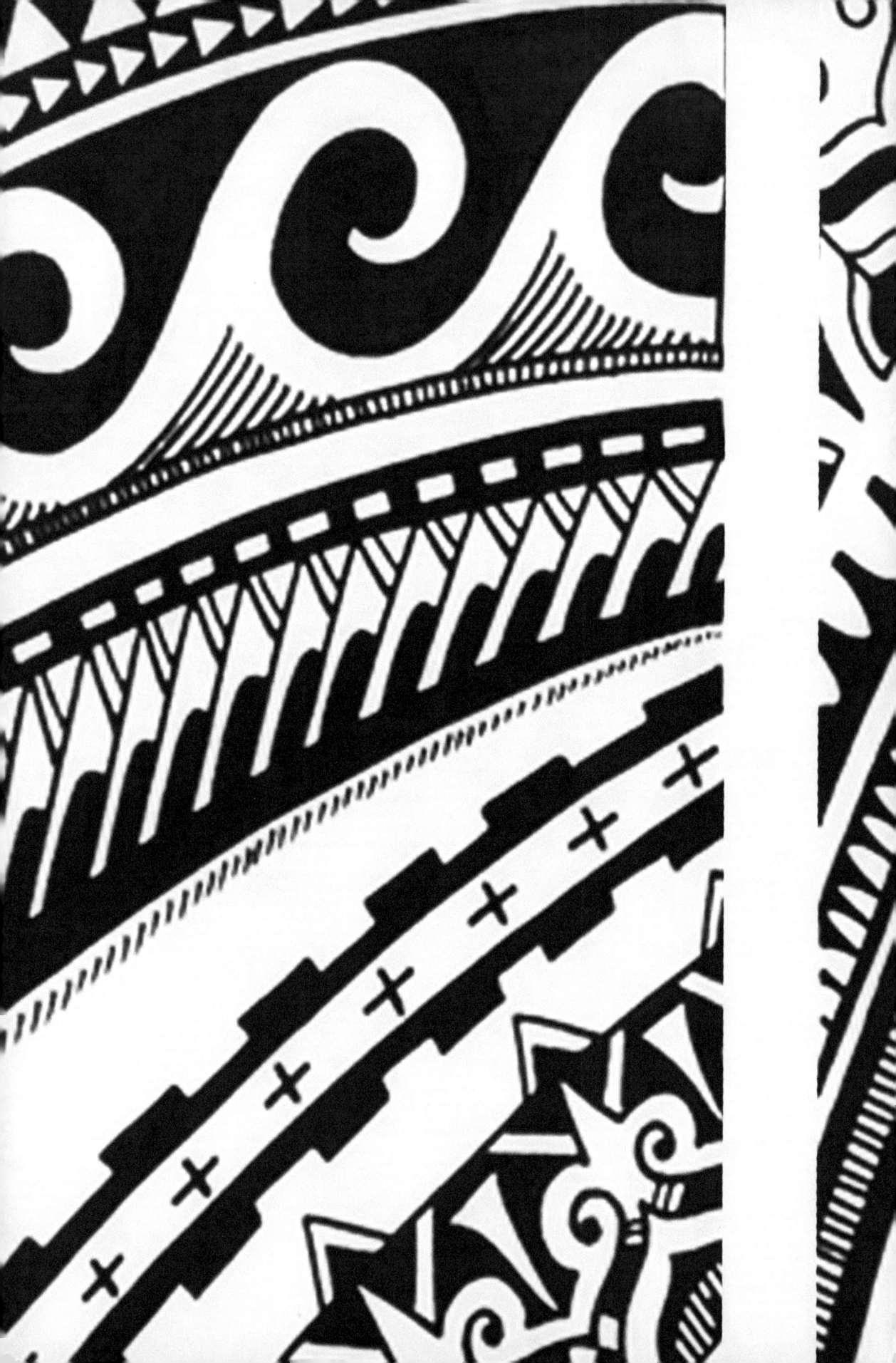

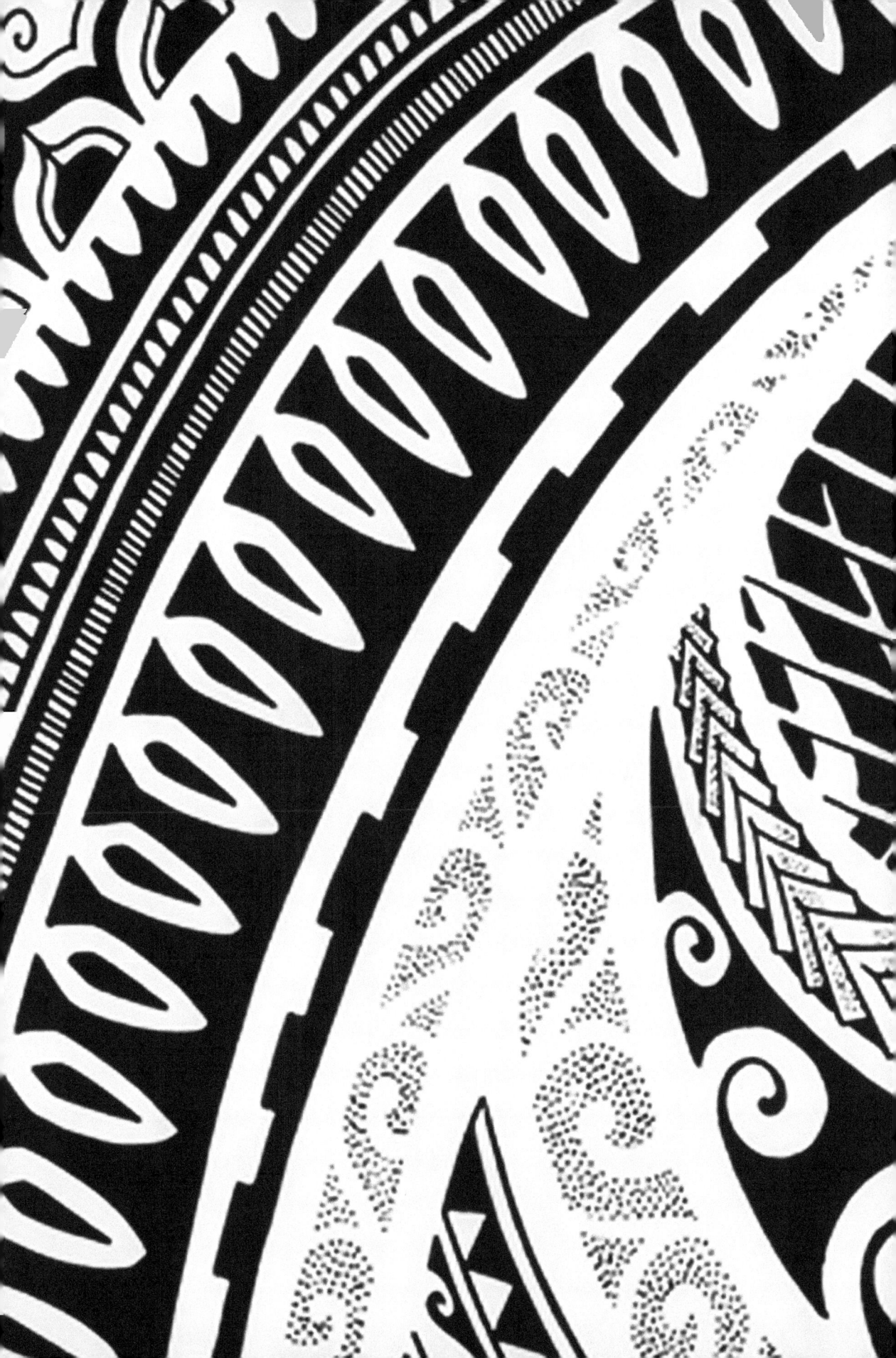

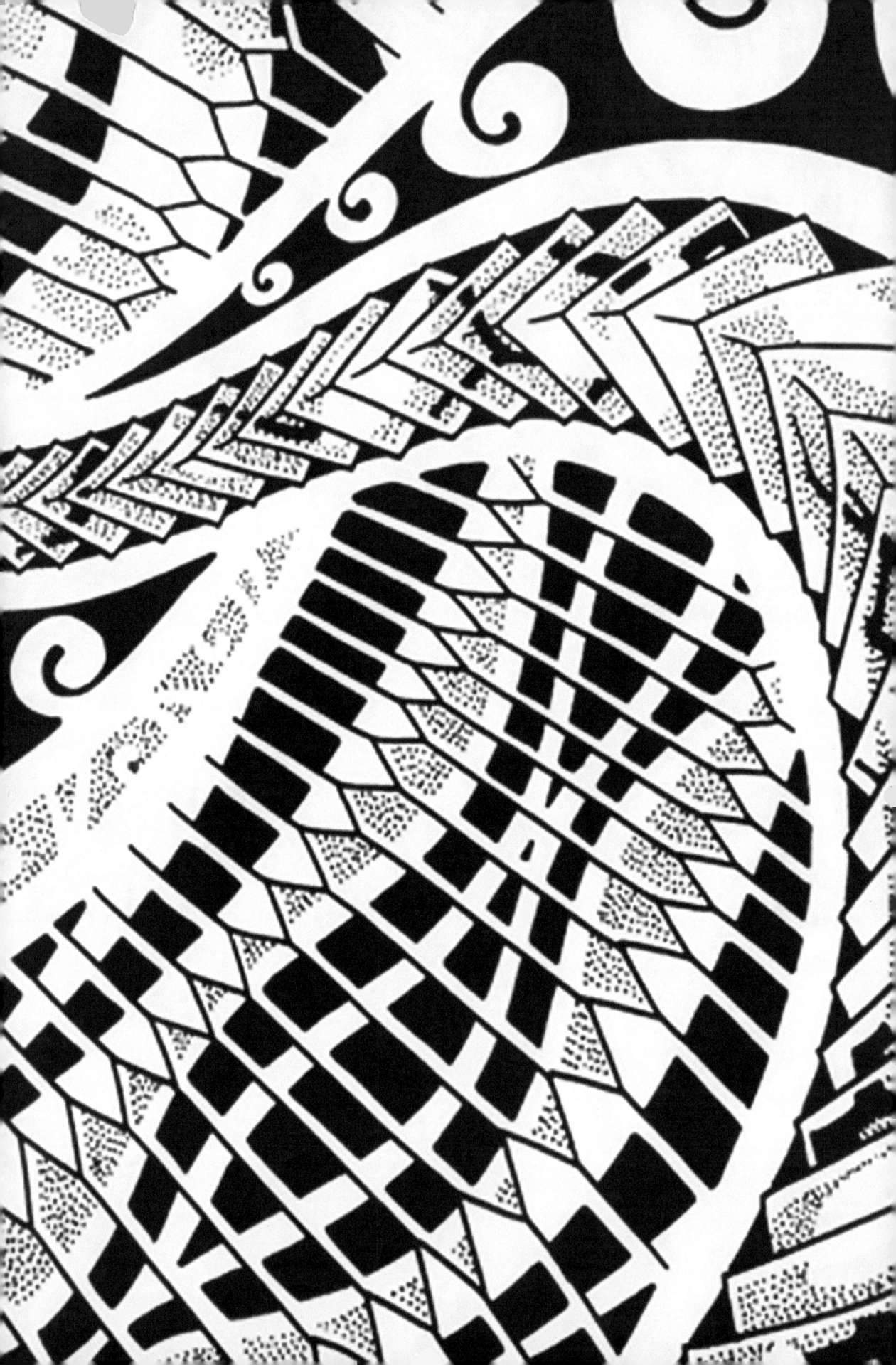

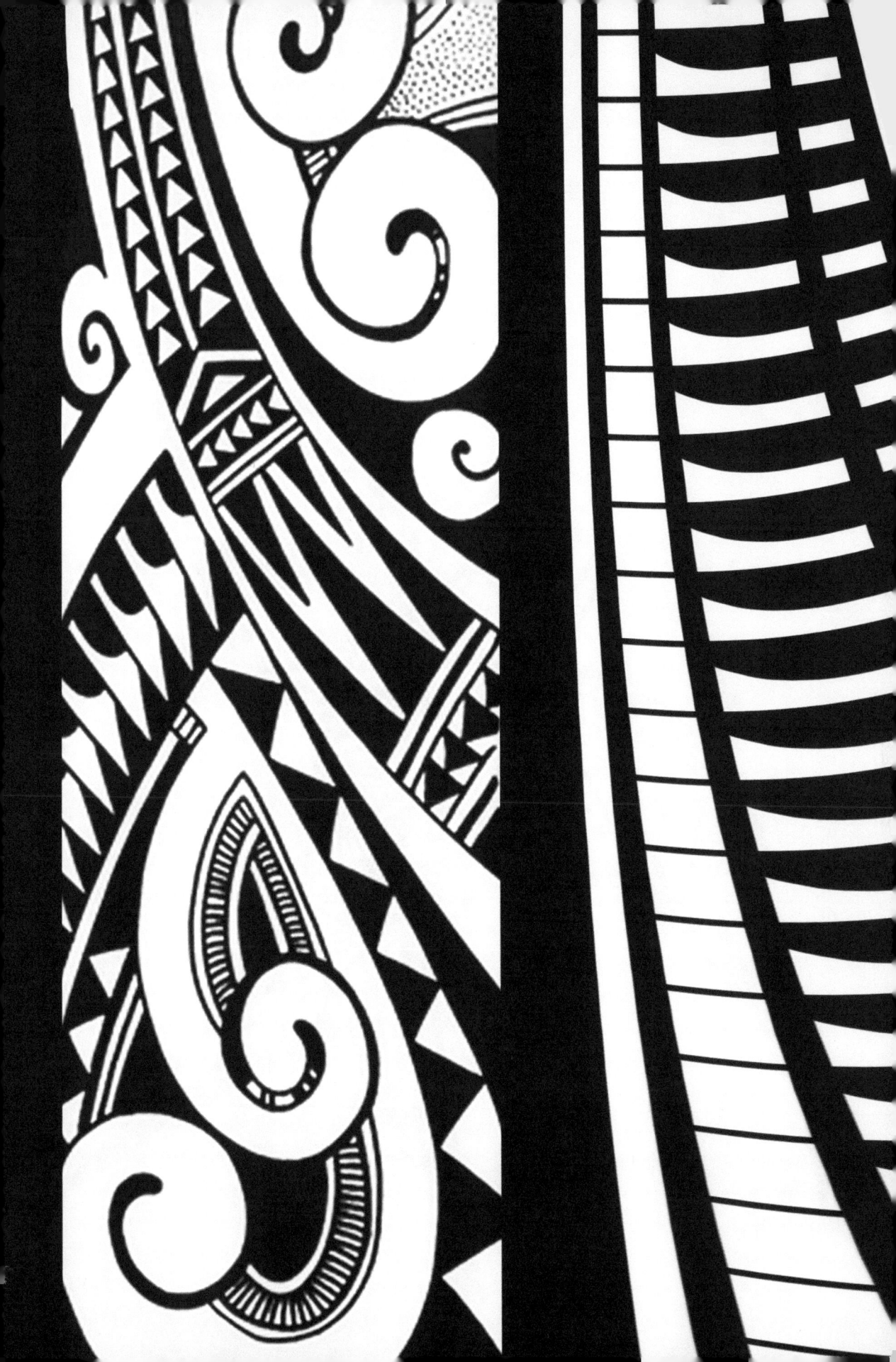

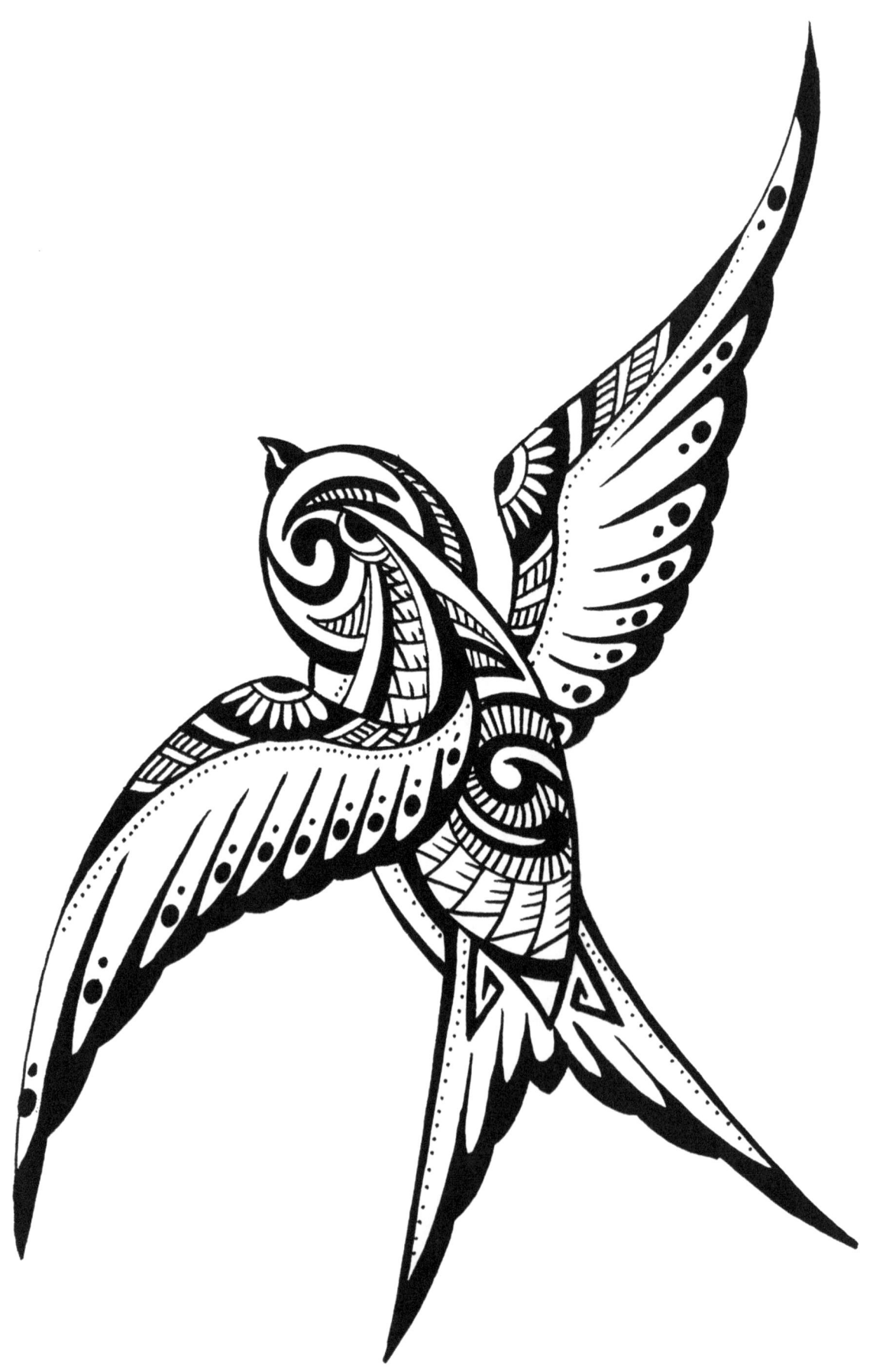

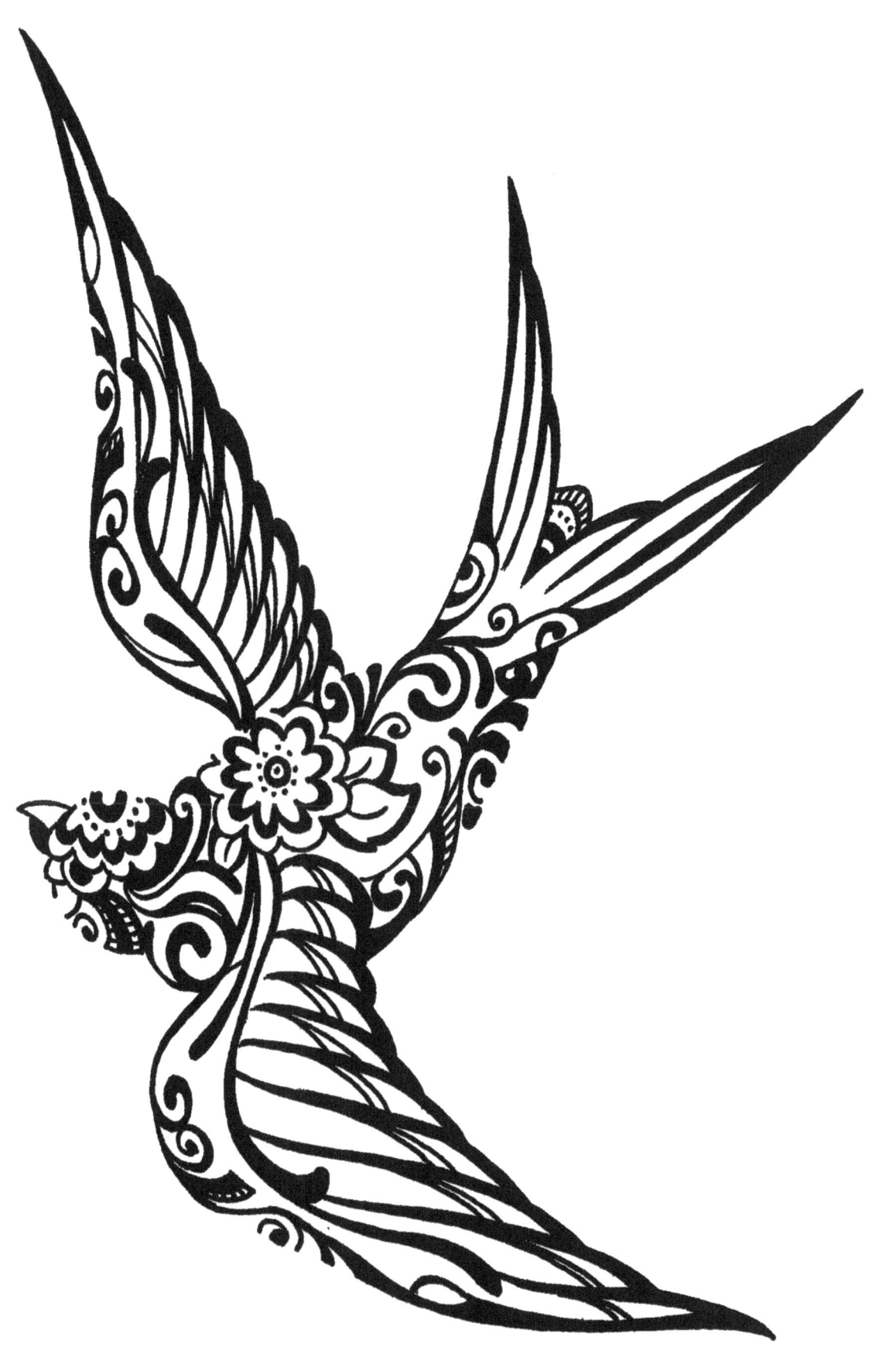

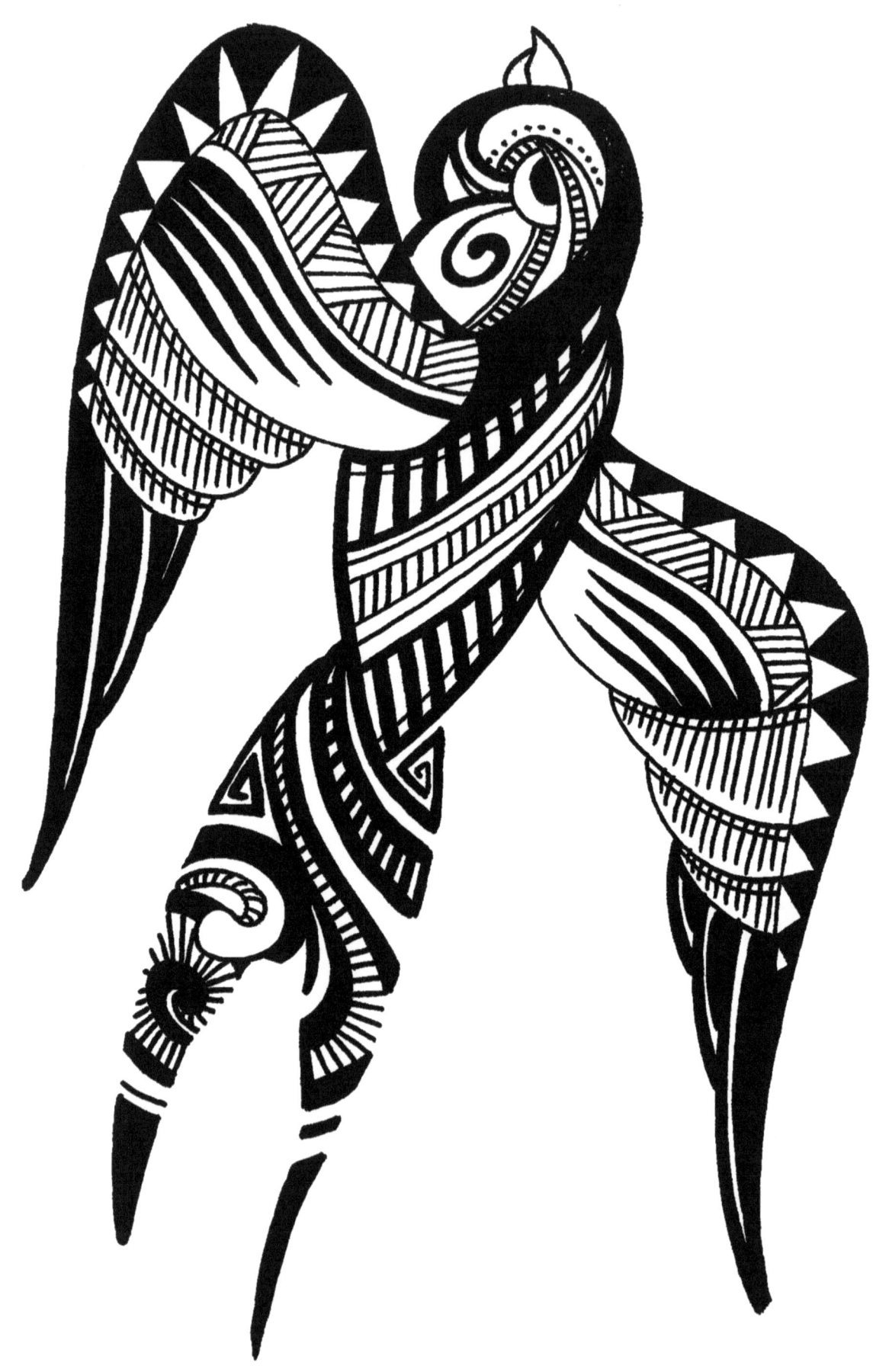

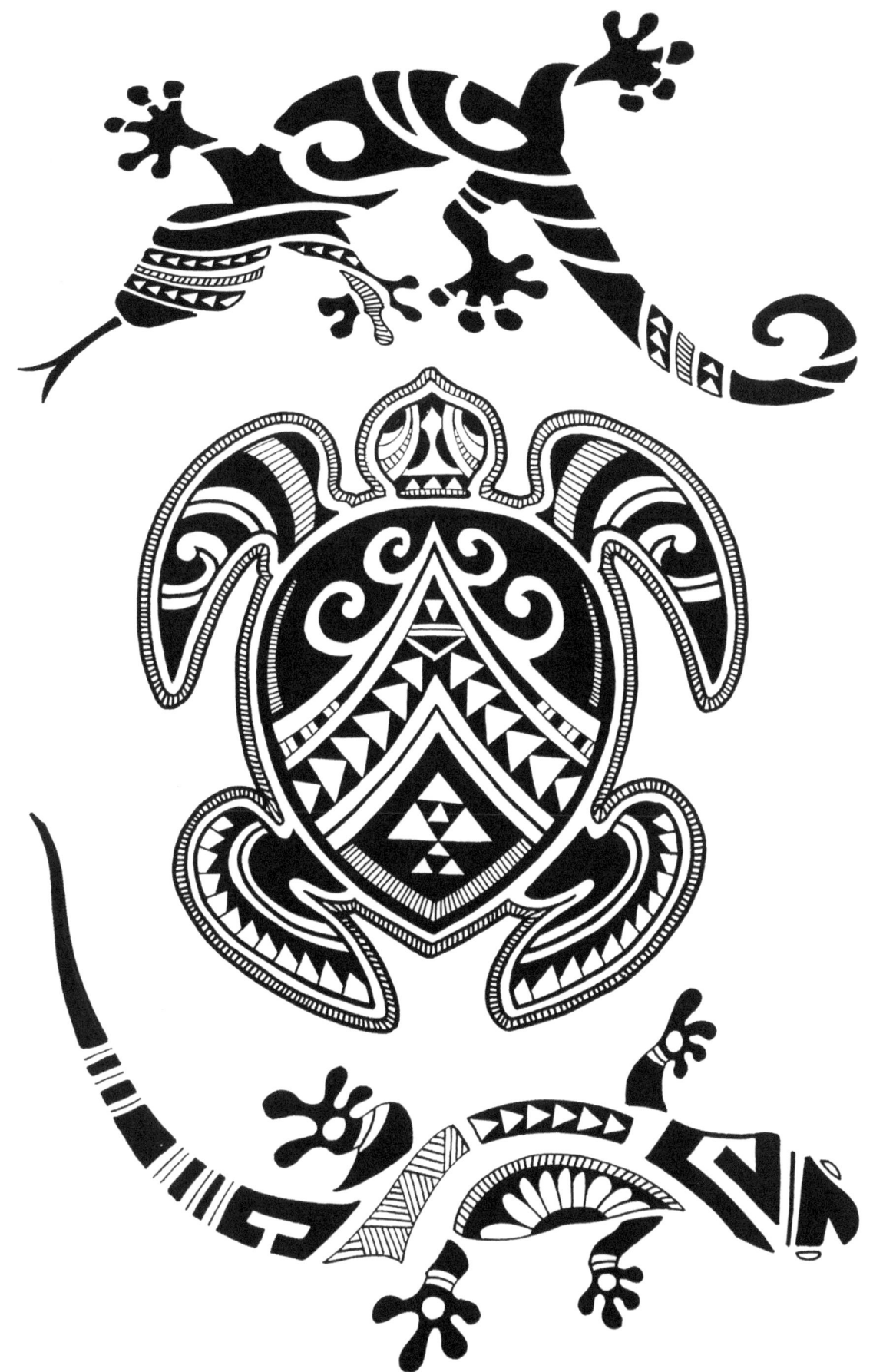

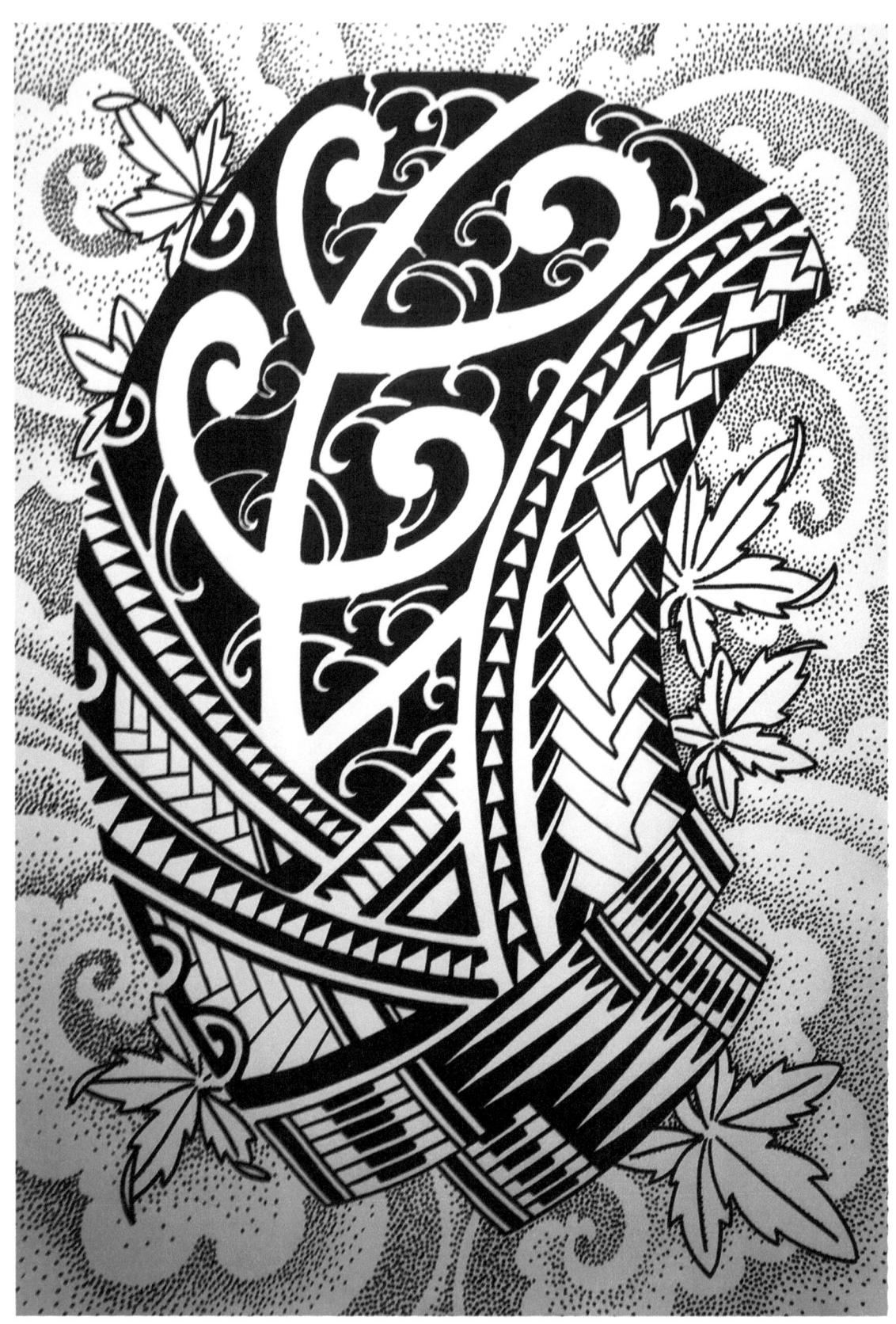

18" x 24"

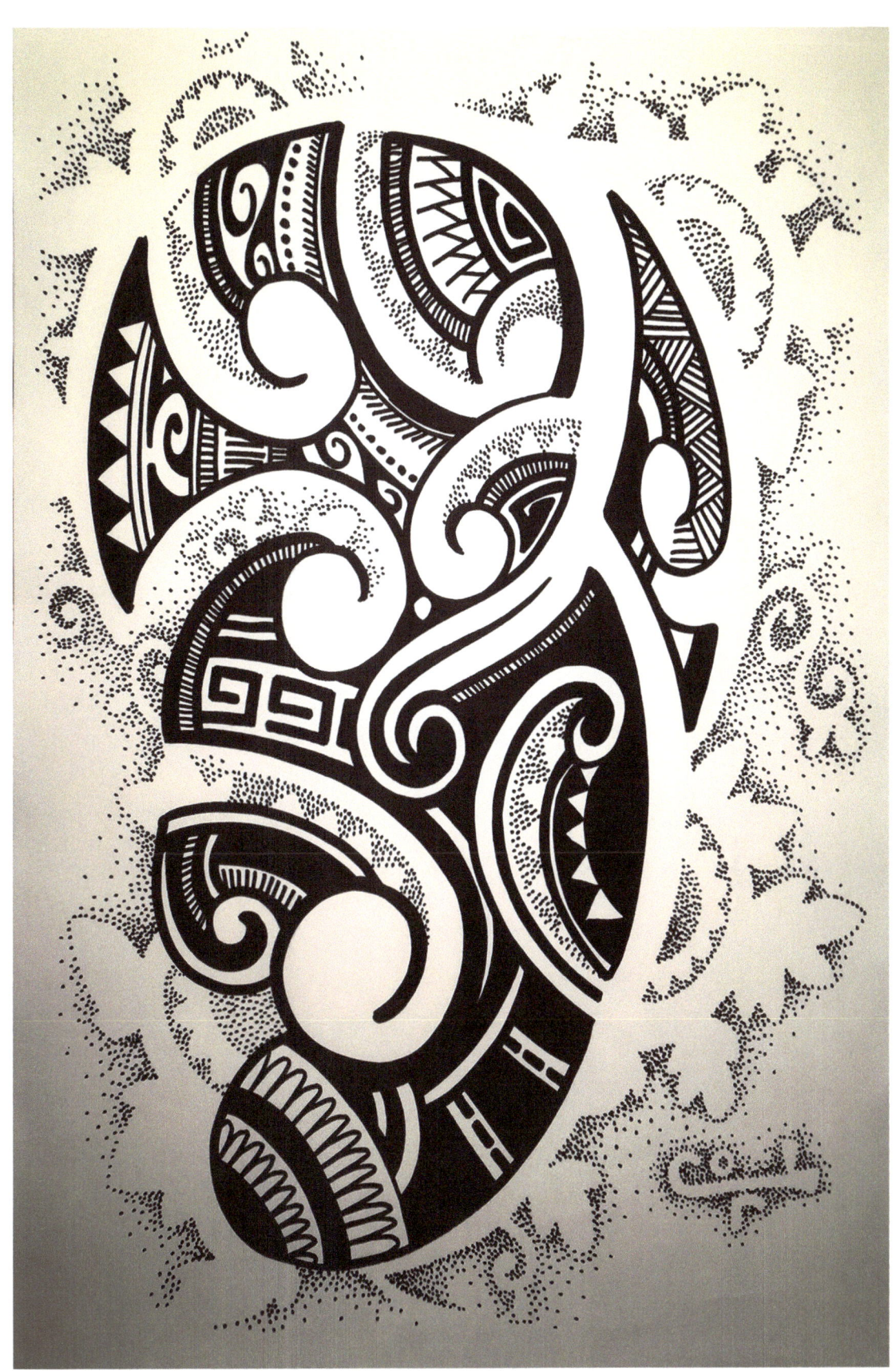

18" x 24"

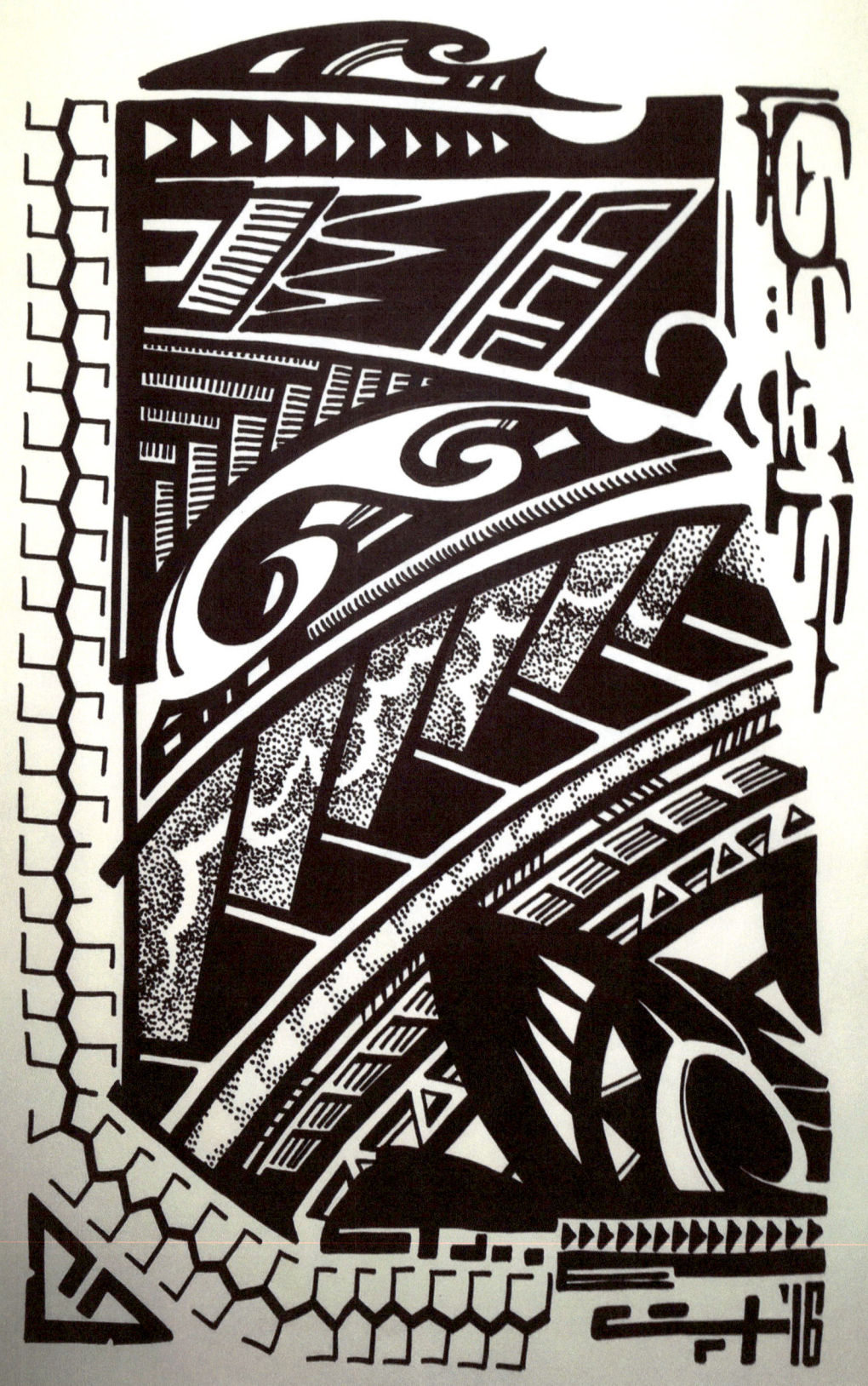

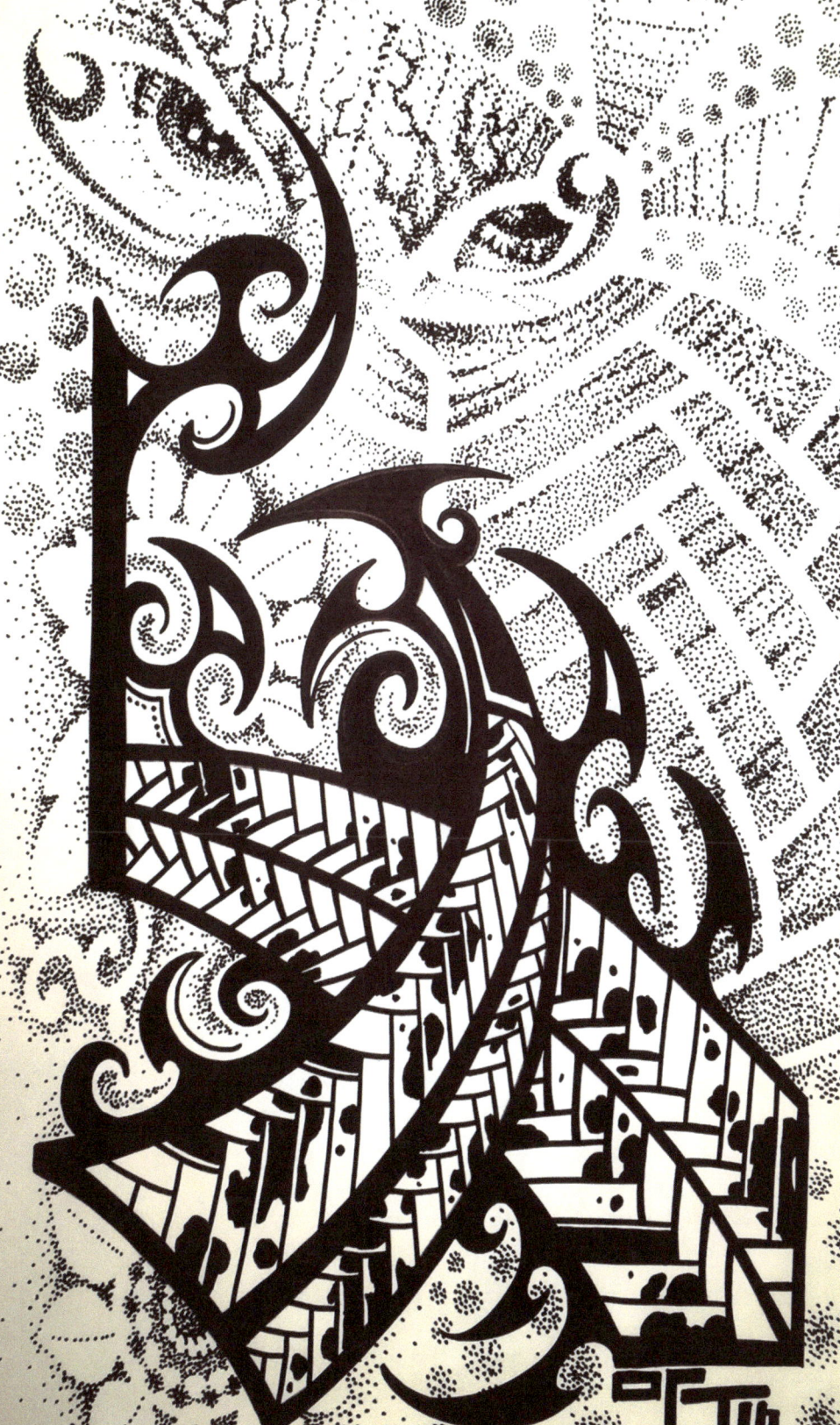

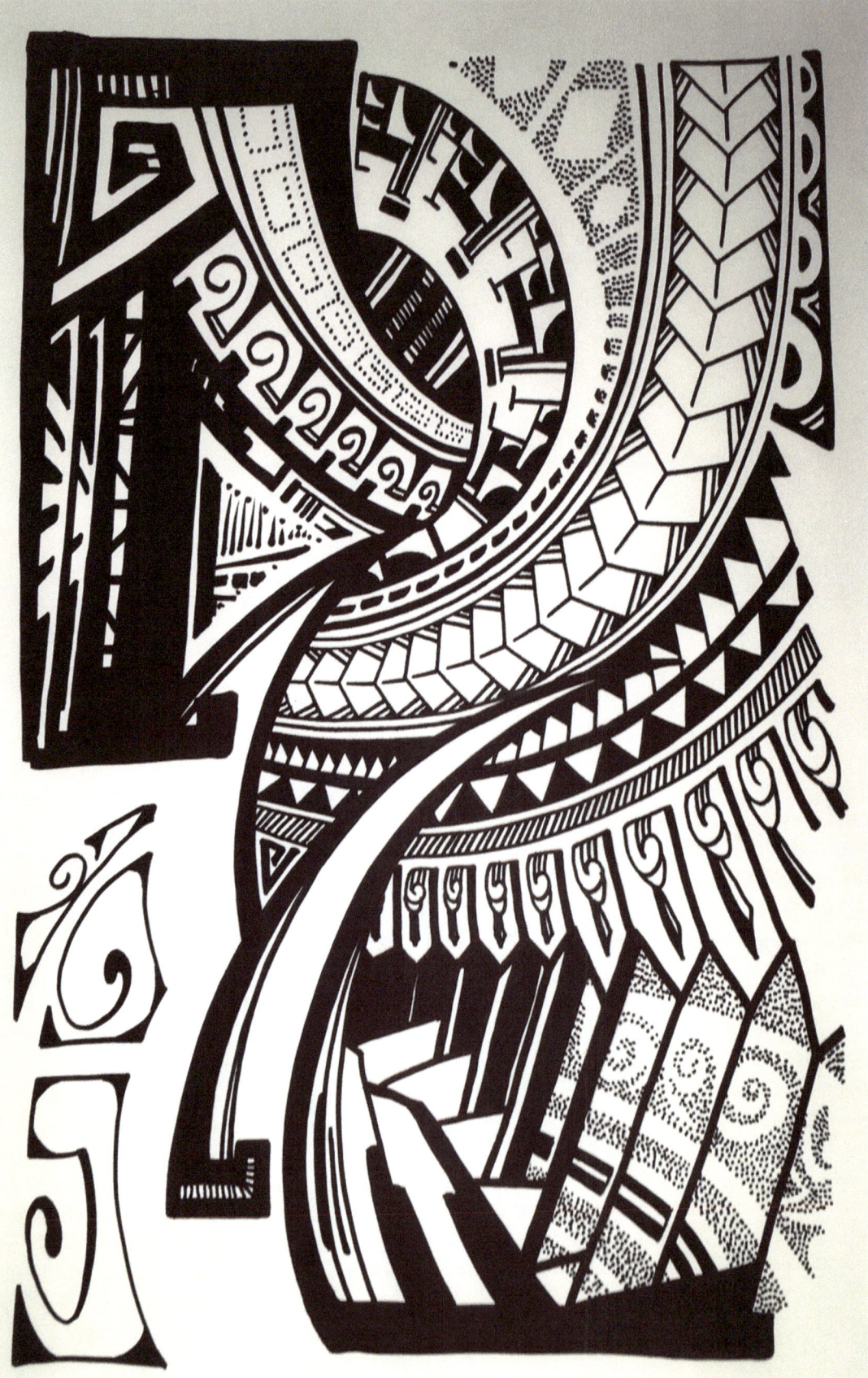

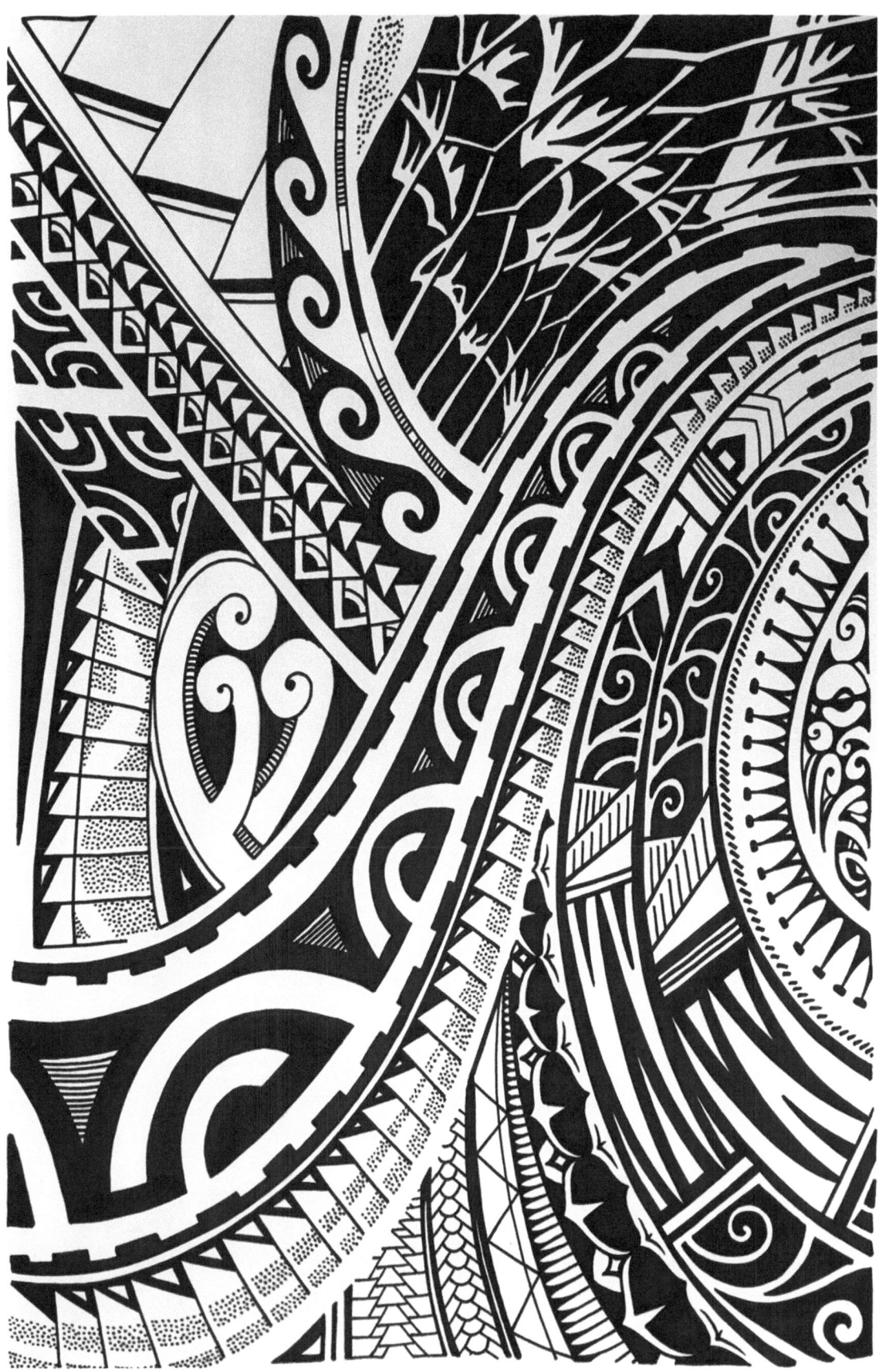

18" x 24"

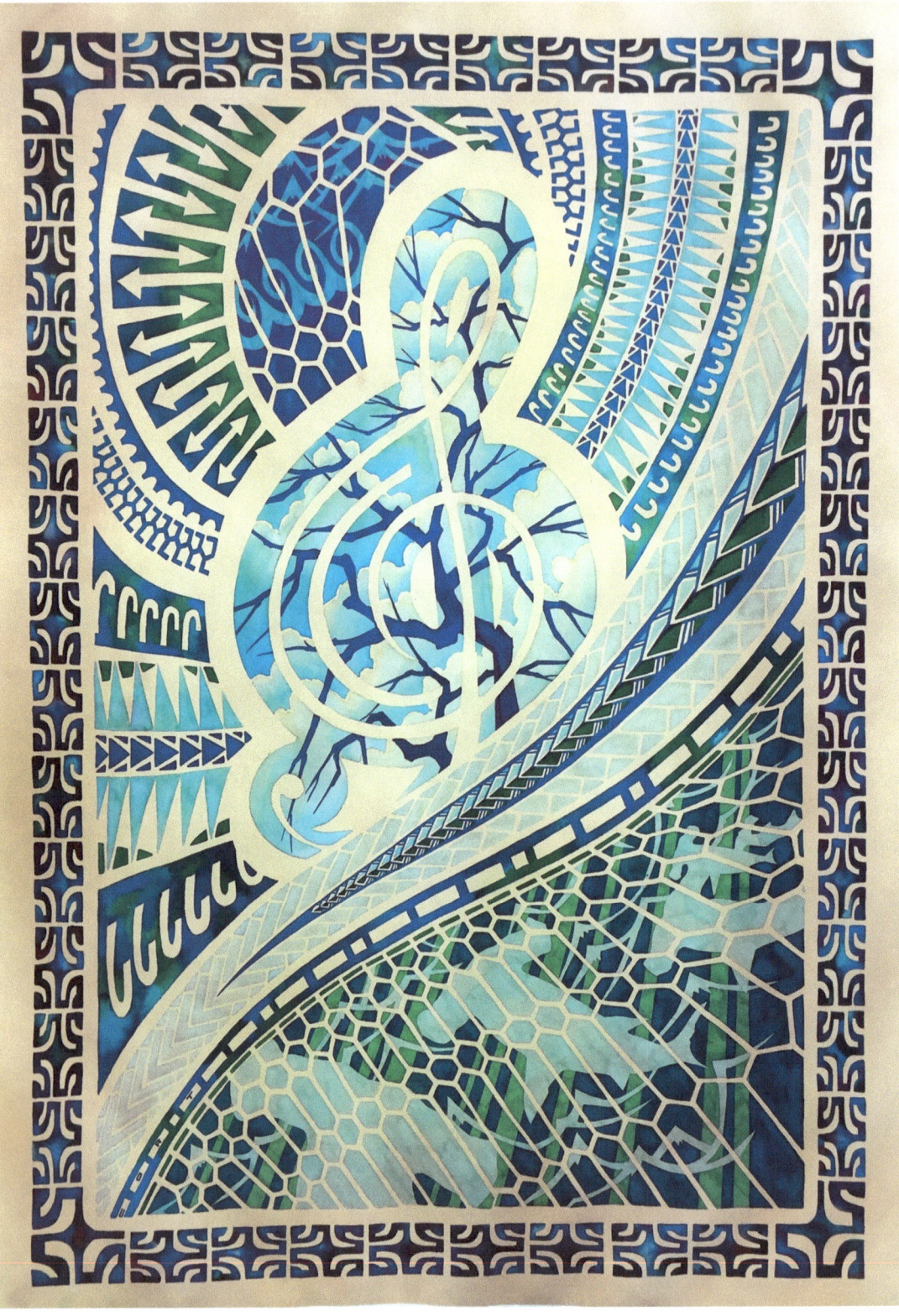

"Circle of Life"
Original size 40" x 52"

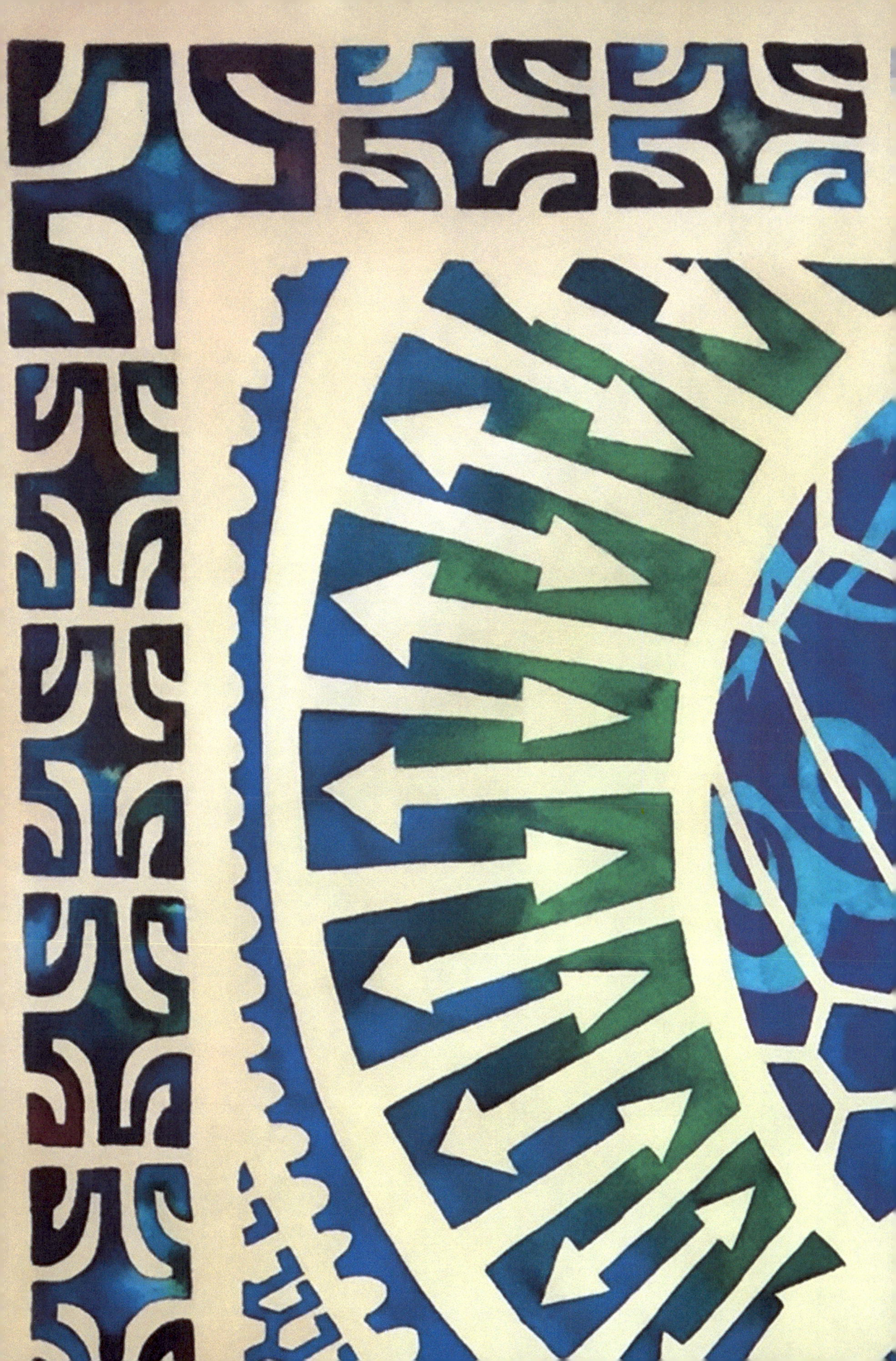

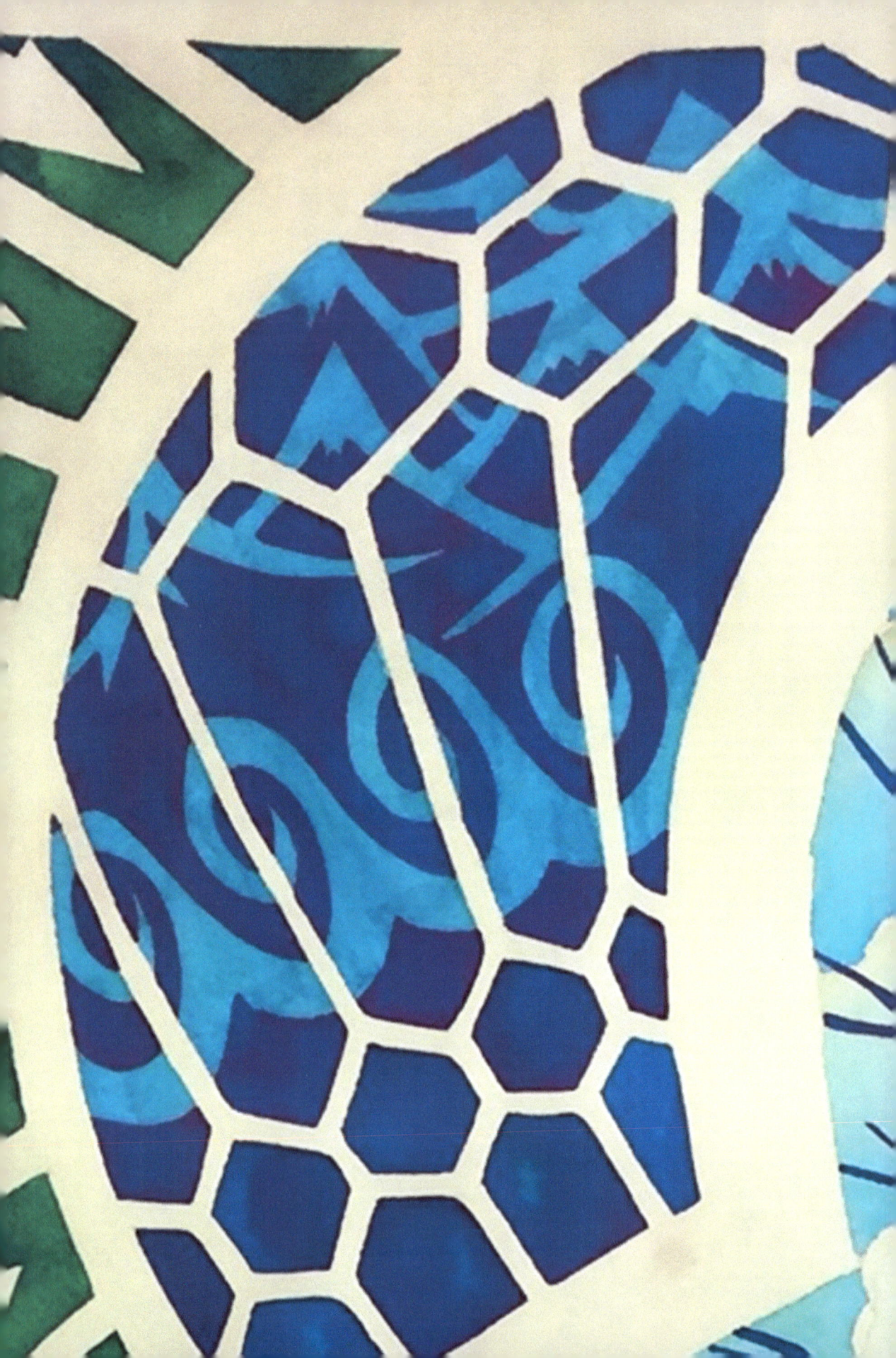

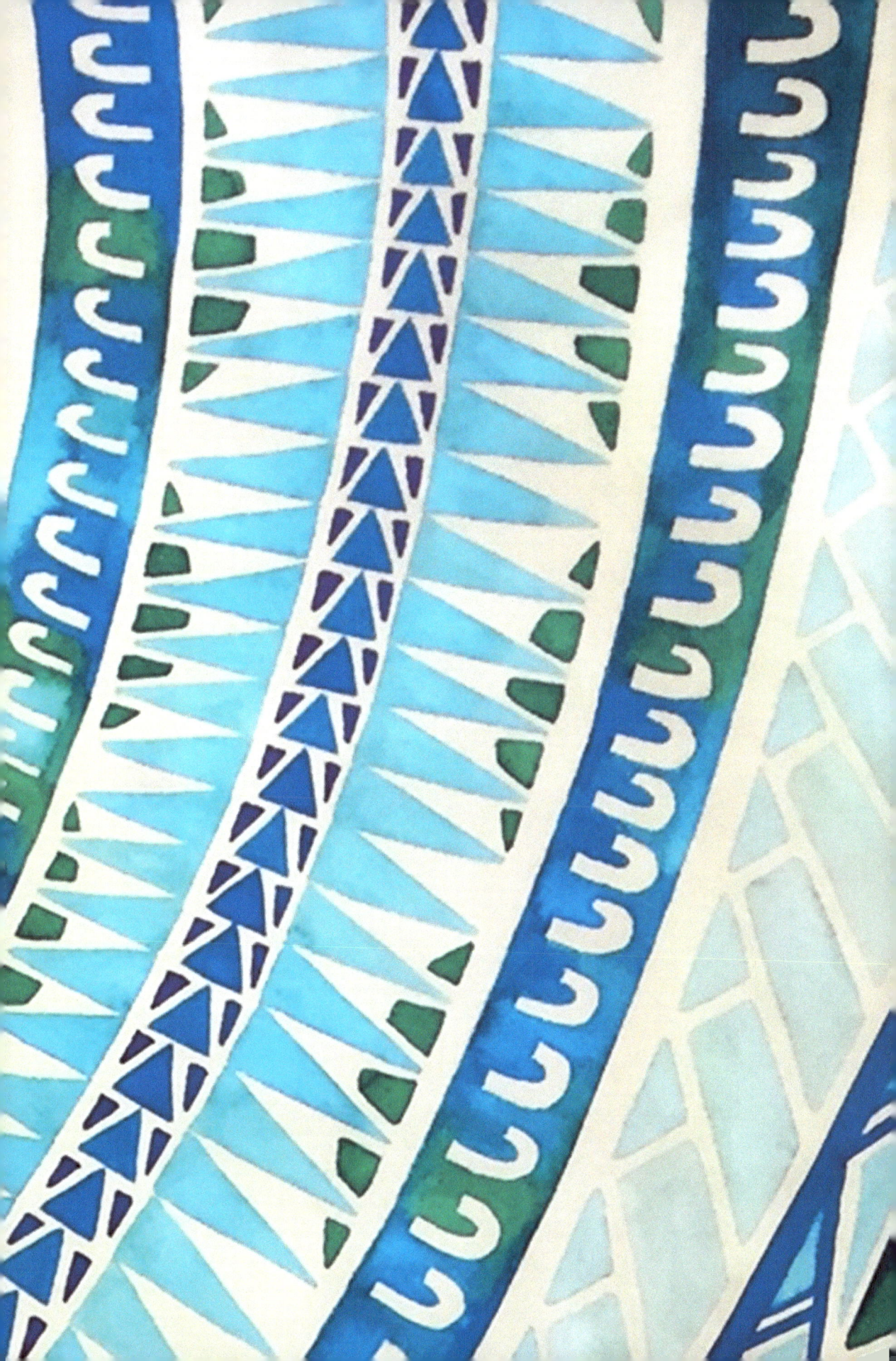

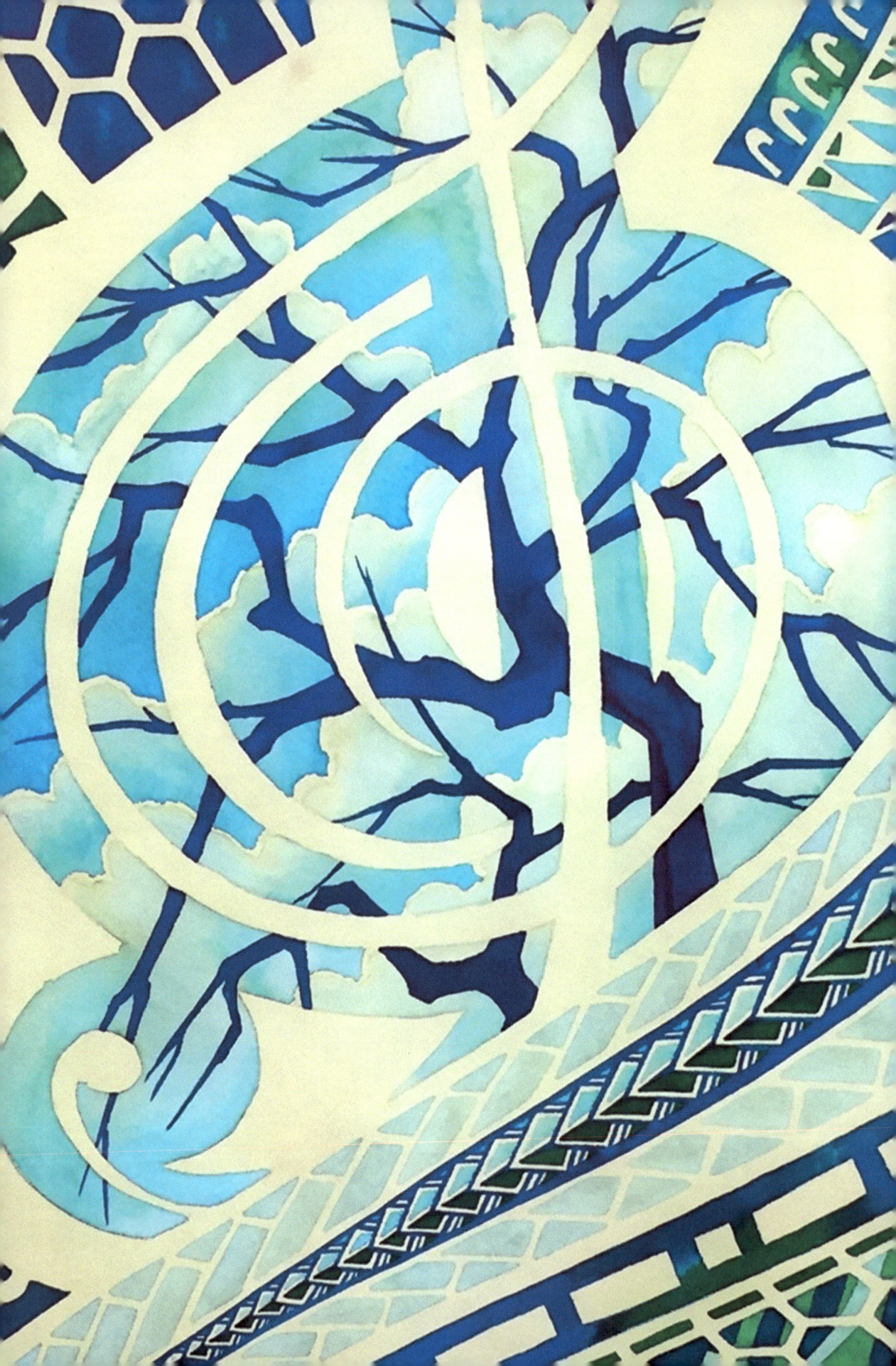

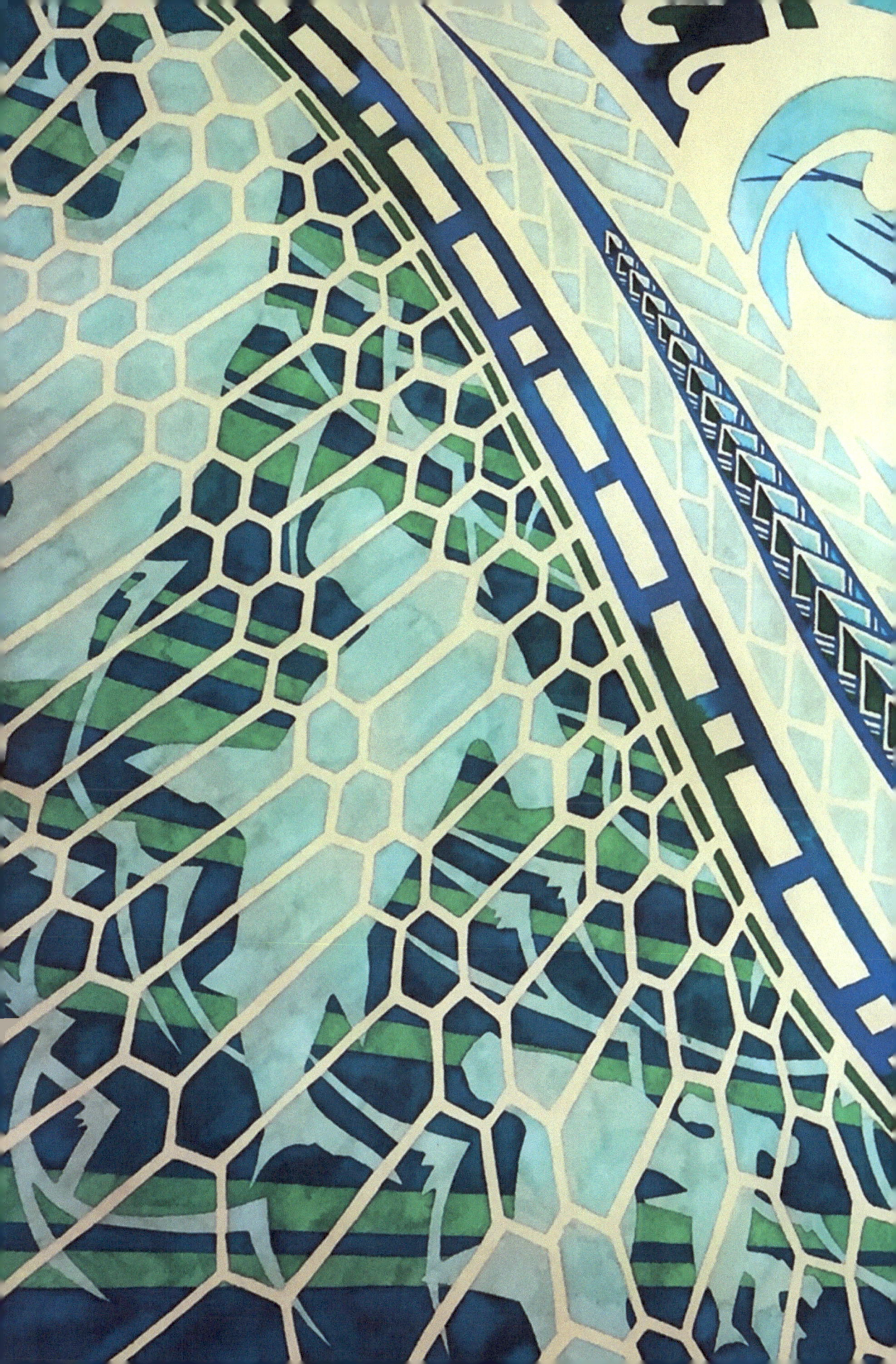

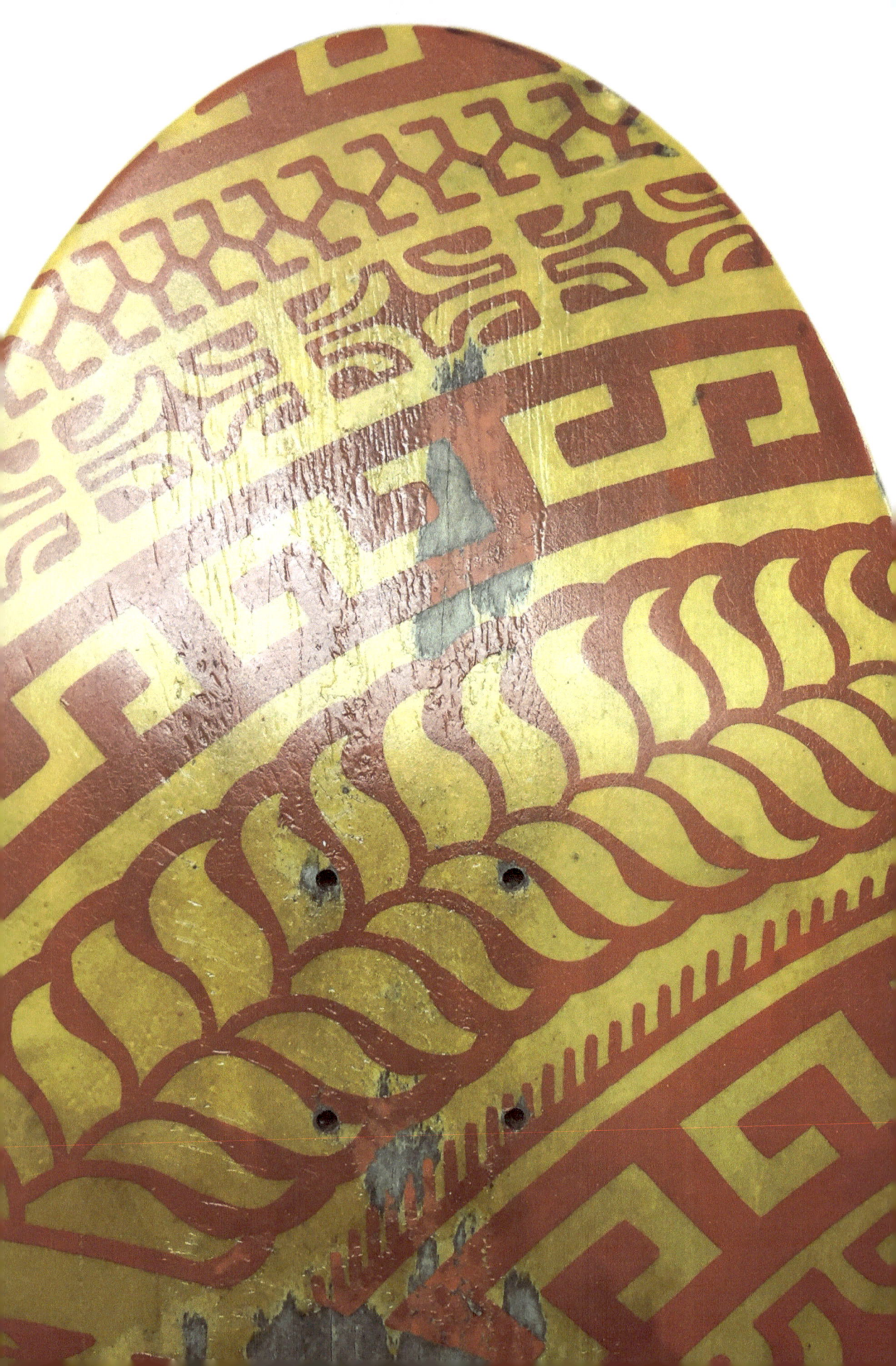

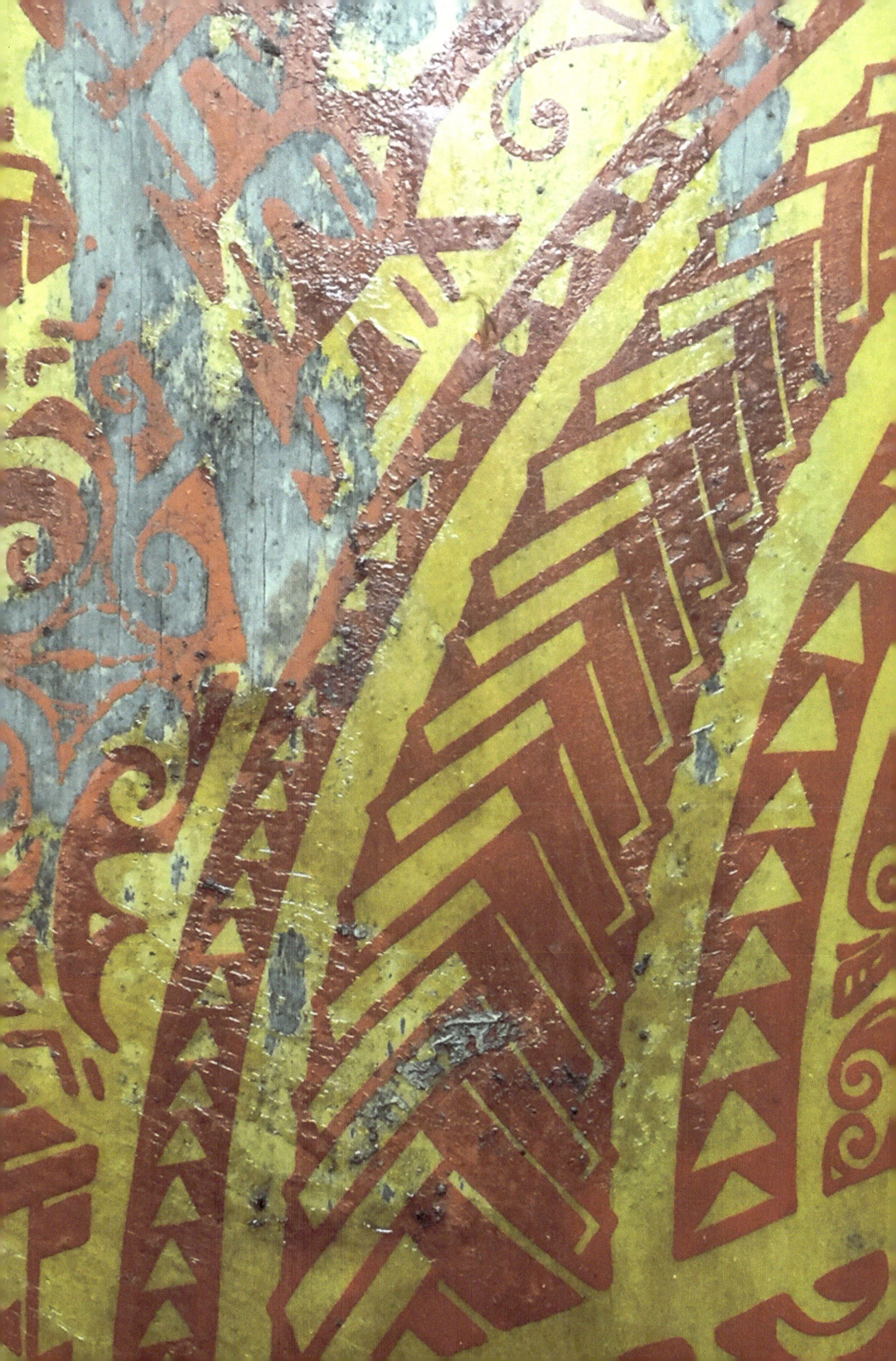

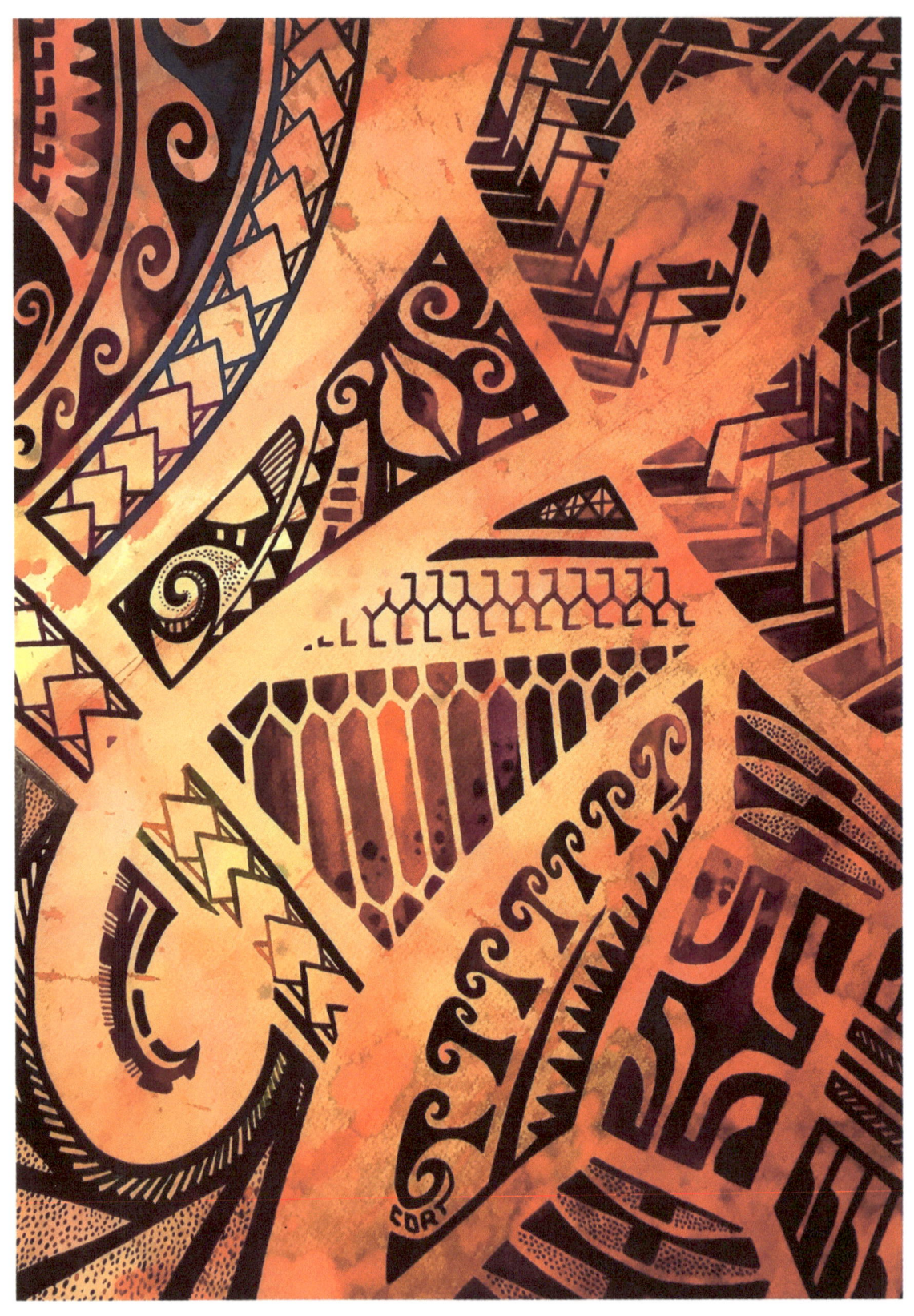

18" x 24" watercolor

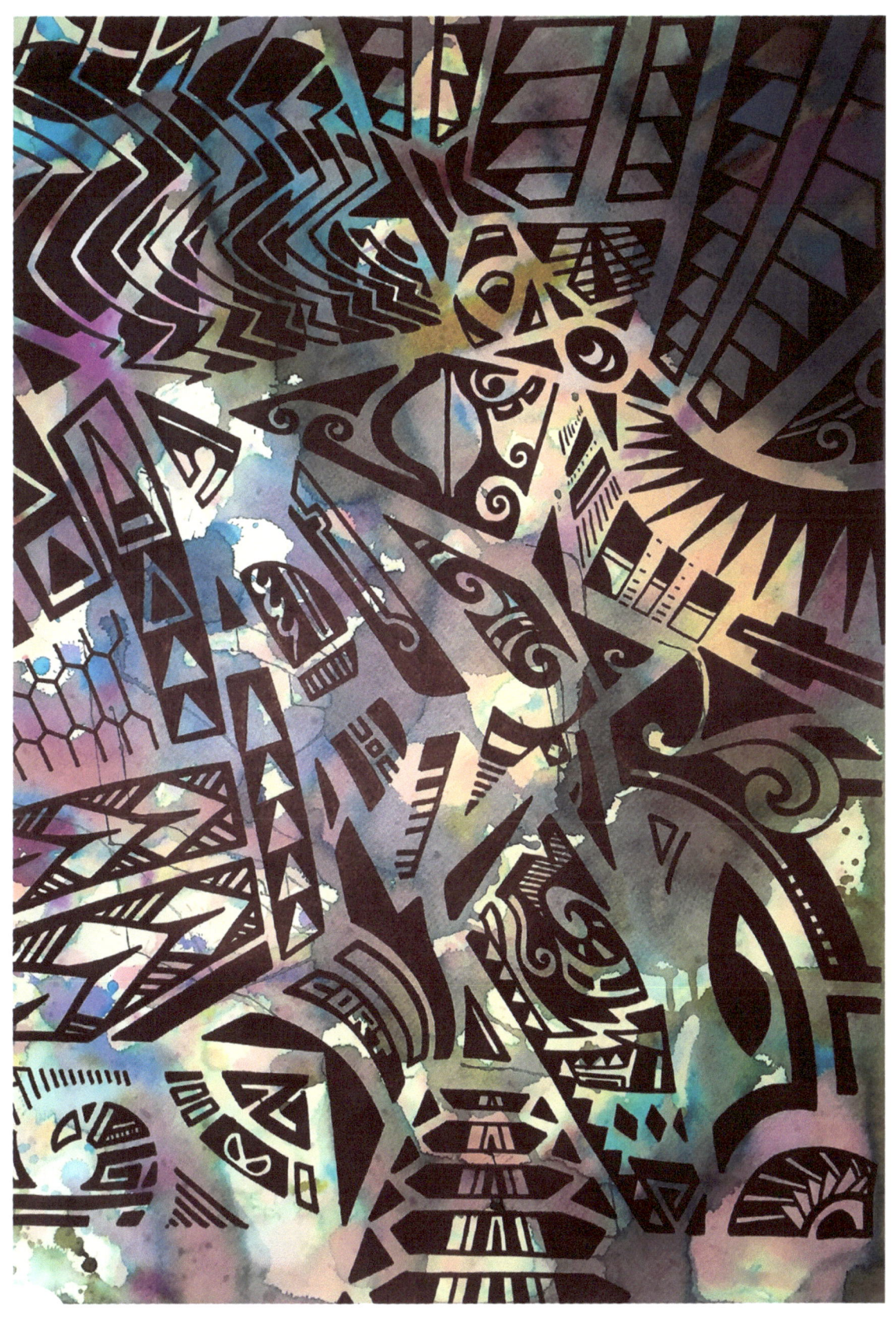

18" x 24" watercolor and marker

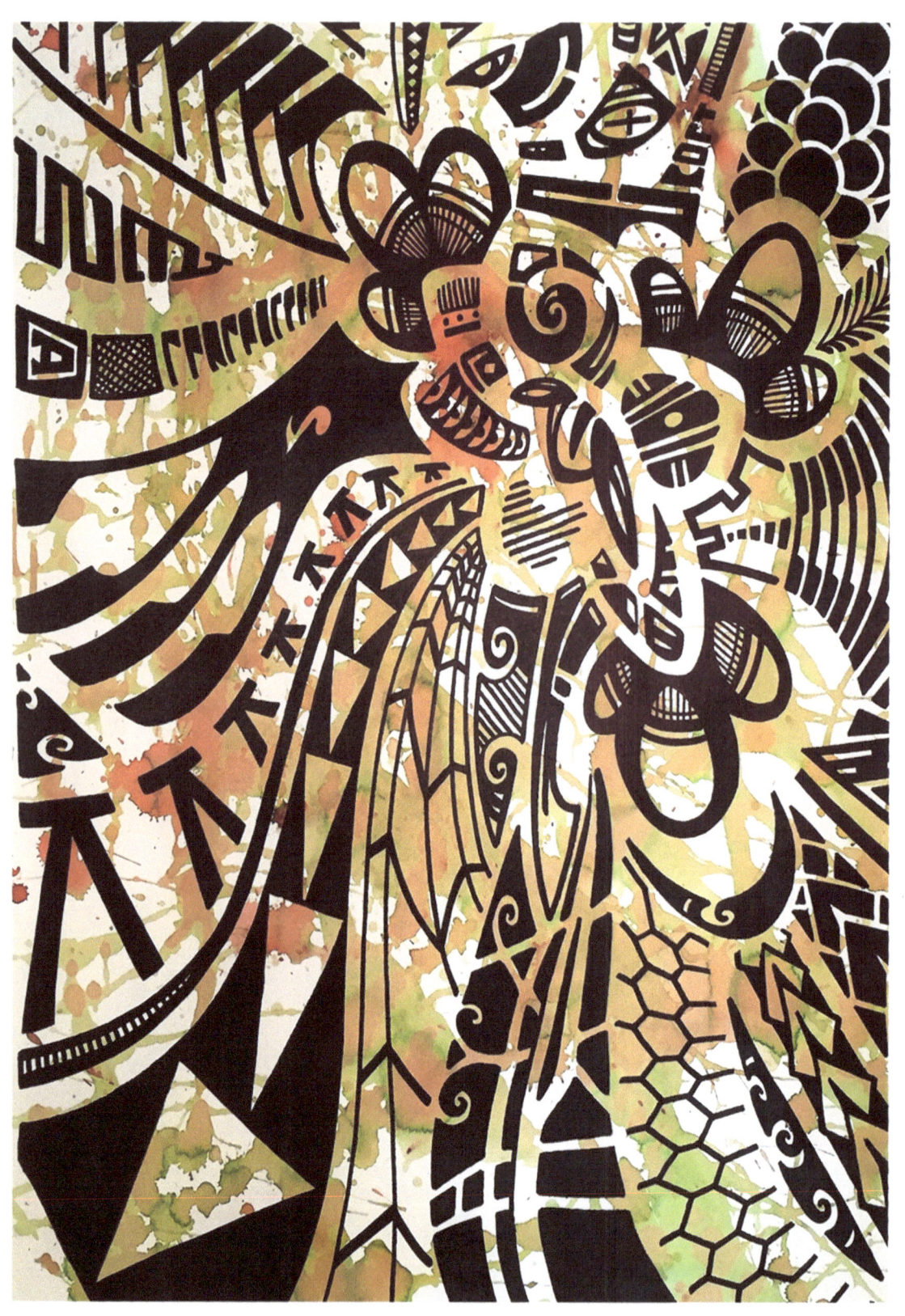

18" x 24" watercolor and marker

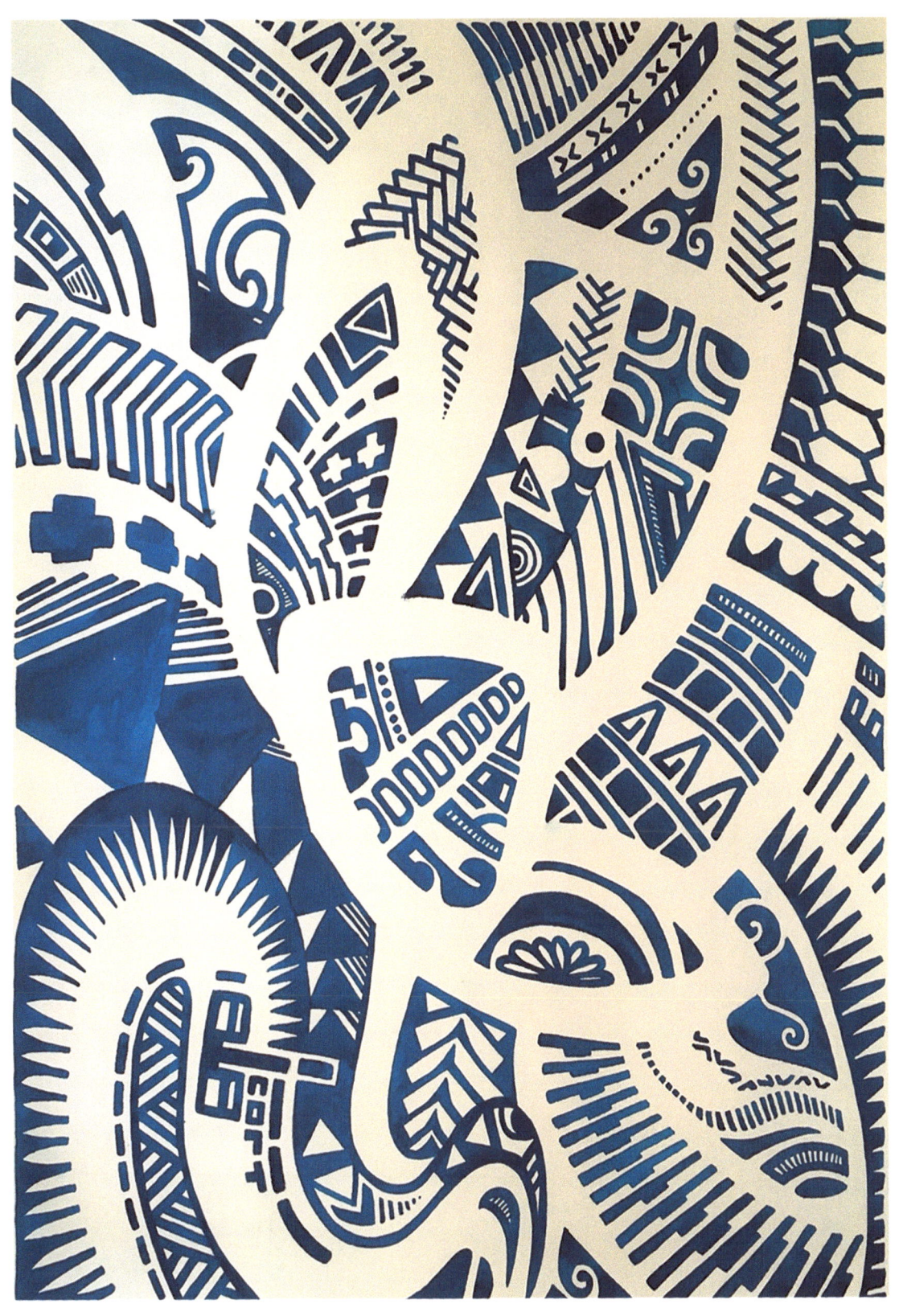

18" x 24" watercolor

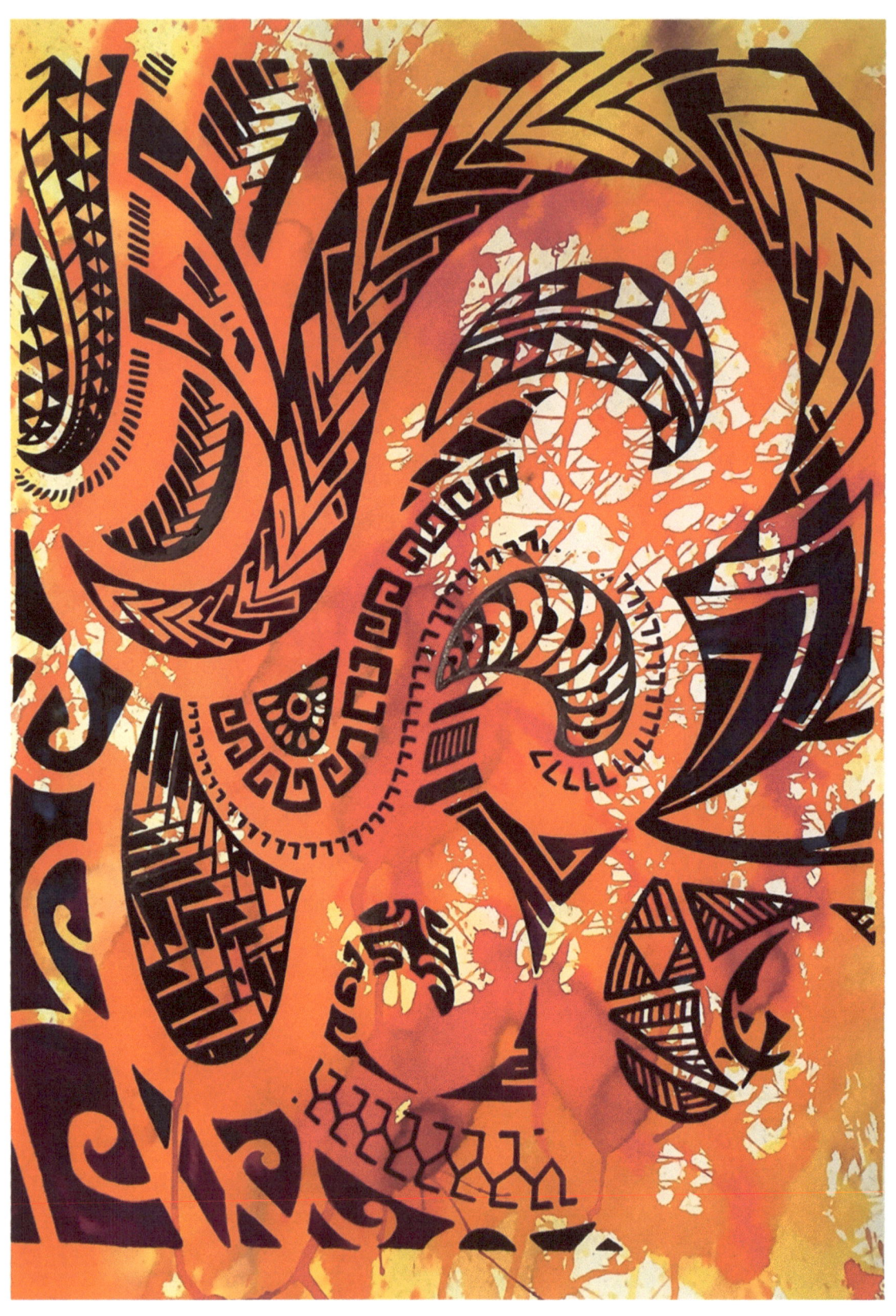

18" x 24" watercolor

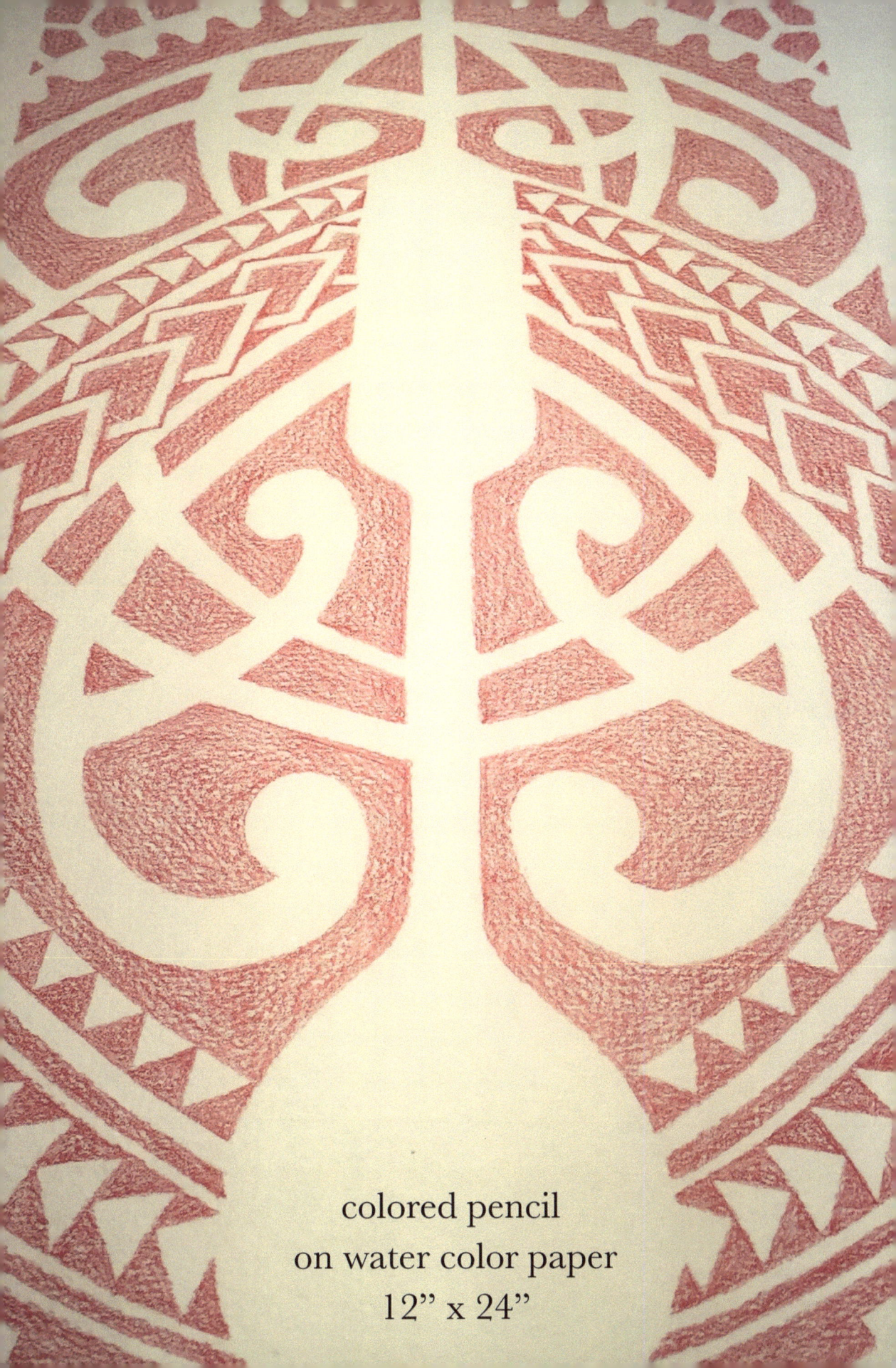

colored pencil
on water color paper
12" x 24"

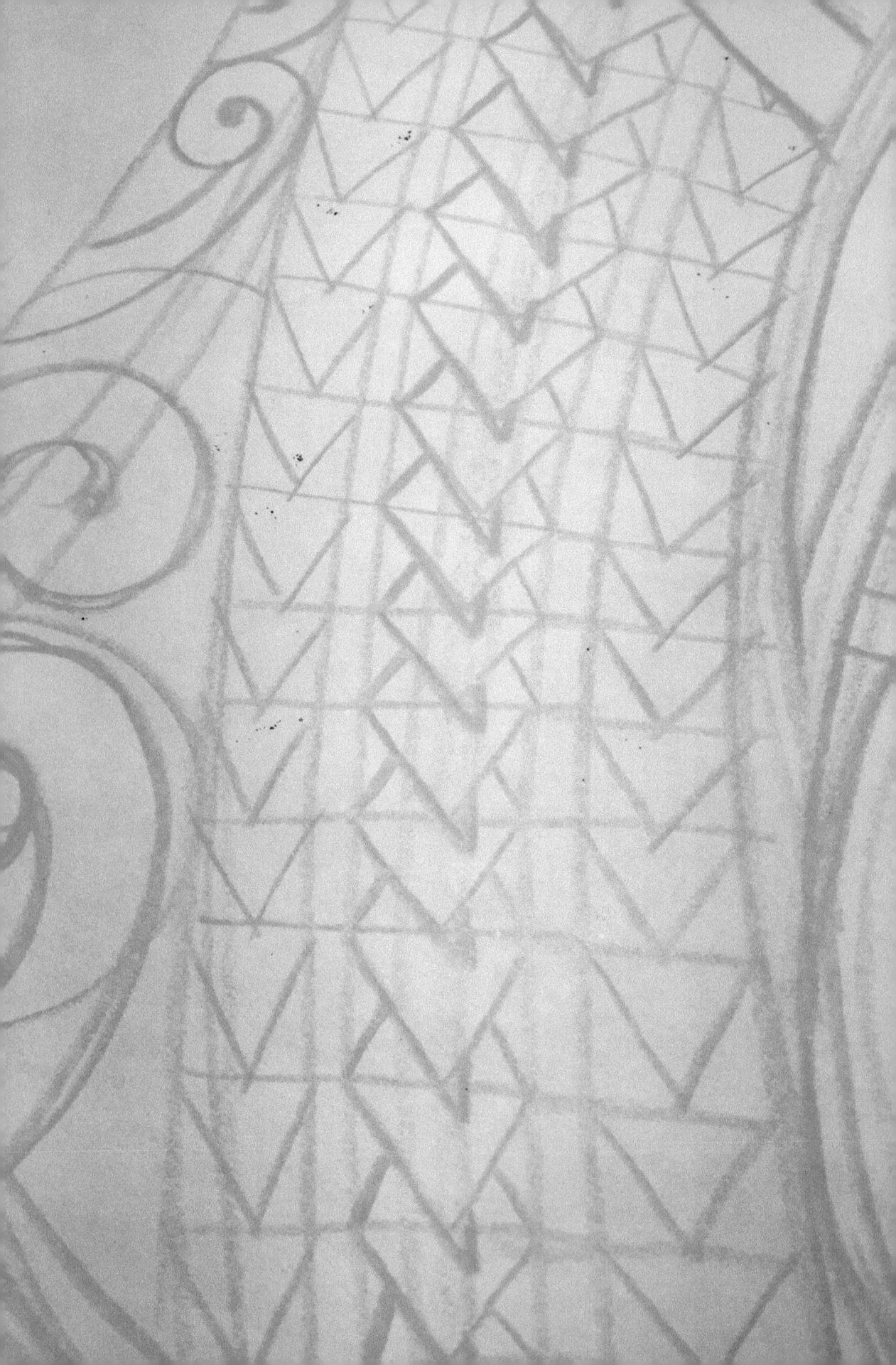

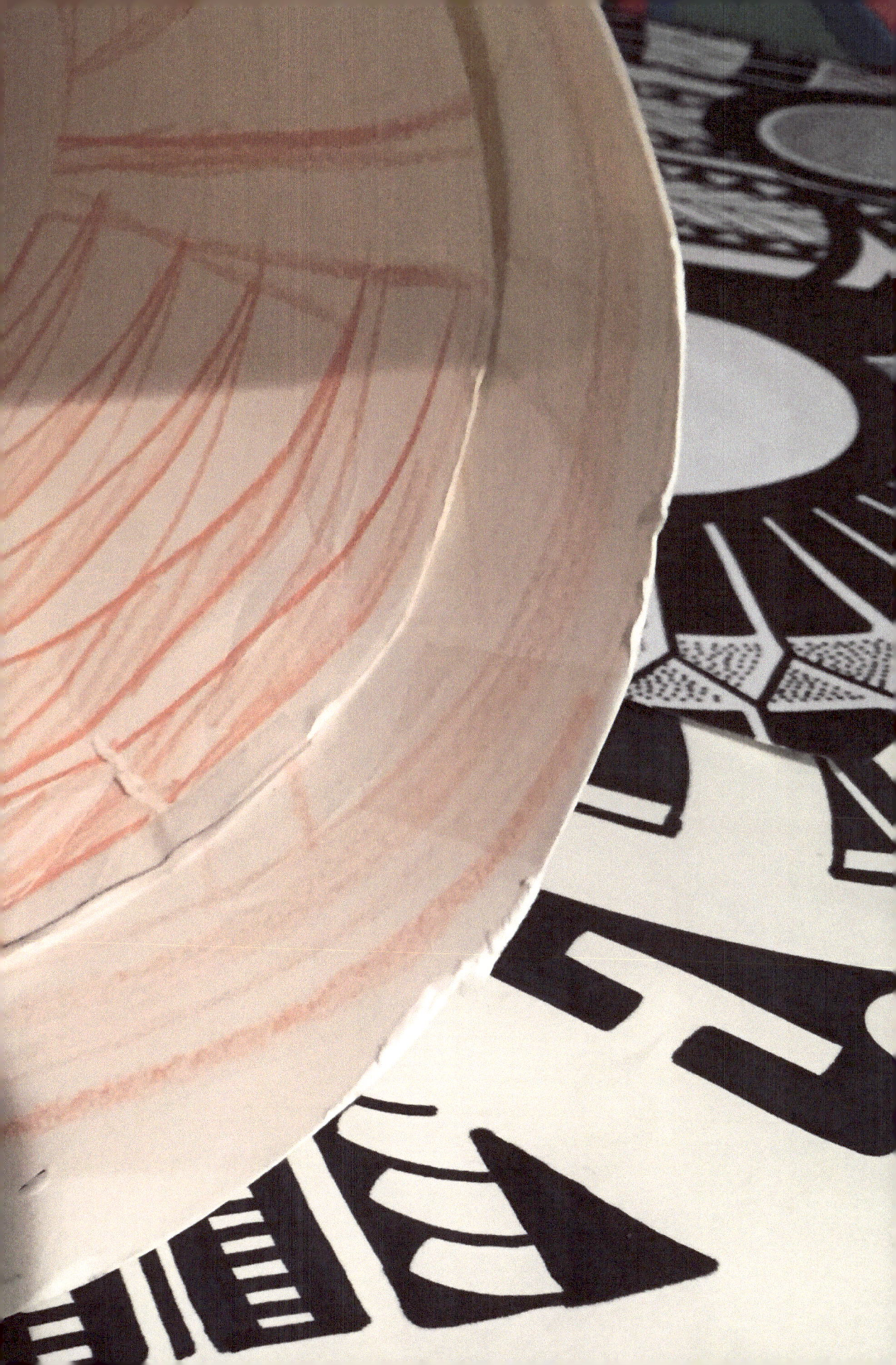

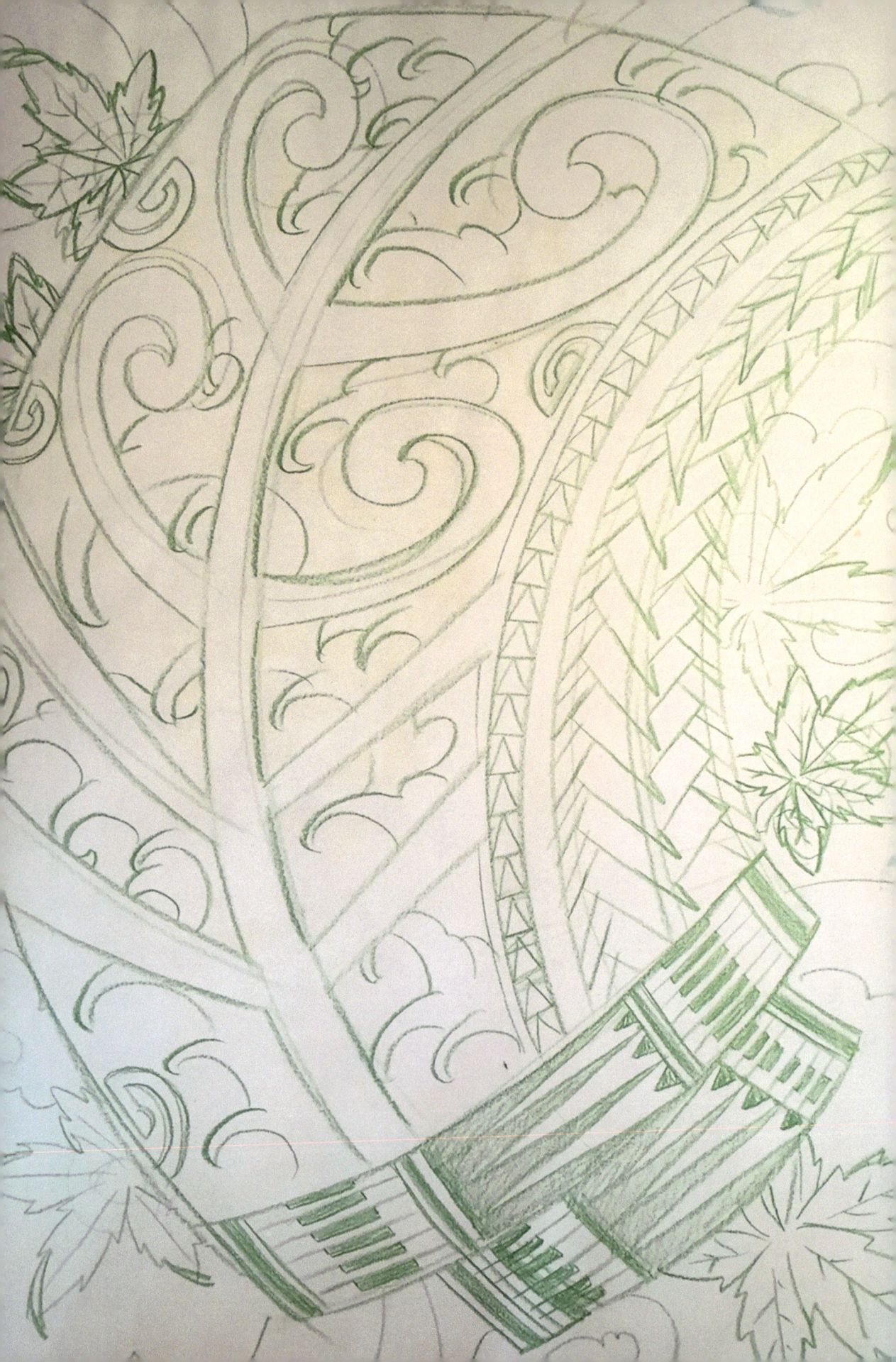

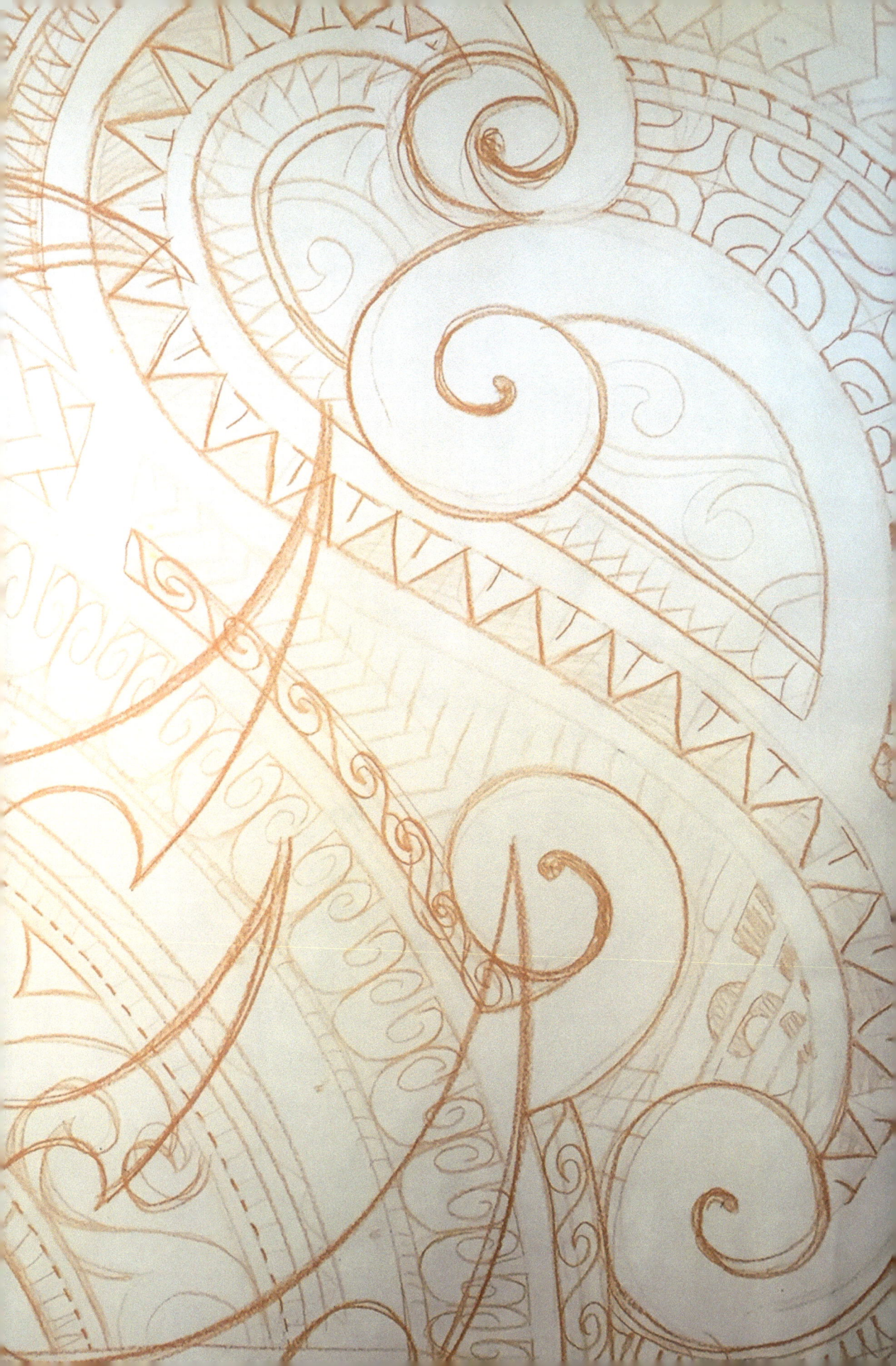

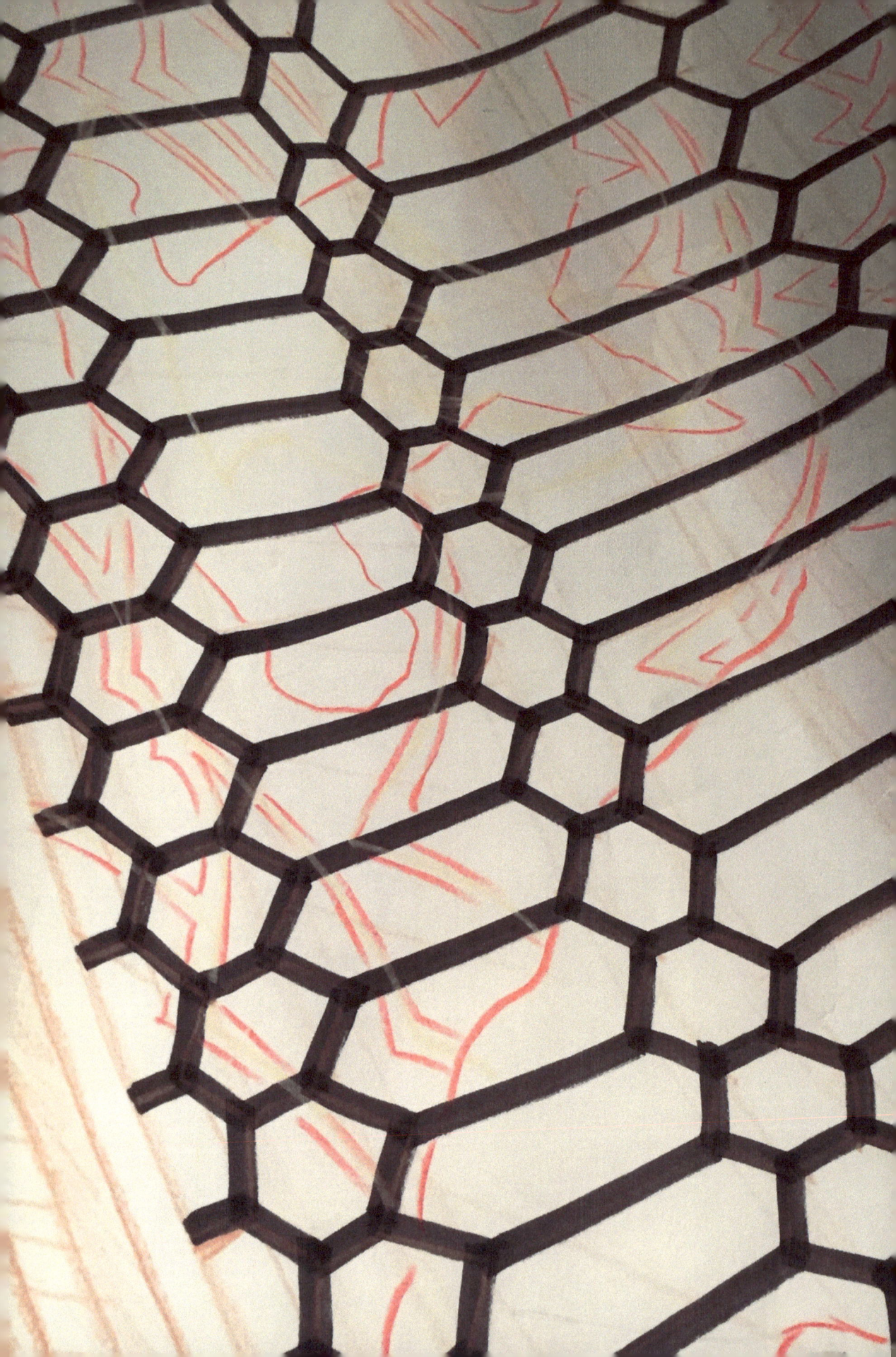

From Japanese style to surreal black and gray, to watercolors and computer art, we have something you will love. Prints ranging in size from 11" x 17" to 40" x 50" will adjust the visual appeal of any room.

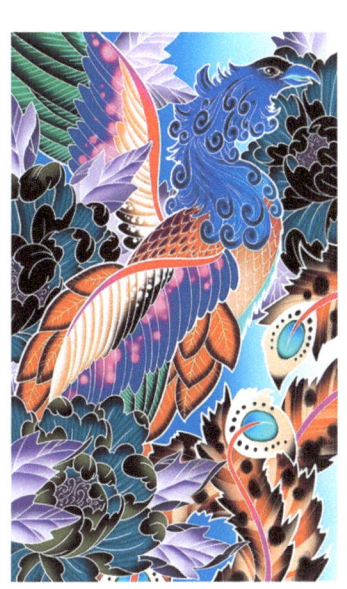
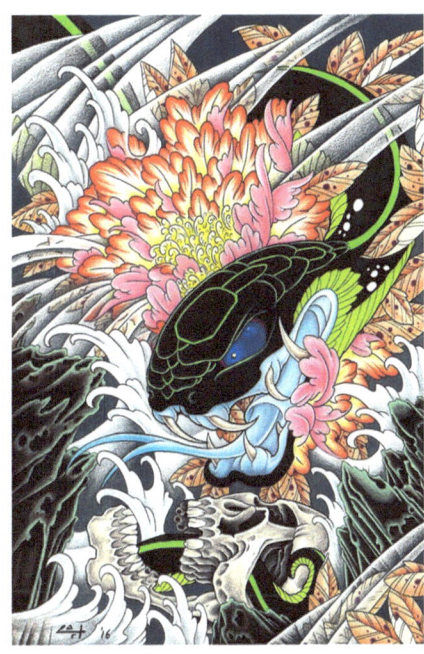
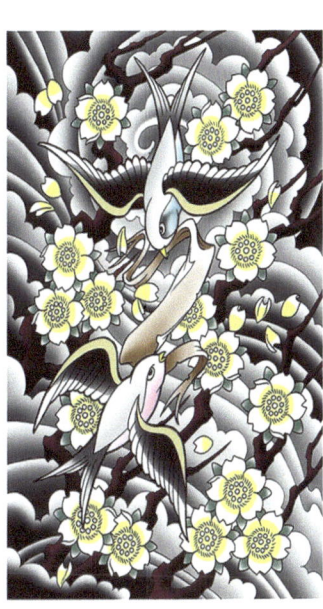
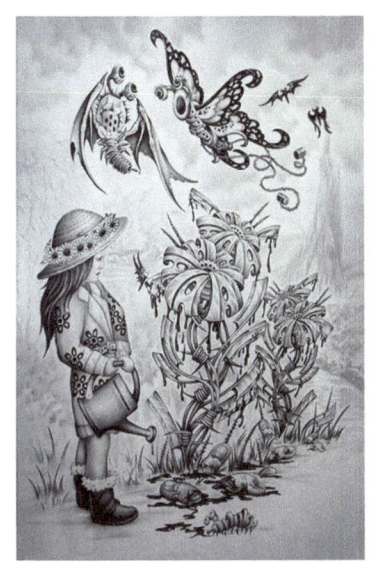
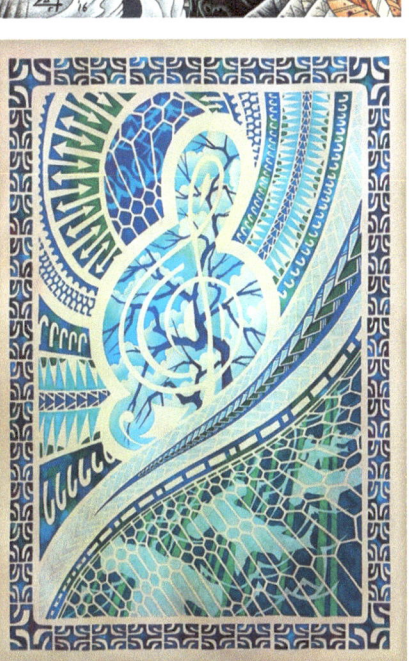
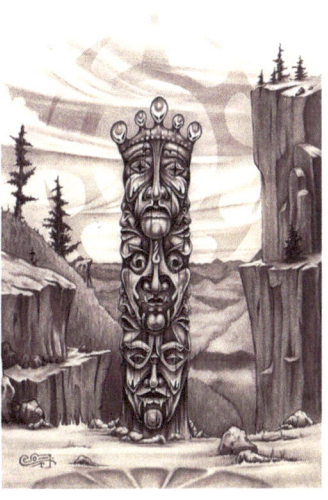

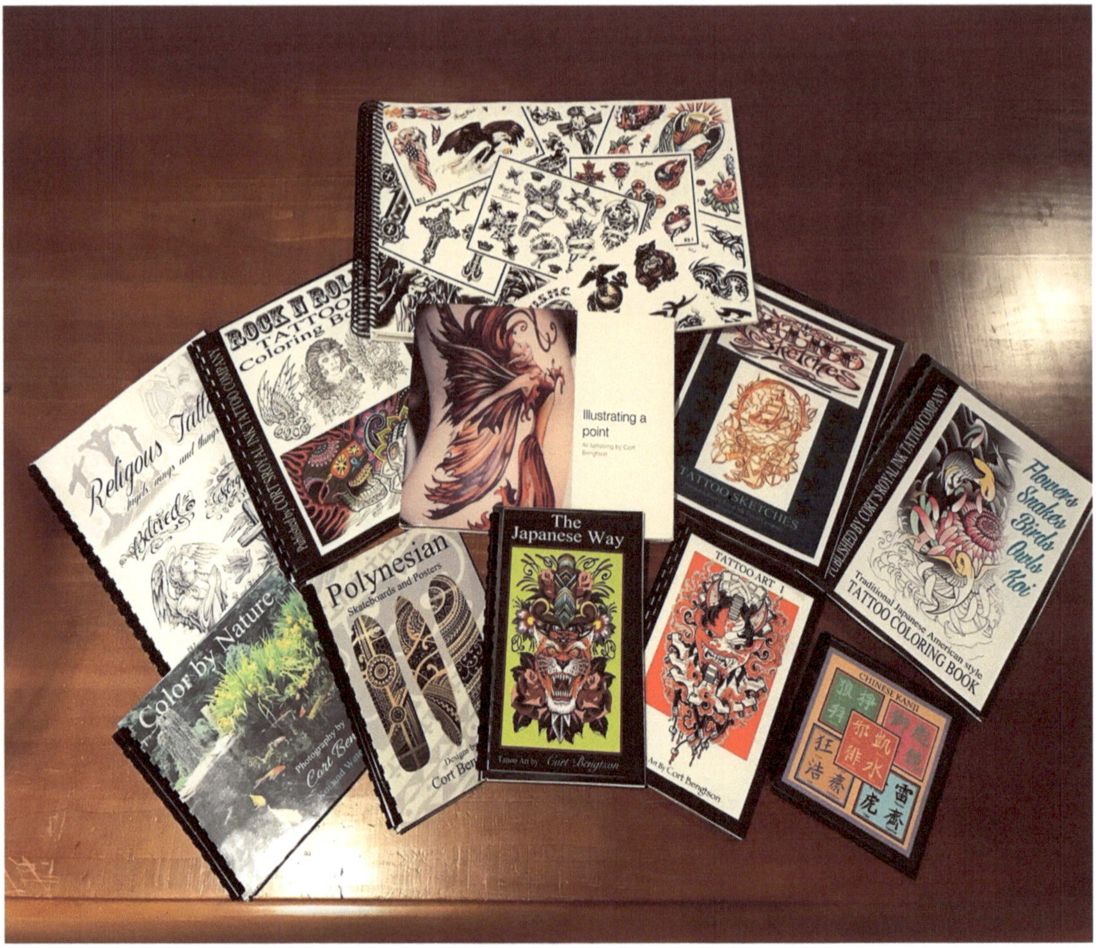

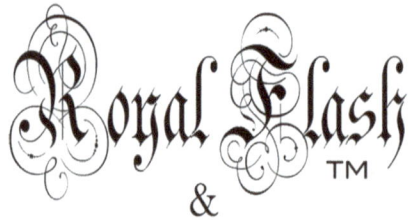

Check out these other great books,
Flash, Prints and original Art from

Royal Flash ™
&
Cort's Royal Ink Tattoo Company

Contact us @   cortsroyalink@aol.com
See whats new @   cortsroyalink on Instagram
COLORKINGTATTOOS.COM

www.ingramcontent.com/pod-product-compliance
Lightning Source LLC
Chambersburg PA
CBHW051911210526
45473CB00006B/1974